POLITICAL CONCEPTS

A Reconstruction

FELIX E. OPPENHEIM

POLITICAL
CONCEPTS

A Reconstruction

THE UNIVERSITY
OF CHICAGO
PRESS

FELIX E. OPPENHEIM
is professor of political science and of philosophy
at the University of Massachusetts at Amherst. He is the author of
Dimensions of Freedom and *Moral Principles in Political Philosophy*
and has contributed articles to the *International Encyclopedia
of the Social Sciences* and the *Handbook of Political Science*.

THE UNIVERSITY OF CHICAGO PRESS, CHICAGO 60637
BASIL BLACKWELL, OXFORD

© 1981 by The University of Chicago
All rights reserved. Published 1981
Printed in the United States of America
85 84 83 82 81   5 4 3 2 1

LIBRARY OF CONGRESS CATALOGING IN PUBLICATION DATA

Oppenheim, Felix E   1913–
  Political concepts, a reconstruction.

  Bibliography: p.
  Includes indexes.
  1. Liberty.   2. Equality.   3. Power (Social
sciences)   4. Public interest.   I. Title.
JC571.076   320'.01'1   80–23846
ISBN 0–226–63184–2

To the memory of my father

PAUL I. OPPENHEIM

1885–1977

Contents

Contents

Acknowledgments

B EAUTIFUL SURROUNDINGS contributed to the pleasure of
writing this book. I am grateful to the Netherlands Institute for Advanced Study in the Humanities and Social
Sciences in Wassenaar, where I was a Resident Fellow
during the academic year 1973/74; to the Rockefeller
Foundation for a Resident Scholarship at the Bellagio Study
and Conference Center in 1976; to the University of Massachusetts at Amherst for a sabbatical leave, which (combined
with a Fulbright lectureship) I spent in Florence; and to the
town of Amherst, a beautiful place in its own way.

Among colleagues who have read this work at various
stages as a whole or in parts, giving valuable advice, my
special thanks go to Terence Ball, David Braybrooke, Carl
Hempel, Donald Moon, J. Roland Pennock, Hillel Steiner,
Warner Wick, and—last but not least—William Connolly in
spite (or perhaps because) of friendly disagreement. Doris
Holden intelligently converted several chaotic-appearing
drafts into ordered typescripts, and William Martel helped
with compiling references and indexes.

Several chapters are based on articles I have previously
published in somewhat different form, and I am grateful to
the publishers for permission to use these materials. Section
1.2 of chapter 1 incorporates pp. 286–87 of "The Language of
Political Inquiry: Problems of Clarification," in Fred I. Greenstein and Nelson W. Polsby (eds.), the *Handbook of Political
Science*, vol. 1 (Reading Mass.: Addison-Wesley Publishing
Co., 1975), © 1975 by Addison-Wesley Publishing Company,
Inc.; reprinted by permission. Parts of chapter 3 closely follow
an analysis originally published as "'Power' Revisited,"
Journal of Politics 40, no. 2 (May 1978): 589–608; reprinted by
permission. Section 3.2 of the same chapter contains material
from "Power and Causation," chapter 6 in Brian Barry (ed.),

Power and Political Theory (London: John Wiley & Sons, 1976), pp. 103–16, © 1976 by John Wiley & Sons, Ltd.; reprinted by permission. Chapter 6 borrows heavily from "Egalitarian Rules of Distribution," *Ethics* 90 (January 1980): 164–79; reprinted by permission of the University of Chicago Press, © 1980 by the University of Chicago. The original version of a greater part of chapter 7 appeared under the title "Self-Interest and Public Interest" in *Political Theory* 3, no. 3 (August 1975): 257–76; reprinted by permission of Sage Publications, Inc.

ONE

Introduction

Il faut chercher seulement à penser et à parler juste, sans vouloir amener les autres à notre goût et à nos sentiments; c'est une trop grande entreprise.

La Bruyère, *Les caractères; ou, Les moeurs de ce siècle*

1.1 PURPOSE AND PLAN

T HIS STUDY endeavors to apply the method of contemporary analytic philosophy to an analysis of selected political concepts. It is not meant to be a dictionary or "vocabulary of politics."[1] The proposing of definitions will here be a device for elucidating some major issues in contemporary social philosophy; e.g., the reconstructionist versus the ordinary language approach in general, the separability versus the inseparability of "facts" and "values," causal versus interpretative models of human action and political interaction.

The title of the book indicates my position on the first of these controversies. To make political concepts suitable for political inquiry, it seems to me necessary to reconstruct them, i.e., provide them with explicative definitions; these must in certain cases deviate from ordinary language to avoid ambiguities and valuational overtones. The proposed explications will be descriptive, so that political scientists with differing normative commitments can nevertheless agree, e.g., that a given rule of distribution is egalitarian (but not necessarily just) or a given policy is in the public interest (whether or not it should be enacted). The aim is to clarify both normative and empirical aspects of political inquiry, and I consider them equally important. However, I advocate no normative doctrines, not even implicitly. Therefore, if the study is to achieve its goal, it should be acceptable to political

1

scientists and philosophers regardless of their ideological convictions.

It is on the methodological level that this study takes a definite position. It espouses not only reconstructionism as opposed to ordinary language philosophy, but also by implication the thesis of the separability of "facts" and "values." It maintains that descriptive concepts and affirmations can and must be distinguished from normative discourse, but it does not subscribe to the "positivistic" views often attributed to the separability thesis. Reconstructionism is also incompatible with the "interpretative" method of explanation.

I am well aware that my approach moves against the tide of current social, and especially political, theory. The emphasis is at present on preserving the many-colored shadings of ordinary language generally and of political discourse in particular; on the "essential contestability" of political concepts; on the impossibility of separating descriptive from normative aspects of what are considered "moral notions"; and on the necessity of interpreting "rule-governed" behavior in terms of the actor's "self-understanding" rather than causally. And so "post behavioral" political science is linked to "antipositivistic" philosophy.

Trends in philosohy, like political ideologies and fashions in jean styles, tend to be short-lived, erratic, and unpredictable. At the time of this writing, the "new left" is becoming senile and a "new right" (going back to old elitism) is emerging in France. Even in philosophy there are signs that the pendulum is swinging back from extreme conceptual relativism to a more analytic approach, if we can judge from an increasing number of articles, especially in philosophical journals.

Be that as it may, it is not with trends but with arguments that I am here concerned. Now, both opposing views have most often been defended in general terms of "how to" interpret political concepts. It seems to me that it is more effective as well as more interesting to "do it," i.e., actually develop reconstructions of specific political concepts. To show the fruitfulness of this approach, it is sufficient to take representative examples. Nor would it be possible to deal with more than a limited number of notions in a study of this kind. I have chosen those of power, freedom, equality and interest. They are among the key concepts of political inquiry, illustrating different aspects and problems of conceptual analysis.[2] I would be pleased if this book were to stimulate the application of such analysis to other areas.

The rest of this chapter will examine the general logical structure of concepts such as those to be defined. Chapters 2–7 will deal with social power, social freedom, egalitarianism, and self-interest and public interest, as well as with a number of concepts related to those appearing in the chapter headings. I shall in each case develop my own reconstruction, provide illustrations, discuss other interpretations recently advanced[3] (in the cases of social power and freedom, in separate chapters), and indicate what seem to me the advantages of my own proposals. Chapter 8 criticizes more specifically certain normative interpretations of these concepts. On the basis of the reconstructions I have developed I hope to be able, in the concluding chapter (9), to argue more effectively for the reconstructionist approach in general.

1.2 EXPRESSIONS TO BE DEFINED

Before we attempt to construct any definition, we must be clear about the expression we are out to define. It must therefore be our first task to formulate that expression in such a way as to reveal its logical structure. As we shall see, many ambiguities in the writings of political scientists and philosophers are due to their failure to be aware of the logical properties of the concepts they are using.

1.2.1 Not Words but Concepts

We are concerned with the analysis of concepts, not with the definition of words. This distinction would not be so important if there were always a one-to-one correspondence between words and concepts. But a given concept—e.g., of freedom—may be labeled be several synonyms—'freedom' or 'liberty' or 'liberté', etc. More important, one and the same word is often used to express two or more different concepts;

e.g., 'freedom' (or its synonyms) applies to at least five concepts of freedom, which we shall distinguish and examine in turn. Concentrating on the *word* 'freedom' tends to obscure the differences between the various *concepts* of freedom.[4]

There is a second reason for not analyzing words: meaning is in general attached, not to words in isolation, but to expressions in which the words typically occur. Words like 'length' or 'influence' are used in certain characteristic phrases like 'the length of x is y units' or 'P influences R to do x'; and it is the meaning of those phrases that needs to be specified rather than the meaning of the words taken by themselves. Only after having laid down the expression to be defined (the *definiendum*) can we determine how best to define it. When the same word in everyday language expresses several concepts, we must construct different expressions for each of them.

A third reason for not dealing with isolated words is that terms like 'power', 'freedom', 'equality', or 'interest' function as nouns in ordinary language. Hence the tendency to commit the fallacy of reification, i.e., to treat such "abstract nouns as though they were proper names and denoted abstract entities (universals, Platonic ideas) in much the same way as proper names denote individuals" (Pap 1949, p. 507; Kaplan 1964, p. 61). Thus, Plato's *Republic* focuses on a search for "justice, a thing much more precious than gold" (I, 336). There is no such *thing* as justice or equality or freedom. All the concepts we will analyze stand for properties, including relational properties, and this is what the corresponding expressions to be defined must bring out clearly.

1.2.2 Property Concepts and Relational Concepts

In logic a property is what can be asserted or predicated of individual entities of some particular kind. Thus, in the expressions 'x is green', 'x is a law', 'x is president of the United States', the words after 'x is...' express in each case properties, regardless of whether, gramatically, they are adjectives or nouns. Democracy, too, is a property concept; i.e., the word 'democracy' stands for a property—namely, one that can be attributed to human organizations like trade unions, universities, or large-scale political organizations. To define the concept of democracy is to say what property it is that we attribute to an organization when we call it democratic. Not 'democracy' but 'x is democratic' (or 'x is a democracy') is the expression to be introduced into the language of political science (and later to be defined). Once 'x is democratic' has been defined, we can say that the noun 'democracy' refers to the property x has when x is democratic. Egalitarianism is another example of a property concept. We shall see that in the expression 'x is egalitarian', the variable x ranges over rules of distribution of benefits or burdens. It is such rules which can be said to have or lack the property of being egalitarian.

The concept of self-interest does not designate a "thing" either. Nor does it refer to a simple property, as does the concept of egalitarianism. Rather, its logical structure is that of a relational property or relation, like that of 'heavier than'. Again, the corresponding terms cannot be taken in isolation but must be considered contextually: 'x is heavier than y'. We see immediately that this is a relation with two variables (or a two-term relation). So is the concept of self-interest. As we shall see, the typical expression to be examined and defined is 'it is in A's interest to do x'.

Whereas the notion of self-interest as we shall construe it is a relation between two terms, the concept of public interest will be interpreted as a three-term relation, like the concept of between, i.e., the expression 'x is between y and z'. Accordingly, we shall take as the *definiendum* of the concept of public interest 'it is in P's interest that A do x'. Another example of a three-term relation is the concept of equality, in contradistinction to the property concept of egalitarianism. Here the expression to be defined is 'A and B are equal with respect to characteristc x', where the variables 'A' and 'B' refer to objects (often persons) and the variable 'x' to characteristics such as age, sex, citizenship, income, ability, need. To say that two or more persons are equal in age or need simply means that they have the same age or need, or that they are substantially similar in such respects (unlike the mathematical concept of equality, which is a two-term rela-

5

tion, as in $2 + 1 = 3$). Here again, it is necessary to specify all three variables. Thus, the statement 'all men are equal' is incomplete, if taken literally, since it includes no reference to a characteristic with respect to which all men are claimed to be equal. One might interpret it as referring implicitly to a common "human nature," a characteristic all men do indeed share. But this is a tautological assertion from which no other factual or normative statement can be derived. That all men are equal (or that all men are "born equal" or have equal natural rights) usually expresses the normative principle that all men *should* be provided by their respective governments with the same benefits; but these must in turn be specified—e.g., equal rights, regardless of certain individual differences such as sex or ability or status.

Social or political power, too, will be construed as a relational concept, referring to relationships of interaction between persons and groups. Accordingly, I shall take as *definienda* expressions like 'P influences R to do x', 'P deters R from doing x', 'P has power over R wrt [with respect to] x'.[5]

Most political scientists agree that power and its related concepts are relational. "But ordinary usage suggests that this is not true. 'Power' is something which one may 'have' or 'not have', 'exercise' or 'not exercise'" (Pitkin 1972, p. 276; similarly, Benn 1967, p. 424). This passage suggests that power should be taken as a property concept. But here, as so often, ordinary language leads us astray. I may "have" a headache or a television set; I do not "have power—period." I have (perhaps) power over my students wrt their reading *Leviathan*. Such expressions are elliptical. When we say that Stalin was powerful or had much power, we mean that Stalin had power over many actors (the Soviet hierarchy, Soviet citizens, Communist parties at home and abroad) and wrt many of their actions.

Hannah Pitkin concedes that "[o]ne man may have power over another or others, and that sort of power is indeed relational. . . . But he may have power to do something all by himself, and that power is not relational at all" (1972, p. 277). Here we have an example of one and the same word, 'power', standing for two very different concepts: one actor's power over another actor's activity, and one actor's power over his own conduct. However, contrary to Ms. Pitkin, the latter kind of power, too, is relational. Even so, the two concepts have a different logical structure. While the former refers to a relation with three variables, the latter expresses a two-term relation. 'P has the power to do (or accomplish) x' is now the expression to be defined. Similarly:

> [P]ower is often said to be a relation . . . , *yet* we talk about the distribution of power, about the power of speech, about seeking power as a means to future enjoyment (Hobbes), or about power as "the production of intended effects" (Russell). (Benn 1967, p. 424; italics added)

In each of these examples, 'power' functions in a relational sense as referring to someone's ability either to do something by himself or to control activities of others. Thus, when we speak of military or economic power, we are using the concept in a relational way to indicate an actor's disposition, e.g., to set the price of oil or to have others buy oil at the set price.

Like the concept of social power, those of social unfreedom and freedom express relations with three variables. Accordingly, we shall take as *definienda* expressions such as 'wrt P, R is unfree to do x'. Here, too, clarity requires that we "fill in" all variables, i.e., that we specify in each case *who* is unfree or free to do *what* wrt *whom*. It is ambiguous, if not meaningless, to say that I am free or that Americans are free or that Italians have more freedom now than they had under Mussolini. What is meaningful and true is that, wrt their government, Italians now have more freedom of speech and less freedom to dispose of their income as they please (because of somewhat more stringent and somewhat better enforced tax laws). If "my conscience" or "my better self" prevents me from doing something or "punishes me" with guilt feelings if I do something, I am not unfree to do so wrt any *other* actor. Whether such expressions refer to some other concept of freedom will concern us later; but surely these are not instances of interpersonal or social unfreedom. It will also be pointed out that the concept of social freedom, unlike that of social unfreedom, refers, at least implicitly, to alternative courses of action open to the respondent. Freedom of religion is not freedom to adhere to the "true" faith, but being left free to adopt one or another religion—or none.

'Freedom' and 'free' function in ordinary language as labels, not only for the three-term relation of social freedom but also (like 'power') for a relation with two variables, namely, freedom of action. In addition, there are three different property concepts of freedom, as we shall see.

1.2.3 Actor and Action Variables

Some further preliminary remarks will clear up possible misunderstandings concerning the variables that occur in the expressions to be defined. Let us take as an example the concept of social power, where I take as the *definiendum* 'P has power over R wrt his doing x'. Here the variables 'P' (the holder of power) and 'R' (the respondent) range over actors, and 'x' ranges over possible actions of R.

Letters like 'P' and 'R' (or 'A' and 'B') often stand for proper names. Now, especially in political contexts, individual actors are often characterized by the office they hold or the role they play. Thus, the actor variables 'P' and 'R' may symbolize the president of the United States or a voter or consumer or lawbreaker, etc. Furthermore, like in game theory, "[t]he decision unit may be an individual, a group, a formal or an informal organization, or a society" (Shubik 1964, p. 8). Accordingly, 'P' and 'R' may also stand for governments and their various branches, interest groups, business firms, nations, and other collectivities. Political science is interested in power relations not so much between individuals as between groups and organizations. To consider groups as actors does not require postulating some metaphysical "group mind."

Formulas like 'P has power over R's doing x' may evoke the specter of behaviorism in its primitive and outdated form. Several of the concepts we have already used are surely not describable in purely behavioral terms. Offices or roles and groups or organizations are definable only by reference to their constitutive rules, e.g., legal norms. Nor does 'doing x' simply refer to observable bodily movements. 'Voting', 'buying', 'occupying a position', etc., are *action concepts* "employed to describe behavior which is done with a purpose such that one can ask, what is its point, aim, or intent.... A specific action concept can be used, only in the context of a certain set of social rules which provide the criteria in terms of which an actor can be said to be performing that action" (Fay 1975, pp. 71, 74). Most actions in the political arena are "speech acts" involving rules of language that speakers and listeners must "understand." Furthermore, the definitions of some of the subcategories of 'power' will refer not only to P's and R's overt behavior, but also to their beliefs, preferences, and choices; and these can surely not be "observed." The same is true of the defining expressions of such concepts as social freedom or self-interest, as we shall see.

We are now ready to formulate, for each of the concepts to be examined, the expression to be defined so as to reveal its logical structure, to construct a suitable definition, to compare it with other interpretations, and to indicate what I believe to be the advantage of my own proposal.

TWO
Social Power

I NEED NOT ENTER the controversy between those political scientists who consider the concept of power of key importance or even as the most basic notion in political science (e.g., Lasswell and Kaplan 1950, p. xiv) and those who tend to minimize its significance (e.g., March 1966, p. 70). I shall just assume that this notion is indispensable for political analysis, not only in its own right but also—as we shall see—because it belongs to a network of other key notions such as influence, deterrence, coercion, punishment, authority, legitimacy, and also unfreedom and freedom.

This chapter will be restricted to an analysis of what I shall call social power, the power concept that occurs most frequently in the context of political inquiry. Furthermore, I shall be dealing here explicitly only with unilateral power relations. In many political and social situations, one actor has power over another in one respect, and the latter over the former in some other respect. We shall see later that such reciprocal power relations—e.g., bargaining, competition, economic exchange—can be analyzed in terms of two unilateral power relations, pointing in opposite directions. Finally, I shall only examine power relations between single actors, not situations of collective power, where an individual can be compelled to act in a certain way not by one of two or more actors, but only jointly. (Goldman 1972 deals with collective power; see p. 225.)

2.1 EXERCISING POWER
I shall make a distinction between the relationships of exercising power and having power, and the former concept will turn out to be a subcategory of the latter.

Definition: P exercises power over R's doing x iff [if and only if] P influences R to do x or coerces R to do x or punishes R for not having done x. P exercises power over R's not doing x iff P influences R not to do x or restrains R from doing x or punishes R for having done x.

The second type of relationship occurs more frequently in the political sphere, and I shall therefore deal more explicitly with negative instances of power. Not performing a specific action also is "doing something"; any instance of behavior can, theoretically, be characterized in either positive (e.g., staying home, obeying the law) or negative (e.g., not going out, not committing larceny) terms.

2.1.1 Influencing
For reasons I shall point out later, I am taking influence as a subclass of power, not vice versa or as exluding power.

Definition: P influences R not to do x iff P performs some action y that causes[1] R to choose not to do x.

Exercising influence, like the other categories of exercising power, refers to a relationship of *interaction*. This is why the defining expression pertains to two actions (of two actors): P's action y and R's action x.[2] As I have indicated, 'action' is to be taken in a large sense. In the area of political interaction, P's influence action y consists in most cases of a "speech act" involving some "communication," these terms to be taken in turn in their broadest meaning. By enacting a law reducing taxes, a government influences taxpayers to buy more consumer goods (intentionally or not—a point to be taken up later). P's action y may also consist in simply occupying a position and playing in that capacity the role of an authority figure in the eyes of R. A policeman in uniform by merely standing at a street intersection may influence drivers to stop at his command.

From the outcome side of the influence relation, R is being prompted by P to do, or not to do, something—again in the largest sense of the word. R's action x may consist of concluding—or breaking—a contract or treaty, of voting for or against a candidate or party or bill, of complying with a law or disobeying it. But this approach might still be considered too "behavioristic." One could object that one actor often influences not another's action, but his perceptions, beliefs, values, decisions. True, P may influence R to change his attitude toward minorities or his beliefs concerning the effect of heredity on intelligence or the value to be given to liberty relative to welfare. Now, the proposed definition by no means precludes us from considering R's beliefs and preferences. However, in a political context these become relevant only to the extent to which they terminate in actions or, as we shall see later, in dispositions to act in certain ways under specified conditions. This is to say that mental states function as intervening variables between P's influence action and R's action of response. Moreover, R's *choosing* to do x—a mental event—appears as an explicit component of the definition of influencing. This is not, strictly speaking, an intervening variable; 'choosing (or deciding) to do x' is to be understood in the sense of making a *final* decision to do so, i.e., as logically entailing that the actor do what he has decided to do, unless prevented.

It follows from the definition of influencing that, before P does y, R has not yet decided to abstain from doing x; he may either intend to do x (e.g., to vote Republican) or be undecided. As a result of P's intervention, R decides not to do x (not to vote Republican but Democratic) and does not do so. In the case of deliberate actions, one's choices are usually determined by a multiplicity of factors, including always by one's own "will." P exercises influence over R's conduct *to the extent that* R's decision is the result of some influence action of P. Theoretically, the clerk's ringing up my groceries is the result partly of the store owner's standing order, to a lesser degree of my presenting the groceries, and to a small extent of his own will. Practically speaking, it is the owner who exercises (or rather *has*, as we shall see later) influence, and hence power, over the clerk's activities.

If R decides to abstain from x independently of P (on his own or as a result of another actor's influence), P cannot have influenced R's conduct—'cannot' in the logical sense, given the proposed definition. Nor does P exercise influence over R's not doing x if R in fact does x—again, by definition. If R voted Republican, R was not influenced by P or by anyone else to vote Democratic. I make this trivial point only to bring out that influence and power are, by definition, successful—but not necessarily successful in the sense that P influences R to do what P "wants him to do" (as we shall see).

P's influence action y usually consists of some verbal communication by which he *persuades* R to choose a certain alternative or *dissuades* him from adopting some course of action. P may do so by providing R with information based on his "honest" (if not necessarily correct) beliefs, or he may mislead him; and he may use rational arguments or play on R's emotions. I consider thus both rational persuasion and deception or manipulation as forms of influence and, hence, of power, and I shall argue later against those who define power as comprising only the latter kind of influence.

Promises of reward and threats of punishment (deterrence) can be considered a special kind of persuasion and dissuasion. By promising R a reward if R does x, P may persuade R to do x, and P may dissuade R from acting in a certain way by threatening him with punishment should he do so: "Offers and threats are interventions, by others, in individuals' practical deliberations. They are intended by their authors to *influence* how a recipient individual behaves, by altering the extent to which he actually desires to do a particular action of a kind which he is able to do" (Steiner 1975, p. 36; italics added). Exchange relationships normally involve mutual promises of reward, and we shall see later that exchange can be analyzed in terms of reciprocal power relations. Unilateral power relations consist more often of *deterrence*, the invocation of negative rather than positive sanctions.

By enacting and enforcing penal legislation, a government usually succeeds in deterring a certain class of persons from acting illegally. It exercises power in that respect over those persons whose compliance with the law is motivated— exclusively or at least primarily—by their desire to avoid incurring the legal sanction. A government exercises no influence over those who break the law or over those who comply for other reasons—e.g., because they consider it their duty or in their long-range interest to obey that particular law, or because they regard governmental enactments in general as morally legitimate.

13

2.1.2 Coercing

Definition: P coerces R to do x iff P performs some action y that
causes R's attempt to avoid doing x to fail. P restrains R
from doing x iff P performs some action y that causes R's
attempt to do x to fail.

'Coercion' is a more familiar term than 'restraint', and for
this reason the former term is often used in a wider sense to
include the latter. Since any action can be characterized
either positively or negatively, any constraining action is
also a restraining one. By constraining you to stay in your
room, I restrain you from leaving. In a political context, instances of coercion can often better be described as restraining situations.

In cases of restraint or constraint, P's action y occurs later
than in situations of influencing. Before P's intervention, R
has not only positively chosen to do x, but also embarked
upon a course of action designed to bring about x. P's action
y impinges not on R's mind, as it were, but on his body or
environment. As a consequence, R gives up his attempt and
ends up not doing x.[3]

The use of physical force is perhaps the first situation that
comes to mind when thinking of coercion, and even of power
in general. Yet, physically coercing someone to do something
or restraining him physically from acting in a certain way
occurs only in unusual circumstances like wars or revolts or
in face-to-face interactions like the guard forcing a resisting
prisoner back into his cell and thereby frustrating his attempt
to escape. "The actual employment of physical force, then,
usually signifies that a policy based on the threat of force has
failed" (Dahl 1976, p. 49).

Attempting something also constitutes an action; but remaining inactive cannot logically be part of the interaction
relationship of exercising power. If the guard pushes the
prisoner into a cell and the prisoner does not put up any
resistance, the guard does not exercise power over him, since
there is no *action* x (e.g., escaping) he attempts to do that the
guard frustrates. Such situations will be covered by the concept of having power.

'Coercion' is sometimes extended to the threat of legal or

moral sanctions. 'If we have an obligation to do something there is some sense in which . . . we are or may be compelled to do it" (Hart 1958, p. 95)—some sense, but not coercion in the technical sense in which I have just defined it. A law imposing the legal obligation to pay income tax may influence taxpayers to pay, but does not compel—in the present sense of 'coerce'—anyone to do so. (Rather, the law makes it punishable not to pay.) Similarly, if P tells R that he will punish him if he does x and if, as a result, R refrains from doing x, this is a case of deterrence, and hence of influence, but not of restraint or coercion.

However, since power is only exceptionally exercised by means of physical violence, it seems practical to follow ordinary usage by extending the meaning of coercion to cover those threats of sanctions often called *coercive threats*. Here, P's threat is so credible and the threatened sanction so severe that R, while theoretically able either to comply or to disobey at the certain price of a severe deprivation, has "practically no choice" but to take the former course of action (see Lasswell and Kaplan 1950, p. 97). Thus, in the typical situation of "your money or your life," R—at least in theory—first attempts to keep the money but soon realizes that to persist in such a course under the circumstances would be irrational. P's promise of a reward that R "cannot refuse" can often be subsumed under coercive threats. A threat ceases to be an instance of mere deterrence (and hence of mere influence) and becomes coercive when it becomes so severe and so credible that any *rational* actor would give in. I quite agree with S. I. Benn "that human action must be interpreted and described in the light of norms of prudence and rationality, without which it would be unintelligible" (1964, p. 240). The concept of rationality is one of the building blocks of our conceptual scheme, and I shall give some indication of the norms of rational choice in the chapter on interests. Here we need only remember that we construe the various power concepts (and those of freedom and unfreedom, as we shall see) as relationships between actor *variables* P and R. That people give in at gunpoint is a statistical generalization which means that *any* actor R of average rationality will probably comply with the demands of *any* P threatening him with a gun. Accordingly, when we see P1 pointing a gun a R1, we predict that P1 will coerce R1 to hand over his money, unless we know that R1 happens to be very strong and courageous—or inclined to take unreasonable risks (cf. Day 1977, p. 269). It is therefore no valid objection against this analysis that men "occasionally act despite the risk of severe deprivation" (Parent 1974, p. 155). P1 did not succeed in coercing R1 if R1 succeeded in "overpowering" P1 or if R1, acting irrationally, did not comply. In that case, P1 probably carried out his threat (but not certainly; R1, while taking an unreasonable risk, might have been "lucky"). Our general criterion is thus: Are the risks and costs of noncompliance so high that it would not be rational to resist? We shall see that the distinction between influence by relatively mild threats and threats of severe deprivation amounting to coercion is of theoretical importance, as it coincides with the borderline between social freedom and unfreedom.

The concepts of influencing and coercing can be used to define that of controlling.

Definition: P exercises control over R's not doing x iff P either influences R not to do x or restrains R from doing x.

'Control' and 'power' are often used interchangeably. To do so is, however, to disregard a form of power not involving the exercise of control, namely punishment.

2.1.3 Punishing

It is true that punishment, unlike influence and coercion, does not involve compliance, but, on the contrary, usually indicates failure to comply. Even so, imprisoning someone for having committed a certain crime must be considered an exercise of power, no less so than dissuading or deterring or restraining him from doing so. We shall see that the concept of punishment is also important as one of the defining characteristics of social unfreedom. "The term 'punishment'... is most commonly and appropriately applied to a situation in which a deprivation or unpleasant experience is deliberately imposed by one party upon another because of an actual or supposed misdeed which is knowingly and intentionally committed by the latter" (Lindesmith 1968, p.

16

217). This characterization may be incorporated into our definitional scheme as follows:

Definition: P punishes R for having done x iff P believes that R committed offense x, and this belief causes P to perform some action y with the intention of depriving R.

We tend to think in the first place of public authorities punishing citizens for having committed a criminal offense. But we should remember, here again, that 'P' and 'R' are general actor variables. E.g., a child may punish his parents for not having given him a lollypop by staging a temper tantrum.

Let us separate the various components of this definition.

a) P believes that R did x. P's belief is usually prompted by something R did (or failed to do), but it is not x that R must necessarily have done. Our definition covers situations in which P punishes R for having done something he did not actually do. But P's deprivatory action y does not constitute punishment, and hence is not an exercise of power over R wrt his having *acted* in a certain way unless y is causally linked to some action x that P accuses R of having done. "Suppose I threaten to beat you up unless you do act A. You refuse to comply and so I beat you up. Here I have failed to control your behavior, but isn't my beating you up itself an exercise of power?" (Goldman 1972, p. 262). Yes, it is, because my beating you constitutes punishment for your not having done x (but not for the reasons given by the author). If I beat you for no reason, I do not punish you and do not exercise power over you, for there is no answer to the question: for having done what? This, I admit, may seem counterintuitive. Here we are faced with a dilemma: should we buy consistency at the price of deviating from ordinary language? I am saying that we should. Other examples may illustrate the advantage of the proposed definition. If I physically restrain you from doing something "just for fun," I am not punishing you either (for anything I claim you have done); but in this case I *do* exercise power over you: I am restraining (or coercing) you. If a terrorist C maims or kills R to instill terror in others, there is *no* power relation—neither punishment nor coercion nor influence. There *is* influence

17

(but again, not punishment) if C, by terrorizing others, induces them to overthrow the government. Of course, often we cannot be sure whether there is some specific action x of R, and, hence, whether there is punishment in particular or a power relation in general.

b) This belief causes P to perform some action y. Whereas P's control action y determines R's behavior, it may seem that, in case of punishment, causality flows in the opposite direction, from R's action x to P's punitive action y. But the proposed definition makes clear that P's action y is more immediately caused by P's own—correct or mistaken—belief that R did x, and only indirectly by some action of R (but not necessarily action x) that gave rise to P's belief.

The difference between control (influence or coercion) and punishment is, rather, that, in case of punishment, R does not act, but is acted upon. P may punish R by literally depriving him of his freedom, his job, some money, food, etc., or by harming R physically. P's punitive action y may also consist of coercing R to perform some *other* action z; e.g., repairing the damage he has done.

c) P does y with the intention of depriving R. While control (influence and coercion) may be exercised unintentionally (as we shall see later), punishment is by definition intentional. What determines whether there is punishment is not R's feeling of being deprived, but P's intention of depriving him. Whether and to what degree R actually experiences the penalty as a deprivation is not relevant. Legislative sanctions are enacted with the intention of depriving anyone to whom they are being applied. Hence, R is being punished by imprisonment even if it so happens that he is pleased to be in jail. What is my reason for this proposal? That P intends to deprive R and that R feels deprived are both factual assertions, not normative judgments. However, to determine whether and to what extent R *suffers* deprivation, I would have to assess whether the negative utility to R of the penalty outweighs the positive utility to him of performing the punishable action. Taking this factor as a defining condition would blur the distinction (to be elaborated later) between the degree of disvalue R attaches to being punished by P and being under P's power, and the degree of P's power over R.

To anticipate: All who are condemned to a prison term of one year are being punished, and to the same degree; but the same punishment is likely to be more disvaluable to R1 who is wealthy and active than to R2 who does not mind being in prison and hence does not suffer from the punishment, and the less disvaluable to R1 the more important to him performing the punishable action x.

d) x constitutes an offense. Taxing and fining are both exercises of governmental power. By imposing a sales tax, government orders buyers, under threat of sanction, to pay a duty. By imposing a fine, government punishes people, e.g., for not having paid a tax. But could it not be argued that taxation constitutes a punishment? Does not government "inflict" a sales tax on people "for having" bought some taxable good? To avoid this conclusion, we must add the further defining clause that the action x that P alleges R to have done constitutes an offense. Offenses or "misdeeds" are defined by man-made rules. We think in the first place of the rules making up a system of criminal law, stipulating that actions with such-and-such characteristics constitute criminal offenses. It is by virtue of such legal rules that officials punish those they find guilty of these offenses. 'X' therefore stands, not for some specific action of R, but for a more general characteristic of that action, e.g., that the action constitutes larceny. However, P may also punish R by virtue of informal, implicit, unwritten rules of ethics, custom, or etiquette; this occurs, e.g., when parents discipline their children. Unlike the concept of controlling, that of punishing refers to normative rules. But like the definition of influencing, that of punishing includes references to mental states: P's *belief* that R did x and his *intention* of depriving R.

Odd as it may seem, it is nevertheless the case that public official P, by condemning R to prison, now exercises power over R wrt an action x of R that has occurred (at least allegedly) in the past and over which P exercised no control. (P may, on the contrary, have tried to exercise control over R's *not* doing x, but P's attempt at dissuasion or deterrence evidently remained unsuccessful.)

Here we see the importance of distinguishing between different power relations that may hold between the same pair of actors. For example: R erects a building in defiance of a zoning law (R does x1), prompting official P to make R remove it (to do x2). Here one and the same action y of P generates three different power processess: punishing R for having done x1, coercing R to do x2, and perhaps deterring R from performing action x3, similar to x1, in the future. It also happens that each of two actors A and B assumes the role of both P and R; i.e., A exercises power over B in one respect, and B over A in some different way. Here is an example.[4] A wishes to challenge a blue law prohibiting swimming on Sundays. On a Sunday, A dons his swim trunks (unless he is also a nudist), calls in the press, dives, and demands that a rather embarrassed policeman B arrest him. Here A influences—or perhaps practically compels—B to arrest him, and B punishes A for having committed the legal offense. (Perhaps A also influences bystanders and others to work for a repeal of that law.) Acts of civil disobedience and resulting punishments thus constitute reciprocal power relations: influence on one side, punishment on the other. These examples also illustrate the importance of specifying the kind of action wrt which one actor is said to have power over another.

2.2 HAVING POWER

People of average rationality tend to refrain from pursuing, attempting, choosing, or even contemplating goals they know others have made unattainable to them or attainable only at great risk or cost. The prisoner who knows that the cell door is securely locked is not likely to try to open it. At least when a policeman is near, drivers are inclined to obey speed laws. Congressmen often refrain from acting in a way they feel sure the majority of their constituents would disapprove. The Polish government is unlikely even to consider joining NATO or the Mexican government the Warsaw Pact, even if the Soviet or the United States government, respectively, does not "lift a finger." There is no exercise of power in these cases; yet there is power, and social scientists are especially interested in such latent relationships of interaction, including situations of "anticipated reactions." The more inclusive concept of having power captures such phenomena. P may thus have power over R's not doing x without R's actually intending or attempting or doing x, and without P's exercising power in that respect through acts of influence, restraint, or punishment. ('For reasons already mentioned, I shall deal explicitly only with negative instances of having power.)

Definition: P has power over R wrt his not doing x iff P has influence over R's not doing x or prevents R from doing x or makes it punishable for R to do x.

2.2.1 Having Influence

Definition: P has influence over R wrt his not doing x iff P performs some action y such that, were R to contemplate doing x, y would cause R to choose not to do x.

As this definition indicates, P "performs some action y" even when he has influence without necessarily exercising it, and we shall see that the same is true of the other forms of having power. Thus, the policeman in our example or the congressman's constituents or the governments of the Soviet Union and the United States all must have "done something" to generate the power they are asserted to have. As mentioned before, 'doing something' must be taken in a broad, nonbehavioral sense. It includes not only such "basic actions" as raising one's hand, but also their immediate consequences and at least some of their long-range effects (cf. Goldman 1970, p. 20), such as occupying an office (after having acceded to it), playing a role (that one has assumed), owning something (that one has acquired), or possessing a skill (that one has developed). Having a disposition should also be included. E.g., P has influence over his son R wrt his not cheating on an examination if it is the case that, were R tempted to cheat, he would remember his father's unerring honesty and thus refrain from cheating.[5] As all these examples also make clear, and as I shall point out again later, the concept of *having* influence and power must be distinguished not only from *exercising* power, but also from the *ability* to exercise it.

In analogy to exercising influence, we may distinguish between having dissuading (or persuading) power and having deterring power, the latter a subcategory of the former. If P campaigns for the Democratic party, he does not exercise influence over those who have already decided to vote either Democratic or Republican. But suppose some of the Democratic voters toyed—or were to toy—with the idea of switching their votes to the Republican party, and that, in such a hypothetical case, they would have been—or would be—influenced by P's campaign speeches not to change their vote after all. P *has* influence over this group of Democratic voters. By erecting a No Trespassing sign on his property, P exercises control over anyone who intends to trespass and is deterred from doing so by the threat of penalty symbolized by the sign. P also has deterring power over all those who, were they to intend to trespass, would finally not do so because of the sign. The legislature, by enacting and enforcing speed laws, has deterring power over two groups of nonspeeders: (1) those whom it thereby deters from speeding (and over whom it also exercises power), and (2) those who do not care to speed but who, were they to contemplate speeding, would change their minds to avoid the penalties. There are three groups over which the legislature has no control: (1) speeders (regardless of whether or not they are apprehended and fined); (2) nonspeeders who, were they to intend to speed, would do so in spite of the risk of punishment; and (3) nonspeeders who, were they to contemplate speeding, would nevertheless keep within the speed limits, but for motives other than fear of sanctions—e.g., because they deem it their moral duty to obey the law without questioning.

This last example has to do with whether authority is a form of power, a widely discussed question. My answer is: it depends. That government P has authority over its citizens R wrt a certain range of their activities means that the latter believe that P is entitled to regulate their conduct within that range and that they themselves have the duty to comply. "[T]he subject does not make his obedience *conditional* on his own personal examination and evaluation of the thing he is being asked to do. Rather, he accepts as a sufficient reason for following a prescription the fact that it is prescribed by someone acknowledged by him as entitled to rule" (Friedman 1973, p. 129). Now, to the extent that R has come to this conviction by himself or as a result of nongovernmental influence (e.g., upbringing, society), government P has authority, but no influence, over R. Indeed, if R contemplated some illegal action, his own general law-abiding disposition would be sufficient to make him comply in the end, and no governmental influence would be required. The Athenian government had authority over Socrates, the prototype of an autonomous person, who had independently formed the moral conviction that he ought to comply even with Athens's illegal measures (i.e., that he should not escape from prison even though he was convinced that his trial was illegal). The Athenian government had no influence over Socrates; it had only the power to punish him. If, on the other hand, R's belief that he ought to comply with governmental enactments had been instilled by government P—through rational persuasion or indoctrination—R is under P's authority *and* influence, and hence power.

2.2.2 Preventing

Just as exercising influence is a subclass of having influence, the concepts of coercing and restraining can be expanded into having coercing and restraining power. For the latter concept (which is, again, the more important one) the simpler expression of 'preventing' is readily available.

Definition: P prevents R from doing x iff P performs some action y that makes it impossible for R to do x.

Analogously, to say that P makes it necessary for R to do x means that P performs some action y such that x becomes unavoidable to R.

Making it—either literally or for all practical purposes—impossible or necessary for a person or group to act in a certain way is perhaps the most widespread form of power; yet it is often disregarded, or not clearly distinguished from actual coercion. Preventing someone from doing something without the latter's attempting to do it occurs more frequently than actually restraining him. If P, instead of erecting a No Trespassing sign, encloses his property by an unscalable wall, he acquires power over all whom he thereby has made unable to trespass. These include also those who do not even attempt to climb over the wall but who, were they to try, would be unsuccessful—if the prisoner first attempts to break out and then the guard pushes him back, the latter exercises power over the former by means of physical coercion. Normally, however, the guard first locks the door, so that the prisoner cannot get out. He thereby *physically prevents* him from breaking out, no matter whether or not the prisoner attempts to escape—in a dictatorship, penalties might be so severe and enforcement so effective that disobedience becomes practically impossible. Situations of so-called non–decision making, where P makes R realize that "it's of no use," also belong to this category, as we shall see.

Repeated persuasion may slide over into *manipulation*. Here R is no longer aware of P's influence action, and becomes psychologically unable to choose or even to perceive certain alternatives that, theoretically, remain open to him. Brainwashing is the most effective form of political control, because it can dispense with the machinery of deterrence.

Prevention covers not only impossibility in the strict sense, but also practical impossibility, i.e., making it so unpleasant or risky that a rational actor would give in. Economic control, whether by government, management or labor, buyers or sellers, consists essentially in closing certain alternatives, in the sense of making those alternatives so costly that it becomes practically impossible to adopt them. Thus, sellers, by imposing the price for a certain commodity, close all alternatives to prospective buyers except "taking it (at the established price) or leaving it" and make those who cannot afford the article at that price unable to buy it. On the other hand, buyers may gain control over sellers by making it practically unavoidable for them to lower the price of their product. Similarly, political parties and pressure groups may gain control over some branch of the government by preventing it from adopting certain policies. Just as there are no fixed boundaries between exercising control by deterrence, coercive threats, and physical coercion, it is not possible to determine in general where having influence ends and prevention begins.

Governmental power over its citizens consists most frequently of making it *legally impossible* for them to perform certain actions. By making divorce illegal, government has power over married couples wrt their not divorcing, without having to exercise power; and it has power in that respect even over those who do not so much as contemplate divorce. Other examples of legal impossibility are declaring certain types of contract null and void, canceling a franchise, not recognizing a foreign government. Just as prevention must be taken to include coercive threats, impossibility in the legal sense has been defined as comprising "not only strict impossibility, but impracticability because of the extreme and unreasonable difficulty, expense, injury or loss involved" (Restatement of the Law of Contracts, 1932, par. 454).[6]

Not enabling someone to do something is not the same as making him unable to do so. That P does not make it possible for R to do x means that it is not the case that P performs an action as a result of which R can do x. This does not constitute power. E.g., if R is locked in a room and P does not unlock the door, P does not gain power over R wrt his staying in the room. Otherwise, it would follow that everyone who fails to let R out has power over him wrt his staying in, and that could mean that practically everybody has power over him. However, abstaining from doing something that is a sufficient condition for making it possible for someone else to act in a certain way may be an instance of doing something that is a sufficient condition for his inability to do so. The prison guard who has the only key to the cell, by not opening it, prevents the prisoner from leaving and has power over him in that respect. The United States government, by not raising immigration quotas in the thirties and forties, prevented potential victims of the Nazi regime from reaching the United States and had power over them in that respect.

Making it possible for someone to do something is not an instance of power either, since it consists of opening a new alternative to him. Sometimes, however, P makes it necessary for R to do what he has enabled him to do. The Soviet government, by granting emigration visas to some of its Jewish citizens, makes it possible for them to leave their country (i.e., to leave or to stay), and then forces them to do so and, consequently, has power over them in that respect.

In analogy to the concept of exercising control, that of having control can now be defined as follows:

Definition: P has control over R's not doing x iff P has influence over R's not doing x or prevents R from doing x.

2.2.3 Punishability

Having punitive power is related to punishing like having influence to influencing, and preventing to restraining. To make it punishable for someone or—more frequently—for a group of persons to perform a certain type of action is to do something such that, were they to act that way, they would suffer punishment for having done so.

Definition: P makes it punishable for R to do x iff P performs some action y such that , were R to do something held by P to constitute offense x, P would punish R for having done x.

In the paradigmatic situation, 'P' symbolizes a government or some of its branches or officials, and 'R' ranges over persons over whom P has authority. What does action y of P consist of? While to punish is to apply a preexisting rule, making a certain kind of action punishable involves the enactment of such a rule. However, by itself, enacting, e.g., a penal law characterizes actions that are illegal, not actions punishable in the behavioral sense with which we are here concerned. By enacting speeding laws, the legislature makes it *illegal* for any driver to speed; i.e., all drivers are liable to be fined if they speed. But the legislature makes speeding *punishable* not for all drivers, but only for those who are actually being fined for having speeded and for those who would be punished if they speeded. At least in theory, it is possible to estimate the percentage not only of speeders, but also of those among them who are being apprehended and fined. If this number is 40 percent, then the legislature has punitive power over 40 percent of all speeders, actual (past and present) and potential (future). Action y of P consists thus both of enacting a rule, such as a law involving some penalty, and of having a general disposition to enforce it, i.e., to punish offenders. That the legislature has a certain amount of punitive power over speeders implies not only that this agency has enacted a measure to the effect that speeders are liable to a fine, but also that it tends to impose the fine on a certain proportion of drivers who speed.

There is a significant difference between having control and punishability. From 'P has influence over R's not doing x' or 'P prevents R from doing x' we can deduce that R does not do x. (And from 'P punishes R for having done x' it follows that R is believed by P to have done x.) But we cannot infer what R will do from 'P makes it punishable for R to do x'. In this case, we can deduce that R will either refrain from doing x or do x and suffer punishment.

Punishability, threatening to punish, and punishing are three different power relations, involving the same power holder, but different groups of respondents. By enacting and enforcing speeding laws, the legislature acquires power—*punitive power*—over those speeders who are fined and over those drivers who would be punished if they speeded. The purpose of enacting and enforcing penal legislation is usually to deter people from violating the law. By means of its speeding laws, the legislature implicitly threatens to punish speeders, and thereby acquires power—*deterring power* over those who comply to avoid the fine and over those who would be deterred by the penalty if they intended to speed. By punishing speeders, the legislature *exercises power* over actual speeders who are actually apprehended. (In a governmental setting, there is usually a "separation of power" between legislators and those officials who apply the laws to offenders.)

We have noticed that P may exercise power over R by threatening to punish him or by promising to reward him; both are instances of the exercise of influence. But there is no such parallelism between punishability and reward-ability—making it rewardable for someone to do something. Punishability is a form of prevention, and hence of having power, since it closes the alternative of performing the punishable action without being punished. But if it is the case that P would reward R were R to do x, P does not prevent R from doing x without being rewarded. R normally has the option of doing x and refusing the reward, whereas he (probably) cannot escape the penalty when he performs a punishable action. Instead of closing an alternative to R, P provides him with an additional one: R has the choice of not doing x, doing x and being rewarded, and doing x and not accepting the reward.[7] Thus, in contradistinction to promising a reward and to punishability, rewardability is not a form of power—except in the case of what we may call coercive rewardability, which makes noncompliance practically impossible.[8]

THREE

Different Interpretations of Power

ON THE BASIS of the analysis provided in the preceding chapter, it will turn out that social power is not synonymous with ability or with social causation. Nor is the proposed explication compatible with certain narrower definitions: power as excluding rational persuasion or offers of reward or unintended control or absence of conflict of intentions or of interests. In the present chapter, I shall argue against these interpretations and in favor of mine.

3.1 POWER AND ABILITY

I had indicated previously (1.2.2) that the word 'power' may refer not only to the three-term relation of social power, 'P has power over R's doing x', but also to the two-term relation, 'P has power to do x'. This means, quite simply, that P can do x.

That I have previously dealt with power only as a relationship of interaction does not imply that I consider the concept of power as ability to be less important in the context of political inquiry. There are, however, several reasons why I think it inadvisable to use 'power' in the sense of 'ability to do something' in our technical language.

First, the defining expression 'P can do x' is here simpler than 'P has the power to do x', the expression to be defined. Using only the former phrase just simplifies matters. Second, using the same word, in this case 'power', to stand for two different concepts easily leads to mistaking one for the other. Third, and most important, there is the danger of confusing 'P has power over R wrt x' not only with 'P can do x (himself)', but also with 'P has the *ability* to exercise power over R wrt x'. And from here it is only one step to *defining* power as the ability to exercise it, as do many authors: "Power is the ability to exercise influence" (Riker 1964, p. 347). Power is "the possession by one actor (A) of the means of modifying the conduct of another actor (B)..." (Barry 1976, p. 70). Power "is the capacity to cause someone to do something he would not otherwise do" (Held 1972, p. 49).[1] True, whoever *exercises* power also *has* power and also *can* have (and exercise) it. But not necessarily vice versa. P may have the resources (e.g., wealth) enabling him to acquire influence over a wide group (e.g., through buying a TV station). But P does not *have* such power unless he actually *does* avail himself of that possibility ('performs some action y...', e.g., acquires a TV station).

Defining power as the ability to exercise it easily leads to a confusion between power and the bases of power, "resources such as wealth, authority, reputation, attractiveness, friendship and physical location.... It is the possession of such resources that confers power or, if you like, that *is* power" (Goldman 1972, p. 229). Such a power resource as wealth confers power; but it *is not* power. Wealth, unlike power, is something one "possesses." For P to exercise and even to *have power without exercising it*, it is not sufficient that he has the resources enabling him to acquire it; he must actually avail himself of such means.

Here are some other illustrations. That the United States has power over Mexico's foreign policy implies not merely that the former is capable of, e.g., deterring or preventing the latter from joining the Soviet bloc; it means that the United States has acquired and now possesses sufficient military and economic resources so that, in the (very unlikely) event that Mexico attempted or even merely contemplated joining the Soviet bloc, the United States *would* prevent or deter Mexico from doing so. Most who have the technical skill and the psychological stamina to hijack a plane would never do so; and only someone who actually hijacks a plane gains control over passengers and crew, making certain actions practically impossible or necessary for them. Governments have the legal authority to lower speed limits and, hence, the capacity to have and exercise power over drivers in that respect. But the government does not *have* such power unless such legislation has been enacted. "To say that the policeman has the power to stop the traffic is to say that *if* some traffic

30

came along and he held up his hand it would stop" (Gibson 1971, p. 105). More precisely: To say that policeman P has power with respect to R's stopping when P raises his hand is to say that P has acceded to and now occupies the office of a policeman so that R would stop upon P's raising his hand, even if R had at first contemplated going on. Before P became a policeman, he supposedly possessed the ability to become one and to control traffic; but he did not have the power to stop cars "any more than the present possible Presidents of 1990 have now any . . . one of the special powers of the President then" (Braybrooke 1973, p. 371).[2]

But why not take power as the ability to realize some outcome as the overarching concept and social power as a subcategory, an approach favored by Alvin Goldman? He takes as the expression to be defined, "S has power w.r.t. issue E" (1972, p. 225), where "'E' stands for an issue, e.g., whether or not it rains at a particular time and place" (p. 223). Roughly, according to Goldman, Smith has power over this issue if rain would occur provided Smith wanted it. One actor's power over another actor can be subsumed under this concept, Goldman argues: "Smith has power *over Jones*, we might say, if and only if Smith has power w.r.t. issues that affect Jones—i.e., that make a difference in Jones' welfare," e.g., if Smith has power over "certain objects or events which [Jones] desires" (p. 260). Later I shall criticize definitions of social power in terms of the respondent's welfare or desires. Here I am only concerned with "power wrt an issue" as the expression to be defined. This formulation cannot bring out what seems to me the important distinguishing feature of *social* power; namely, that it refers to an interaction relation, a relationship between some action y of P and some possible *action* x of R ("were R to do or attempt or intend x . . ."). Nor does it enable us to make the other important distinction I just illustrated, that between the power an actor has and his ability to acquire (and exercise) it.

3.2 Power and Causation
3.2.1 Power Identified with Causation
"[F]or the assertion, 'A has power over B', we can substitute the assertion, 'A's behavior causes B's behavior'" (H. Simon

1957, p. 5). Does my own definition of exercising control by the disjunction of influencing and coercing make this concept coextensive with social causation? It has been held that I have "construe[d] 'influence' and 'coercion' so broadly as to cover virtually any social interchange in which the behavior of one person determines the behavior of another. It is difficult to see what kind of social behavior would *not* qualify as an exercise of power" (Ball 1978, p. 615). This is a weighty criticism; if warranted, we could dispense with the concept of exercising power (in the sense of control) entirely, and use only that of social determination. My reply is that there are many kinds of social causation not covered by either the concept of influencing or that of coercing as I have defined them. We have seen that there is neither influence nor coercion, and hence neither control nor power, in all situations in which R's behavior, while determined by the behavior of others, cannot be causally linked to the behavior of a *determinate* person or group, but in which the causal chain must, at least for practical purposes, stop at impersonal factors such as inflation, unemployment, overpopulation, lack of resources—to take just a few calamitous examples. Nor is there a control relation when P causes R, not to *do* something, but to be better or worse off. Only when P's depriving R is an instance of punishment is there exercise of power (but not of control). There are also instances of interpersonal causation not involving actions of either P or R—e.g., driver P has a blowout, which causes R's car to collide with P's. Here the causal relation holds, strictly speaking, not between P and R, but between P's tire and R's car. But we do say, in a loose way, that P caused R's accident. However, the causal relation is not one of coercion or control or power, since there is no action of P (nor of R).

The concept of power, as I have defined it, is therefore not synonymous with social causation; nor is it the case that "power relations are logically a subset of causal relations" (Dahl 1968, p. 410), since there can be causation without power. There can also be power without causation. True, whenever P *exercises control* over R's not doing x, P performs some action y that causes R not to do x. But if P *has* power over R's not doing x without actually exercising it, R's not doing x is not the causal result of any action P does perform. Here causation is not actual, only hypothetical. The advantage of the concept of having power is precisely that it covers situations in which R neither does nor attempts nor even contemplates doing x, and where there is no punitive or restraining or deterring or dissuading action on P's part. Power and causation are overlapping categories.

3.2.2 Cause as Defining Condition of Exercising Power

Exercising power is the area where power and causation overlap. The word 'causing' does, indeed, occur in the defining expressions of 'influencing', 'coercing', and 'punishing'. To assert that R's action x was influenced by some action y of P is not merely to describe what R did, but also to provide at least a partial *explanation* of P's conduct. (Why did R do x? Because P influenced him to do x.) I shall indicate later that my use of 'causing to do' does not commit me to the "covering law model" of explanation in the area of human action in general and of political interaction in particular. At this point the question arises: in what sense do I use the word 'cause'? Here we must distinguish between cause as sufficient and cause as necessary condition, and between strict and probabilistic causality.

That a certain event C causes another E means either that C is a sufficient, or that it is a necessary condition for the occurrence of E, or that it is both. A sufficient condition of a given event E is a set of circumstances such that, if C obtained, E had to occur. A necessary condition of a given event E is a set of circumstances C without which E could not have occurred. For example, if a metal wire is heated, it will lengthen (and if it does not lengthen, it was not heated); heating is a sufficient condition for an increase in the wire's length, but not a necessary one: suspending a heavy load from the wire would have the same effect. Conversely, the presence of oxygen is a necessary, but not a sufficient, condition of fire.

When dealing with human affairs, we do not use the concept of strict causality, but speak of cause in a probabilistic sense. Given the notions of sufficient conditon and necessary condition a probabilistic interpretation, we can say: A prob-abilistically sufficient condition for an event E (e.g., R's doing x) is a set of circumstances C that make E highly prob-able, and a probabilistically necessary condition of E is a set of circumstances C without which the occurrence of E would be highly improbable. If I say that P influenced R to do x, there are two assertions I am making with certainty: (1) that P did y, and (2) that R did x. I also assert (3) that P's action y was at least one of the causes of R's doing x; but this I assert not with certainty, but with a relatively high or low degree of probability. That P exercised influence over R's action x is then a probabilistic causal explanation of R's conduct. That P will influence R to do x involves three predictions, all of them of a probabilistic kind: (1) R will probably do x; (2) P will probably do y; (3) R's action x will probably be the causal effect of P's action y. Similarly, that P will punish R for having done x means that P will probably find R guilty of having done x, and that this belief will probably cause P to perform some action y that will probably deprive R.

Even more obviously, the concept of having power refers to causality in the probabilistic sense. To assert that P has power over R wrt his not doing x means that P performs (or has already performed) some action y such that, were R to intend or attempt or do x, this action y of P would probably cause R to change his mind or to become unable to do x or to suffer punishment for having done so.

3.2.3 Control: Sufficient Condition

It is in the sense of necessary condition that most writers implicitly refer to causation when interpreting the notions of exercising or having control (or power when used as a synonym of control), "A has power over B to the extent that he can get B to do something that B would not otherwise do" (Dahl 1957, p. 203); i.e., had B acted otherwise (had he not done x), A would not have had power over him. Similarly, "Presumably, we observe the influence of A over B by noting the differences between the way B actually behaves and the way he *would* behave if A were not present" (Simon 1957, p. 66). "Power . . . is a capacity to cause someone to do some-thing he would not otherwise do" (Held 1972, p. 49; see

Benn 1967, p. 424). If R would have acted differently had P not intervened, then P's actual influence or coercive action y was a necessary condition for R's actual conduct.

This interpretation makes it possible in certain cases to ascertain and even to measure the degree of P's control over R by the magnitude of the deviation of R's actual behavior from what he would have done, had P not intervened. Yet, the assertion that P influenced or coerced R to do x is perfectly compatible with the contrary-to-fact assumption that R would have acted the same way without P's control action. Someone who asserts that the United States, by dropping the A-bomb on Hiroshima, influenced Japan to capitulate, claims only the following: Given that the United States government dropped the bomb, it became highly probable that Japan would decide to give up. That is to say, the former event was a probabilistic sufficient condition of the latter. The claim is not, and it need not be the case, that Japan would have continued to fight had Hiroshima not been destroyed. Japan might have come around on its own to surrender, or the Soviets might have deterred the Japanese from going on. This interpretation not only captures what we mean, but has a practical advantage in the context of empirical research. Sufficient conditions are usually easier to establish than necessary ones, at least in the area of human interaction. From the fact that the United States dropped the A-bomb (as a threat of still greater harm), Japan's capitulation could be predicted fairly safely; and this was actually the expectation of American policymakers. The hypothesis that Japan would otherwise not have capitulated is much more difficult to substantiate and need not be established to ascertain that the United States exercised influence, control, and power over Japan in this instance.

Similarly, John F. Kennedy, by means of the televised debates, influenced a sufficient number of voters in his favor to make him win the election. To verify this statement, we need only to show that his television performance was a probabilisitically sufficient condition for their vote. It would be much more difficult to demonstrate that, without these debates, a sufficient number of voters would have voted against him to defeat him; nor would it be necessary to establish this hypothetical fact to substantiate the hypothesis under consideration.

Here is a counterexample. Election officer P places R's name on the voting register. This is a necessary condition for R's voting and also for his voting Democratic, but not a sufficient condition for either. By registering R, P does not influence R to vote (R may abstain), let alone to vote Democratic. P makes it merely possible for R to vote, and we have seen that enabling someone to do something is not an instance of control.

Coercion seems to be different from influence in this respect. If R actually attempts to do something that P hinders him from accomplishing, does not that imply that R would have carried out what he had set out to do, had P not interfered? It would therefore seem that "a further requirement for a person being coerced is that he would have chosen differently had he not been threatened" (Bayles 1972, p. 19); hence, P's coercive action must be a necessary as well as a sufficient condition for the failure of R's attempt.

Now, in the dramatic cases that immediately come to mind, such as the gunman's coercive threats, we do indeed suppose that the victim would have kept his purse had there been no coercion. But we cannot, and need not, make this assumption in every instance. There are situations in which, even if P had not restrained R from doing x, R might have suddenly decided to give up his attempt to do x, either as a result of his own change of mind or because someone other than P influenced or coerced him not to do x. And if we subsume threats of severe deprivation under coercion, such threats should not be interpreted differently depending on the degree of their severity. Coercion, like influence, requires only that P's action y be a sufficient condition for the failure of R's attempt to do x. Thus, while P's placing R's name on the voting list is a necessary but not a sufficient condition for R's voting, denying R's request for registration is a sufficient condition for R's not voting but not a necessary one, since R might have abstained anyhow. In this case P restrains R from voting and exercises power over him in this respect.

Similarly, 'P prevents R from doing x' means that some

action y of P is a probabilistically sufficient condition for R's inability to do x, that is, for R's not doing x even if he attempted to. P's erecting a high wall makes it highly probable that R cannot trespass. But P's action need not be a sufficient condition for R's not actually trespassing. If R does not attempt to trespass or does not even contemplate trespassing, his lack of inclination is a sufficient condition for his not doing so, and it is trivially true that he does not trespass (unless accidentally). Yet P's action y is not a necessary condition either for R's not doing x or for R's inability to do so. Indeed, even if P had not erected the wall, R might not have trespassed, perhaps because he did not attempt (and perhaps did not even contemplate) doing so; and R might not have been able to trespass, perhaps because he had broken a leg. All these hypothetical cases are compatible with the assertion that P made it impossible for R to trespass (i.e., prevented him from doing so) and had power over him with respect to his not trespassing.

We may, accordingly, restate the definitions of the concept of control as follows: P exercises control over R's not doing x iff P performs some action y that is a probabilistically sufficient condition for R's decision not to do x or for the failure of R's attempt at doing x. P has control over R's not doing x iff P performs some action y such that, were R to intend to do x, P's action y would be a probabilistically sufficient condition for R's deciding not to do x or for his inability to do x.

3.2.4 Punishability: Necessary and Sufficient Condition

In contrast to exercising and having control, punishment and punishability involve causation in the sense of both necessary and sufficient condition. The concept of punishment implicitly refers to three such relations. (1) R does something (drives) that causes P (a policeman) to form the belief that R did x (speeded). Had R not acted in a certain way, P would probably not have believed that R did x; and the fact that R acted that way made it likely that P would interpret R's conduct as an instance of x. However, this causal connection is not, and need not be, mentioned explicitly in the definition of the concept of punishment. (2) P's belief that R did x causes him to perform some action y (impose a fine on R). Without P's belief that R did x, P would probably not have done y; and having formed that belief, it became probable that he would. (3) P's action y causes R some harm. Without P's punitive action, R most probably would not feel deprived (probably, but not certainly; someone other than P might have harmed him instead, whether or not as a punishment for his having done x or something else); and the fact that P did y made it highly probable that R would feel worse off.

The definition of punishment may thus be restated in more precise terms as follows: P punishes R for having done x iff P's belief that R committed offense x is a probabilistically necessary and sufficient condition for R's being deprived.

The same considerations apply to the concept of punishability: P makes it punishable for R to do x iff P performs some action y that is a probabilistically necessary and sufficient condition for the following: were P to believe that R committed offense x, this would be a probabilistically necessary and sufficient condition for his performing some action y that would deprive R (strictly speaking, that would be a probabilistically necessary and sufficient condition for R's being deprived).

3.3 POWER AND PERSUASION

According to the proposed definitional scheme, persuasion is a form of influence and influence a form of power. Some writers would go along that far, but would be reluctant to draw the logical conclusion that persuasion is a form of power. At least persuasion by rational argument is not, they argue. "[T]o offer a man good reasons for doing something is not to exercise power over him, although it may influence his decision" (Benn 1967, p. 424). According to this interpretation, influence and power are overlapping categories: power comprises coercion and influence by means of deterrence and deception, but to use truthful information to modify someone else's choice is not an exercise of power.

This categorization has been defended, often implicitly, by appeal to common usage. "The president's implied or threatened use of his power to veto legislation may influence congressional action; but this is not to say that he therefore has power *over* their actions" (Ball 1975, p. 212). But ordinary language is here, as so often, an unsure guide. We *do* ordinarily say that the president exercises power over those congressmen whom he succeeds in dissuading from voting in favor of some bill by signifying his intention to veto it or sending a message recommending its rejection, whether by rational or irrational arguments. We do consider the controllers of mass media as exercising power over those whom they persuade, either by "honest" or "dishonest" means, e.g., to vote for a certain candidate. Later we shall examine another reason for this use of language: that to manipulate or coerce or punish is somehow wrong (at least prima facie), whereas to persuade by means of rational arguments is laudable.

There is a similar tendency to subsume under *coercion* not only coercive but even mild threats of punishment.[3] It would then follow that, if I keep within the speed limits to avoid a fine, I am being coerced to slow down or am restrained, rather than deterred, from speeding. From here it is only one step to take threats of sanctions as the defining characteristic not only of coercion, but of power itself. E.g., "A power relation can exist only if one of the parties can threaten to invoke sanctions" (Bachrach and Baratz 1970, p. 21). But the equation deterrence = coercion = power would leave out three other power processes: influence through persuasion, physical coercion, and punishment.

From the point of view of an effective language of political inquiry, the decisive question is: what is more important, the differences between rational persuasion on one hand and deception/deterrence/coercion on the other, or the similarities between all these relationships of interaction? Different political scientists may give different answers, depending mainly upon their research topic. But all will agree that we need a single concept bringing together all methods by which one actor determines another actor's conduct, whether he uses rational persuasion or other devices.[4] What label we choose does not matter. The term 'power' is readily available.

It has been objected that

> any definition of power which, focusing exclusively upon supposed "similarities," glosses over—or renders otiose by fiat—the differences between (say) rational persuasion and coercive manipulation, leaves the political scientist ill-equipped to *describe* (much less evaluate) what he sees. (Ball 1978, p. 616)

My reply is that to subsume both rational persuasion (e.g., by the physician) and coercive threats (e.g., by the gunman) under the concept of exercising power is not to "gloss over" the dissimilarities between these two subcategories, let alone "to ignore or obliterate them" (Ball 1978, p. 618) (just as to speak of killing is not to ignore the difference between murder and execution).

The question still remains which distinction is more important, that between persuasion by reason on one hand and all other forms of influence *and* constraint on the other, or that between influence by whatever means on one hand and coercion on the other. From the point of view of political inquiry, it seems to me the latter difference is more significant, because it coincides with the distinction between social power and social freedom. We shall see that, by restraining R from doing x, P not only exercises power over R in that respect, but also makes R unfree to do x. By influencing R not to do x, whether by rational argument or by other means, P, while again exercising power over R's not doing x, does not restrict R's freedom either to do or not to do x.[5]

3.4 Power and Exchange

I have defined influence (and hence power) as including both threats of punishment (deterrence) and offers of reward (inducement), and coercion as comprising both coercive threats and irresistible offers. So do other writers. "[A]s an inducement to accept an offer approaches a high level, it approaches coercion proportionately" (Held 1972, p. 57). Similarly, in the words of the United States Supreme Court, "The power to confer or withhold unlimited benefits is the power to coerce or destroy" (United States v. Butler, 297 U.S. 1 [1936]).

Others have argued against considering rewards of any kind as coercive. "[C]oercion involves threats and threats refer to harms, not benefits" (Bayles 1972, p. 23; see also Nozick 1969, p. 458). "The mere gaining of a good, no matter how great, does not force one to do anything" (Gert 1972, p. 36). But it seems to me that offering water to someone stranded in the desert, provided he acts in a certain way, amounts to threatening him with severe deprivation if he does not and constitutes an exercise of power through coercive threats. (See 2.1.2.)

Still others hold that promises of reward (except perhaps irresistible ones) should not be subsumed under power (Benn 1967, p. 425; Easton 1953, p. 144). Again, it is probably the negative connotation of 'power' that accounts for the tendency to associate this word with threatened deprivations but not with promised benefits. From an analytic point of view, it is surely more consistent to subsume invoking positive as well as negative sanctions under power. Whether the bribing of some official by an aircraft manufacturer coerces or merely influences him to buy its planes is arguable; that it is an exercise of power is beyond doubt. "[C]ompliance is compliance whether it is induced or coerced" (Barry 1976, p. 92; see Baldwin 1971, pp. 19–38).

Not considering inducements as forms of power easily leads to denying that exchange relations constitute power relations. This view is often defended by the argument that exchange is a symmetrical relation, whereas unilateral power is asymmetrical.

The latter is undoubtedly true. Unilateral power relations are asymmetrical, like 'father of' (if A is the father of B, B is not the father of A), not symmetrical, like 'married to' (if A is married to B, B is married to A). 'Power' is asymmetrical for the simple reason that, if P has power over R's doing x, it is *logically* impossible that R has power over P wrt *the same action* x, since x is an action of R, not of P. 'Power' is sometimes considered asymmetrical for a different reason, namely, because power consists of "interactions in which abilities to produce intended effects and to derive benefits are unequally distributed. This is precisely what is meant by 'asymmetric' relations" (Eckstein 1973, p. 1146). No, it is not.

'Asymmetrical' and 'symmetrical' are *formal* properties of relations, and like all logical properties, they hold independently of the meanings of the words denoting the related items.[6]

While it is generally agreed that unilateral power is an asymmetrical relation (sometimes for the wrong reason, as we just noticed), it is sometimes claimed that reciprocal power relations are symmetrical. "Political reality obviously includes a number of symmetrical, reciprocal influence relations: for example, bargaining, the exchange of leadership for support, and arms races" (Alker 1969, p. 9). Similarly, Eckstein maintains that buyer-seller exchange relations are symmetric (1973, p. 1147). Here again, a failure to be clear about the logical structure of the various power concepts leads to a mistaken view. Reciprocal influence and control relationships are not symmetrical either. Exchange relations, for example, do not consist of one symmetrical relation, but of two asymmetrical relations, involving two different actions (of the same pair of actors). A induces B to do x1, and B induces A to do x2. Both A and B assume here the roles of both P and R, but wrt two different actions. Thus, in a commercial transaction, A offers his product to B to influence B to pay him a certain sum, and B offers A a certain price to influence A to sell him the product.[7] Similarly, one can interpret conflict situations like "Soviet-American nuclear deterrence as two *separate* and relatively successful influence attempts" (Baldwin 1978, p. 1235; italics added). Similarly, the employer induces prospective employees to perform some specified task by promising them some specified remuneration, and the latter induce the former to hire them in exchange for doing the work. (After the contract of sale or employment is concluded, each party can *deter* the other from violating the contract by appeal to public authority.) By joining a private association, "the member agrees to submit to organizational authority in return for whatever benefits he derives from membership" (Cartwright 1965, p. 16), and the managers of the organization induce prospective members to join and submit to its regulations by promising these benefits. The same analysis applies to the exchange of bribes for police protection or of testimony for immunity from prosecution. Even the holdup situation can be analyzed in terms of reciprocal influence: the gunman induces his victim to hand over the money by promising to spare his life, and the victim persuades the gunman to let him live by promising to hand over the money. It makes no difference from the present point of view whether the benefits are unequally distributed or whether the exchange results in an equilibrium. Hence, I do not agree that "interdependence and mutual influence of equal strength indicate lack of power" (Blau 1964, pp. 117–18). On the contrary, "*all* exchange relationships can be described in terms of conventional power concepts" (Baldwin 1978, p. 1229; italics added)—namely, in terms of two power relations pointing in opposite directions, both of them asymmetrical and both involving influence by inducements.

3.5 Power and Intention
3.5.1 Power Defined as Intentional Control
I have defined punishment as involving P's intention to deprive R. On the other hand, the proposed definitions of influence and coercion do not refer to P's intention. Yet control, and hence power in general, has often been defined as involving P's intentional influence or coercive action; e.g., power is "a relationship in which one person or group is able to determine the actions of another in the direction of the former's own ends" (Easton 1953, p. 144). Power, at least "[i]n the narrow and more common sense of exercising power over another" (Bayles 1972, p. 26), requires that "X intends that Y do A" (p. 24). "[T]here can be no *un*intentional or 'unconscious' *exercise* of power" (Ball 1975, p. 202; italics in original). "The central idea in the concept of power, I suggest, is connected with getting what one wants" (Goldman 1972, p. 222).

No doubt, the paradigmatic case of exercising control, especially in the political sphere, is: R wants to do x; this is contrary to some purpose of P; P therefore wants R not to do x; P therefore, by deliberately performing some action y, influences or coerces R not to do x. According to Benn, to speak of unintended power would lead to "some odd results. Instead of suffering a *loss* of power, the crashing financier who brings down thousands with him in his fall would be exercising a power that is perhaps greater than ever before" (1967, p. 426). Nor would Benn characterize as powerful the careless smoker who unintentionally starts fires (1967, p. 426) (and presumably thereby compels others to flee). According to Ball, if R's action x is based on his *mistaken* belief that P wants him to do x, there is a power relation only if "C has (1) deliberately inculcated this belief, or has (2) knowingly taken advantage of a pre-existing belief of R's that C knows to be mistaken" (1975, p. 202). It is surely contrary to common usage to say that P exercises control over R if he causes him to do not just something P does not intend that he do, but something *contrary* to P's desire. "[I]f the unintended effect the parent has on the child is to stiffen the child's determination to be as different from the parent as possible, such influence would not be taken as an instance of power" (Partridge 1970, p. 26). Or take the manufacturer who cuts his prices and thereby practically compels his competitors to lower theirs, which is the opposite of what he would want them to do (Bayles 1972, p. 26); or Hitler's bombing of English cities, which stiffened their inhabitants' resistance.

But here again, ordinary language is inconsistent. We do in certain cases say that P exercises power by persuading R to do x even if P does not intend to do so or does not even know that he does. There is the example of "[t]he boss who comes to work in a grumpy mood [and who] may not intend to induce his secretary to treat him gently" (Dahl and Lindblom 1953, p. 96), but who does. Karl Marx, through his writings, influenced the actions as well as the beliefs of political leaders of subsequent generations and often in directions of which he would probably have disapproved. Partridge, while hesitating to subsume such cases under power, does characterize as a power phenomenon the unconscious tendency of elite groups to persuade lower strata to adopt their own customs and ideas (1970, p. 36). And even Benn wonders whether "a ruling elite that neither knows nor cares about the effects of its actions on other classes" does not exercise power over them (1967, p. 424). Or take the pollsters who predicted that Truman would lose the presidential election of 1948 and thereby quite unintentionally influenced voters—to disconfirm that prediction. Did they not exercise power over voters who voted for Truman because of these polls? Or consider some other cases of unintended deterrence: Senator R votes against foreign aid because he erroneously believes that the majority P of his constituency will not reelect him if he votes in favor of it. Driver R slows down in the mistaken belief that driver P in the car behind him is a policeman. We are inclined to say that the constituents exercised power with respect to Senator R's vote, and driver P over driver R's slowing down, even though R's belief that P wants him to act in a certain way is mistaken and not deliberately formed by P. Similarly, if coercion is defined as the use of threats "to change B's behavior in accordance with A's intentions" (Wertheimer 1972, p. 222), we will have to deny that an oil-producing country that raises oil prices and thereby unintentionally prevents developing nations from buying fertilizer exercises power over them in that respect. Yet, we are inclined to regard such a relation as one of power. Here are some examples of P's preventing R from doing x (and thereby acquiring power over him) without intending to do so. The winner in an athletic competition has power over the losers. The buyer of the last theater ticket has power over those standing in line behind him. A country occupying conquered territory has power over other states wrt not extending *their* power over the region it has occupied. Even cases in which P causes R to act contrary to P's intentions are sometimes subsumed under power. Dahl characterizes such instances as "negative influence" (1976, p. 43) or negative power (Dahl uses the terms interchangeably).

Taking common usage as guide confronts us then with a dilemma. If we define exercising control as intentional influence or coercion, we cannot capture the "power" of such actors in our examples as the ruling elite, the pollsters, the erring senator, or countries raising oil prices. This definition is surely too narrow. But the proposed interpretation may be considered too broad, since it applies to our examples of the crashing financier and the careless smoker. It also covers situations in which P causes R to act contrary to P's desire, and that is its major defect. It could be corrected by modifying our definition as follows: 'P exercises control over R's doing x' means that P influences or coerces R to do x *unless* x is *contrary* to what P wants R to do. (Situations in which R is merely made by P to do something P did not intend would constitute power relations according to this modified definition.) This solution strikes me as complicated and awkward.

From the point of view of an effective language of political inquiry, there are strong reasons against the narrow interpretation of the concept of power. Intending (or desiring or wanting) to bring something about and, in particular, intending that others act in some specific way is too ambiguous a notion to be included in the defining expression of another concept if it can be avoided. Intending something implies predicting that it would occur if one acted in a certain way, but an actor can normally foresee only a limited range of the consequences of his contemplated action. In order to ascertain that P exercised power over R's doing x, the researcher would have to determine whether R's doing x was among the consequences of P's action y that P foresaw—and intended. This is often difficult, especially in the case of influence. While the act of communicating is usually done with some intention, the message being communicated may have an effect quite different from that intended by the sender, as some of our examples illustrate. It may be practically impossible to figure out whether the effects P's communication had on R's behavior corresponded to P's intentions.[8]

Furthermore, the unintended effects of political decisions on the political actions of others are often of particular interest to political scientists. I agree therefore that "a realistic or adequate study of political or social power cannot afford to discount unintended effects" (Partridge 1970, p. 25). However, "[s]ince most people are interested in the desire for power, undesired power is easily forgotten" (Gibson 1971, p. 104).

3.5.2 Power Defined in Terms of P's Preferences
A variant of the view that power requires R's behavior to conform to P's intentions has been proposed by Jack Nagel: "A power relation, actual or potential, is an actual or potential causal relation between the preferences of an actor re-

garding an outcome and the outcome itself" (1975, p. 29). As we are concerned with a particular kind of outcome, namely, another actor's behavior, "[t]he statement 'A exercised power over B' is to be construed as 'A's preferences caused B's behavior'" (p. 30).

Now, "preferences" do not by themselves cause "outcomes." My wish that you do something does not cause you to do it—unless one believes in telepathy. My desire that you do something may motivate *me* to do—e.g., say—something that will in turn cause you to do it. Nagel acknowledges that the causal link between P's preference and R's response is often an indirect one, that P's desire that R do x may motivate P to perform some action y that in turn constitutes "the proximate cause of B's response" (p. 28). But there are situations in which P, while wanting R to do x, does not perform any overt influence action y; but R does x just the same, as he realizes that this is what P wants him to do and anticipates P's negative reaction should he fail to conform to P's desire. E.g., Senator R votes against foreign aid, as he believes—this time correctly—that he would otherwise be defeated by his constituents P in the next election. Nagel holds that, in such cases of "anticipated reactions," the intermediate variable "A's behavior (influence attempt)" is to be replaced by "B's anticipation of A's future reaction" (p. 28). It is to capture such situations that Nagel considers it necessary to "define power as the causation of outcomes by preferences" (p. 24).

It seems to me that cases of anticipated reactions are covered by the proposed definition. R's belief that P would, e.g., punish him if he failed to do x is necessarily based on and hence caused by something P did. Some voters must have somehow expressed their views on foreign aid or a lobbyist told Senator R about it, so that he became aware of their opposition and voted accordingly. Nagel himself quotes Shannon and Weaver as pointing out that communication as a form of action must be interpreted very broadly as including "all of the procedures by which one mind may affect another" (p. 33). But if 'P's influence action y' is interpreted that broadly (and I pointed out that I think it should be), then the proposed definition surely applies to anticipated reactions.

Furthermore, Nagel's definition, while unnecessary to cover anticipated reactions, leaves out situations that must be subsumed under the concept of power. Nagel indicates correctly that, according to his definition, there is no power relation between P and R if R *mistakenly* believes that P wants him to do x and acts accordingly, since R's action x is then not the outcome of P's preference (p. 33). Yet, as I pointed out, the concept of power should apply at least to cases in which P has no preference as to what R should do.

3.5.3 Power Defined as Implying
Conflict with R's Intentions

Writers like those examined in the two preceding sections interpret power as conflict of wants, wills, intentions, or preferences. Looking at the power relation from the point of view of R rather than of P, they conceive power as P's ability to cause R to act not only in conformity with P's will, but also contrary to R's own original intention. Thus, Max Weber defined power as "the probability that one actor within a social relation will be in a position to carry out his own will despite resistance" (1947, p. 52). Similarly, according to Benn, one of the main features of power is "a conflict of interest or wishes engendering a resistance that the initiator overcomes" (1967, p. 424). Now, we have seen that P may, e.g., influence R to do x without intending to do so. In such a case there is no conflict between the wishes of P and R. But the question still remains whether power, intended or unintended by P, implies a shift of *R's* intentions.

The actual exercise of coercion does indeed involve a conflict of P's and R's wills. There is an attempt at resistance on R's part that P overcomes. But none of the other forms of power requires a change of R's intentions. P may exercise influence by shaping as well as by changing R's desires. If P persuades R to vote Democratic, P exercises power in this respect not only if R originally intended to vote Republican, but also if R had no preference and was undecided. Exchanges like commercial transactions that, as we saw, are best interpreted as two separate and reciprocal power relations need not involve changes of intentions either. At least when prices are set in advance, as in stores, customer and store manager influence each other to sell and to buy, respectively, at the fixed price, and that is precisely what each is out to do from the start. And whenever P has control over R's doing x without needing to exercise it, R does what he originally intends to do. Wrt not committing murder, government has control over everyone under its jurisdiction except murderers, including all those who have no intention of committing the crime but who, were they to contemplate such an action, would change their mind in view of the law and its enforcement. Most citizens obey most laws of most governments not so much because they are being deterred by threats of sanctions from doing what they really would like to do, but because they consider the government's power legitimate and therefore intend to comply from the start.

Let us remember in this connection that the concept of intention is rather ambiguous. In one sense, even the victim of a holdup does what he wants to do under the circumstances, namely to hand over the money rather than risk his life; and this is also what the holdup man wants him to do. In another sense, the victim acts against his will, i.e., under duress; he would obviously have preferred to keep the money.

One last objection. If 'P exercises power over R's doing x' implies that P causes R to act against his will, then P's power act y is a necessary condition for R's doing x; i.e., had P not done y, R would have acted differently, namely in accordance with his original intention. I explained why I think that power had better be defined in terms of sufficient rather than necessary condition. If so, then power relations do not necessarily involve a change in R's intention. These various considerations lead me to the conclusion that power relations should be conceived as holding independently of the intentions not only of those who are in a dominant position, but of their respondents as well.

3.5.4 Power Defined as Involving
Conflicts of Interest

A slightly different approach is that of Steven Lukes: "[P]

exercises power over [R] when [P] affects [R] in a manner contrary to [R]'s interests" (1974, p. 27) but not necessarily contrary to R's original intention, since—as Lukes points out (and as we shall see)—one may be mistaken about one's interests so that they differ from one's desires. Like Nagel, Lukes claims that his conceptualization captures situations other definitions fail to include—in this case, manipulation and so-called nondecisions. By manipulating R, P does not influence R to act contrary to his intentions but "exercises power over him by influencing, shaping or determining his very wants" (p. 23), causing him thereby to act contrary to what would be in his interest. A nondecision is—in the words of Bachrach and Baratz, who introduced the term—"a decision that results in the suppression or thwarting of a latent or manifest challenge to the values or interests of the decision-maker" (1970, p. 44), e.g., a policy that keeps potential issues a group might raise from reaching the political arena. Here, the dominant P does not "perform some action y" but remains inactive. Nor does the suppressed group "do x"; it does not raise the issue, realizing the uselessness of such an attempt. Yet, there is a power relation also in this case, according to Lukes, since there is a *"latent conflict* . . . between the interests of those exercising power and the *real interests* of those they exclude" (Lukes 1974, p. 24). As an illustration, Lukes refers to Matthew Crenson's study of non–decision making in the cities, which points out that United States Steel for a long time effectively stopped the issue of pollution from being raised in Gary, Indiana, without doing anything. The company's "mere reputation for power, unsupported by acts of power" was "sufficient to inhibit the emergence of the dirty air issue" (Crenson 1971, p. 124; quoted by Lukes 1974, p. 43).

My objection is that manipulation and nondecisions, like anticipated reactions, can readily be subsumed under the proposed definitional scheme. While anticipated reactions are instances of *exercising influence,* manipulation and nondecisions seem to me clear cases of *having power* by means of *prevention.* Indeed, to manipulate someone is to make him incapable of becoming aware that a certain alternative is in fact open to him and, hence, to make him psychologically unable to pursue such a course. That the manipulated person or group is made to act against its interest need not enter the definition of power and need not even always be the case. As to non–decision making, Lukes himself characterizes it as the use of power "to *prevent* politicians, officials or others from raising issues or proposals known to be unacceptable to some group" (Lukes 1974, p. 37; italics added; cf. also Bachrach and Baratz 1970, p. 16).

The terminology ("nondecision") may well account for some confusion here. We have seen (2.1) that, in principle, any action can be characterized positively or negatively, e.g., staying home or not going out. Not raising an issue is not a "nondecision," but—usually—a decision not to raise it. By not taking any action on pollution, United States Steel did "perform some action y" that made it impossible for citizens of Gary "to do x"—namely, to bring up the question so that, were they to intend or attempt to do so, they would give up as soon as they realized the impossibility of prevailing in face of the company's obstruction, however passive. Again, in Luke's own words, United States Steel "effectively *prevented* the issue from even being raised" (1974, p. 42; italics added). By preventing R from doing x, P has power over R in that respect, regardless of whether it would have been in R's interest to do x.

On the other hand, Luke's definition, like those of Nagel and others discussed previously, fails to include instances that should be regarded as power relations. Rational persuasion is often used to make someone act in accordance with his interest, e.g., when a doctor convinces his patient to stop smoking.[9] That is perhaps the reason Lukes does not consider rational persuasion an instance of power, in contrast to my proposal. Also, P may deter R from acting against his interest or coerce him to pursue it. We need only think of J. S. Mill's "public officer" who restrains someone from crossing an unsafe bridge by "seizing him" and turning him back. We sometimes want to be compelled to do what we know to be in accordance with our interest. And we have seen that, in exchange situations involving reciprocal power relations, there need be no conflict of interest between the parties.

In summary, each of the definitions examined seems to be

too narrow. While power relations often involve conflicts of wants or interests, not all of them do. The proposed definition refers neither to the intentions nor to the preferences nor to the interests of either P or R—merely to their actual or potential actions. It covers persuasion (rational and deceptive), inducement, and deterrence (including manipulation and "nondecisions").

FOUR
Social Freedom

L IKE THE CONCEPT of social power, that of freedom will be taken here as referring to a relationship of interaction between two persons or groups, i.e., to situations in which one actor is, wrt another actor, free to act in any of several alternative ways. This is the meaning most frequently attached to "freedom" in political writings. Constructing an adequate explication of interpersonal or social freedom will enable us to distinguish this notion more clearly from such other concepts as freedom of action or so-called positive freedom, as well as from a variety of normative usages of the word 'freedom' and its synonym 'liberty'.

4.1 Social Unfreedom

I shall first examine the concept of social unfreedom because it is the simpler one, because it is connected with the concepts of social power we have analyzed, and because it will in turn help to define the concept of social freedom. I shall spell out what it means to say that one person or group is, wrt another, unfree to act in a certain way. There are two ways in which an actor can make another unfree to do something: he may make it either impossible or punishable for him to do so. The defining expression will indicate these two methods.

Definition: Wrt P, R is unfree to do x iff P prevents R from doing x or would punish him if he did x.

Analogously, we might say that, wrt P, R is unfree not to do x (or that it is mandatory for R to do x) iff P makes it either necessary for R to do x or punishable for R to abstain from doing x. However, I shall deal explicitly only with the former expression, as 'wrt P, R is unfree to do x' dovetails with 'P has power over R's not doing x'—the expression on which we focused in chapter 2.

4.1.1 Preventing

Clearly, someone who either restrains or prevents me from acting in a certain way (or coerces me to do something or makes it necessary for me to do so) does limit my freedom in that respect. By making R unable to do x, P not only has control over R's not doing x, but also makes him unfree to do x. If the guard either restrains or prevents a prisoner from breaking out, the latter is, wrt the former, unfree to leave. Similarly, the owner who encloses his property by a high wall makes everybody unable, and unfree as well, to trespass. The same relationship of unfreedom holds between the gunman who uses coercive threats and his victim. Offers "one cannot refuse" also render the person to whom they are made unfree to disobey. The same is true of legal impediments. If divorce is not legalized in a given country, its citizens are, wrt their government, unfree to divorce, including those citizens who do not contemplate such a step.

Unfreedom is not synonymous with inability. A person is not unfree to do what he cannot do unless his inability is caused, at least in part, by another person or jointly by several individuals or a group, intentionally or not (as I shall point out later). A kleptomaniac may be psychologically unable to refrain from stealing, but he is not unfree to refrain—wrt any other actor. As J. P. Day points out, his behavior is compulsive, but not compelled (by anyone else) (1977, p. 262). Someone who lacks the skill to wiggle his ears or to play the violin is not interpersonally unfree to do so. On the other hand, a prisoner, unable to leave his cell, is under the power of the guards who would push him back if he tried to break out *and* unfree to do so wrt the guards. What if P has made it difficult rather than impossible for R to do x? Has he made him unfree to do so? Here we must remember what we said about impossibility in connection with control. Strict impossibility shades over into difficulty, unpleasantness, and risk; hence, unfreedom is, like control, a matter of degree. (This aspect will be examined in 4.3.)

Whether an actor's incapacity to act in a certain way is the result of the intervention of some other person or group or is due to other factors is often a matter of controversy. That the high cost of television time renders this medium inaccessible to most does not appear to constitute a limitation of freedom of speech. Or could it be considered an instance of social unfreedom after all? If the rate has been set by a few monopolistic networks, is it then not true that those who cannot afford the media are unfree to use them—unfree wrt the broadcasting companies whose rates have made them unable to take advantage of their facilities? (I am assuming that monopolistic prices are set by specifiable actors, but nonmonopolistic prices by "the market.") Were workers in the mid-nineteenth century just unable to earn a living wage because of the generally prevailing economic, social, and political conditions? Or were they also unfree to earn more, and if so, wrt whom? Wrt the employers who did not offer higher wages? Wrt the government because it failed to enact minimum wage laws? Was the inability of many to find employment in 1929 merely the result of the Depression, or was the Depression in turn a consequence of Herbert Hoover's policies? If so, the unemployed did not merely lack the possibility of finding work; they were also unfree to secure employment—wrt Herbert Hoover and whoever else caused the Depression.

It might be argued that goverments, by not introducing social legislation, failed to enable workers to earn higher wages and on this account made them unfree to do so. However, we have seen that, by not enabling R to do x, P does not necessarily make R unable to do so. Only when P makes it impossible for R to do x is there power and—we may now add—unfreedom. So the question is: did the legislators, by not enacting minimum wage laws, merely fail to enable workers to secure an adequate living standard, or did the course taken by the former prevent the latter from earning more and make them unfree to do so? Similarly, did the American government in 1929 merely abstain from adopting measures of full employment, or did its policy make it impossible for many to find jobs?

Professor Macpherson considers "an important source of unfreedom the capitalist property institutions whose necessary . . . result was the coercion of the non-owning class" (1973, p. 99). Given the proposed definitions, coercion by *institutions* is not an instance of social unfreedom, unless their existence is in turn "the result of arrangements made by other human beings," as the author claims in another passage (p. 98). To deny this, he holds, is to "suggest or imply that the poverty of the poor is entirely their own fault" (p. 100). But this is not implied. Poverty can be viewed as the "fault" not of either the poor or the wealthy, but of economic and political institutions not shaped by the actions of any particular group or class. (Even Marx explained low wages in contemporary industrial society as the necessary consequence of an economic system in which capitalists were enmeshed no less than wage earners.) Whether poverty under capitalism constitutes unfreedom depends, then, on the general theory of the causes of poverty one adopts. Some tend to explain poverty and unemployment in terms of anonymous causal factors inherent in that, or perhaps any, economic system; others are inclined to lengthen the causal chain to arrive at specific persons or groups whom they *accuse* of being the cause of what they consider to be instances of unfreedom. Thus Macpherson "counts as deprivations of an individual's liberty the indirect interference imposed by withholding from him the means of life or means of labor" (1973, p. 118). The words 'interference' and 'imposed' point toward specifiable actors who, moreover, not merely failed to enable the individual to secure the means of life and labor, but 'withheld' them from him, i.e., made it impossible for him to secure them. The choice between such rival explanatory theories is then likely to be affected by ideological and normative considerations. Conceptual analysis cannot provide general objective criteria to distinguish between agents and other causes of inability, and to decide when the causal chain becomes too long to be subsumed under the concept of unfreedom. Since 'unfreedom' has a negative valuational connotation in ordinary language, there is a tendency to apply the term to any situation of which one disapproves. On the basis of the proposed "value-free" language, to deny that poverty or unemployment under capitalism is an instance of social unfreedom is not to justify capitalism; and to hold that it is implies no condemnation of that economic system.

4.1.2 Punishability

Unfreedom is often taken as applying only to prevention. E.g., "An individual is unfree if, *and only if*, his doing of any action is rendered impossible by the action of another individual" (Steiner 1975, p. 33; italics added). It seems to me that, if another individual (or group) makes it punishable for the former to perform a certain action, he must also be considered unfree to do so. Wrt P, R is unfree to do x not only to the extent that P makes it impossible for R to do x, but also to the extent that P would carry out an explicit or implied threat of punishment if he found R guilty of having done x. One might object that I myself previously considered punishability a form of prevention and that 'prevention' can therefore be taken as a synonym of 'unfreedom'. The reply is that P, by making it punishable for R to do x, makes it impossible for R to do x *without being punished*, but does not prevent him from doing x.

It has, in fact, been objected that "[t]he existence of a threatened punishment does not in itself create unfreedom. To say that a man is unfree to perform an activity he in fact performs is logically most cumbersome" (Cassinelli 1966, p. 34). It seems to me that this interpretation of social unfreedom does not even deviate from common usage. We do say currently that a speeder does something he is officially unfree to do. Nor does this common use of language seem cumbersome to me. (Incidentally, a conclusion cannot be "logically cumbersome," but only logically false—or true, as this statement is, given the proposed definition.)

This interpretation of unfreedom has also been criticized for implying "that a man can be socially unfree to do something he has already done" (Parent 1974, p. 157). I do not claim that P, by punishing R at time t2 for having done x at time t1, makes R *retroactively* unfree to do what he did. From the fact that R is being punished for speeding at t2, I infer that R *was* unfree to speed when he did (at t1), not that he is *now*, at t2, unfree "to do something he has already done." If R was not caught speeding at t1, it follows by definition that R was not unfree to speed *on that occasion* (but free to speed or not to speed, as we shall see). At t1, we can only say that R is unfree to speed with a certain degree of probability, depending on the likelihood that he will be fined. And so is everyone else. Another driver who stays within the speed limit at t1 is just as unfree to speed as R who speeds, unfree to the extent of the probability of the counterfactual statement: were he to speed, he would be fined. If punishment is certain, his unfreedom is maximal; but if the law is not being enforced at all, he is not unfree to speed (but free to do so), no more so than if there were no legal speed limit. If the Highway Department applies speeding laws to 40 percent of all speeders, it follows that *everyone* is to a degree of 40 percent unfree to speed—speeders (any speeder has a 40 percent chance of being fined), would-be speeders, and those who do not consider speeding, including nondrivers (there is a 40 percent probability that any of them would be fined if he speeded). Everyone is also under a legal obligation to keep within the speed limits—to 100 percent. The higher the degree of law enforcement, the closer the correspondence between the range of behavioral unfreedom and of illegal behavior.

Does it sound odd to say that someone did something that, we found out later, he was unfree to do (more precisely, unfree to have done), or that he is doing something now that, it will turn out later, he is unfree (more precisely, he will have been unfree) to do? We do not hesitate to affirm that one actor was punished by another for an action he performed previously, or to predict that the latter will punish the former for what he is doing now. In our ordinary language, there is unfortunately no transitive verb referring to unfreedom analogous to 'punishing' (or 'influencing', 'deterring', 'coercing'); one does not say, 'P unfrees R'. We can say that P makes R unfree to do x by preventing R from doing x or by making it punishable for R to do x. Here P's action y is temporally prior to R's potential action x. But it would indeed by odd to say that P, by punishing R now for having done x, makes R now unfree to do x or to have done x. Ordinary language leaves us no choice but to put ourselves in the shoes of R, rather than of P, as it were, when referring to actual punishment as an instance of unfreedom, and to say, if P punished R for having done x, then R was, wrt P, unfree to do x. It becomes then more practical to use, as the defining expression in our restructured language, 'wrt P, R is unfree to do x' to cover prevention and punishability, including actual punishment.

The application of legal sanctions by government to citizens who act illegally is only one kind of social unfreedom through punishability. Such relationships hold among all kinds of persons or groups. Wrt a union, a company is unfree to withhold certain benefits from union members if otherwise the union would picket the company. Members of an organization who would be expelled if they did not conform to certain, perhaps unwritten, norms are unfree to deviate from such rules wrt the organization or its leadership. Wrt Saudi Arabia, the United States is unfree to increase its military aid to Israel if Saudi Arabia would in that case further increase its oil price, and the more unfree, the higher the price. On the other hand, the United States is not unfree to acquire oil from Saudi Arabia if that country would in that case ask for a higher price, because that would not constitute a punishment of the United States for wanting to acquire the oil. Rather, this is a bargaining situation. On the other hand, if I tell B that I am "not free for dinner" because I have accepted A's dinner invitation, this is not to be taken literally. Wrt A, I am not unfree to dine with B, since presumably A would not hinder me from going with B or punish me if I did. 'I am not free for dinner' does not refer to interpersonal unfreedom at all (nor to unfreedom in any other sense). It means that I have a prior engagement and subscribe to the principle that promises should be kept. Perhaps "my conscience" would "punish me with guilt" if I broke my engagement with A; but my superego is not *another actor*.

4.1.3 Social Unfreedom and Control

Social unfreedom and control are overlapping categories.

a) Influence is an instance of control, but not of unfreedom. This is contrary to the view of Plamenatz that P makes R unfree to do x "either by making it impossible for him to do so or else by supplying him with a motive for abstaining from it" (1968, p. 111). It is not the case that supplying R with a motive of whatever kind for abstaining is an instance of unfreedom. Only supplying him with a motive for avoiding the penalty is. But even that is not a defining condition of unfreedom. If it is punishable for R to do x, R is unfree to do x, regardless of whether he does x at the risk of penalty or whether he abstains—and for whatever reason. If P supplies R with a motive to vote Democratic and thereby succeeds in persuading R to do so, R, while in fact voting Democratic, is not unfree to vote Republican—certainly not wrt P and probably not wrt anyone else, since presumably no one would have restrained him from voting Republican or punished him, had he done so. This conclusion follows from the proposed definition, and it does not matter whether P uses rational arguments or deceptive devices to influence R's action, or whether he does so by means of threats of punishment or offers of reward. I do not agree that "threats of punishment involved in law enforcement constitute impairments of freedom" (Dryer 1964, p. 447). The threat of punishment may deter someone from acting in a certain way, but does not make him unfree to disregard the threat. True, the threat is often evidence for the prediction that the threatened penalty would be applied in case of disobedience; but it is the probability that the threat would be carried out, not the threat itself, which makes R unfree to disobey. Suppose there is a local speed limit ordinance that is practically never enforced. By means of the "30 m.p.h." sign, the town may deter some drivers from going faster, especially if they mistakenly believe that the law is being enforced. These drivers, while deterred from speeding, are under the township's control in this respect, but are not unfree to speed, since they would not be punished if they did. It is of course in the behavioral sense that they are not unfree to disregard the speeding law they are under a legal duty to obey. Similarly, by promising to reward R for doing x, P may influence R to do x, but he does not make him unfree to abstain from doing x and to forego the reward. "Interventions of an offering or threatening kind effect changes . . . in individuals' relative desires to do certain actions. . . . [But] neither the making of threats nor that of offers constitutes a diminution of personal liberty" (Steiner 1975, p. 43).

b) Punishability implies unfreedom but excludes control. Suppose driver R does not believe that the local speed limit is being enforced, but that this belief is mistaken. R speeds and is being fined. R is, wrt the town, unfree to speed, because it has made speeding punishable; i.e., it enforces the ordinance. The same holds if R is unaware of the law. Ignorance of the law neither excuses nor alters the fact that one is unfree to violate it—to the extent that it is being enforced. And if R knows of the speed limit and if he slows down because he is a "law-abiding citizen" rather than to avoid the penalty, he is also unfree to speed. While his slowing is in this instance not controlled by anyone else, it is still the case that, were he to speed, he would be fined.

That P makes it punishable for R to do x implies that the prediction that P would punish R if R did x is warranted, not that R makes a correct prediction to that effect. But P has no control over R's conduct. If R did x, P could not logically have had control over R wrt his *not* doing x (nor could anyone else). If R did not do x, P may have had control over R's inaction—not by making it punishable for R to do x, but by deterring R from doing x by means of the implied threat of punishment. (It is also conceivable that some sadist first persuades someone to perform a certain action and afterward punishes him for having done so.)

There is thus an important difference between control on the one hand and unfreedom through punishment on the other. That P exercises or has influence over R wrt his not doing x or that P restrains or prevents R from doing x implies that R does not do x.[1] In contrast, from the hypothesis that P makes it punishable for R to do x, we cannot infer anything as to R's actual behavior; that is, we cannot infer whether R will do x and be punished or whether R will refrain from doing x. Benn and Weinstein ask, "[I]f I decide against a course of action to avoid threatened penalties am I free or unfree . . . ?" (1971, p. 196). Free or unfree in what sense? To disobey? If the prediction is warranted that the threatened penalties would be applied, I am no doubt unfree to disobey, regardless of whether I decide for or against that course of action, and regardless for what motive.

To repeat: Both threats of punishment and offers of reward

are, if successful, instances of exercising influence, and hence of control, but not of unfreedom; and punishability constitutes unfreedom, but not control. On the other hand, rewardability implies neither control (as we saw in the chapter on power) nor unfreedom. Why is it that rewardability does not make R unfree to *abstain* from performing the rewardable action (unless the reward is coercive), just as punishability (even when not coercive) makes R unfree to *do* what is punishable? The difference is this: If it is the case that, were R to do x, P would reward R for having done so, R has the choice of (1) not doing x, i.e., not complying and foregoing the reward; (2) doing x and accepting the reward; and (3) doing x and declining the reward. Thus, if Paul says to Roberta, "I will give you a present if you . . . ," he does not make her unfree to refuse. But if P has made it punishable for R not to do x, there are only two alternatives open to R: (1) not doing x, i.e., not complying (and being punished); and (2) doing x, i.e., complying (and not being punished). The alternative of performing the punishable action and escaping punishment has been excluded by P—to the extent that P would in that case punish R.[2] Thus, if Paul would in fact take Roberta's ring from her if she refused, R is unfree to say no. Only if P's promise of a present amounted to a coercive offer would R be unfree to refuse. But why, one might ask, do I make a distinction between coercive and noncoercive rewards, but not between coercive and noncoercive punishments? Coercive rewards amount to coercion, hence to unfreedom; noncoercive rewards are instances of influencing. On the other hand, any punishment constitutes unfreedom, no matter how mild. How are we to interpret what H. Steiner has called a "throffer" (1975)? P says to R, "Do x and you get one hundred dollars; don't do x and I take one hundred dollars—from you" (or "I kill you"). I would say that R is, wrt P unfree not to do x, but free either to do x and to accept one hundred dollars, or to do x and to refuse the reward.

c) Preventing is the area where control and unfreedom overlap. If P makes it impossible for R to do x, P has control over R wrt his not doing x *and* R is, wrt P, unfree to do x. To take some previous illustrations: The guard both has control over the prisoner wrt his not leaving the cell and makes him unfree to do so. Where divorce is illegal, citizens are, wrt their government, unfree to divorce as well as under its control in that respect. Similarly, certain big corporations are, through price-fixing, in control of consumers wrt their buying the products at the set price, and the latter are, wrt the former, unfree to procure them at lower prices. Coercive threats and coercive offers are instances of both control and unfreedom. I do not agree with the second sentence of the following statement:

> When H points his pistol at T and says, "Your money or your life," we can predict that T will almost certainly hand over his money, because we know that this is what almost everybody does in such a case. But it neither follows nor is true that T is unfree to keep his money in this situation, as he would be if H forced him to hand it over, or cowed him into handing it over. (Day 1977, p. 264)

If this were just an ordinary threat, it would be a case of mere influence and T would not be unfree to keep his money. But more likely, pointing a gun does constitute a credible threat of the severest kind of deprivation, one that makes it practically impossible for R to resist and hence that makes him unfree to do so. There is a second reason I would consider this a clear case of interpersonal unfreedom. H has made it punishable for T not to hand over his money (assuming, of course, that H would take T's life if he did not comply).

Another fluid border of relevance in this connection is that between deception and manipulation. We have seen that influence, even by deceptive means, does not make the influenced unfree to act contrary to what he has been persuaded to do. But deception may amount to manipulation, so that the manipulated becomes psychologically incapable of perceiving other alternatives that are in fact open to him. If so, the manipulated becomes, wrt his manipulator, unable, and *for this reason* unfree, to act differently. In spite of the difficulty of applying these distinctions in certain concrete cases, they are of theoretical importance, since they mark the separation between control without unfreedom (through influence) and control with unfreedom (through preventing).

I have argued (3.5) in favor of extending the concept of control (and power) to cases where P, even unintentionally, makes R unable to do x. Correspondingly, if P unintentionally prevents R from doing x, he makes him unfree to do so as well. Other writers interpret such situations differently. "[S]omeone who makes it impossible for another to do certain things is not said thereby to impair another's freedom, unless it is his intention to make it impossible for him to do them" (Dryer 1964, p. 447). "If a person became enmeshed in a trap that had been set to snare game, we would at least hesitate to say that he was deprived of liberty, precisely because the relevant intention was missing" (White 1970, p. 192). I think that we would hesitate not for this reason, but because we might not know who had set the trap and hence wrt whom the person was unfree to get out of the trap. Even so, he became unfree to leave, unfree wrt whomever did set the trap and regardless of the latter's intentions. I conclude that even unintended preventive actions are instances of unfreedom as well as of control.

4.2 Social Freedom

"Like a vacuum, freedom clearly represents the absence of something" (Gill 1971, p. 1). Accordingly, our first impulse might be to consider social freedom the contradictory of social unfreedom and to hold that one is free to do what one is not unfree to do. If government has not made divorce illegal, are married couples not free to divorce? Are we not free to drive within the speed limits and even to exceed them if they are not enforced? But there are counterexamples. Government has not made it impossible or punishable to pay taxes; hence, we are not unfree to pay them. But neither are we free to pay. Rather, we are unfree to withhold payment; in other words, paying taxes is mandatory. Like unfreedom and control, social freedom refers to relationships between two actors P and R; but unlike these concepts, freedom pertains to two or more alternative actions open to R, doing x or not doing x, or doing either x or z. I am unfree to do this; I am free to do this or that.

Definition: Wrt P, R is free to do or not to do x iff wrt P, R is neither unfree to do x nor unfree not to do x.

In other words, P does not make it impossible or punishable for R to do x, and does not make it impossible or punishable for R not to do x. Wrt the United States government, voters are free to vote or to abstain.[3] Analogously, 'wrt P, R is free to do x or z' means that P does not prevent R from doing x or z, and does not make it punishable to do either. In the United States, voters are free to vote Republican or Democratic.

Social freedom, like punishability, and unlike influence and prevention, does not refer to the actor's actual behavior. From 'wrt P, R is free to do x or z' we cannot infer whether R will do x or z.

4.2.1 Freedom to Do What
with Respect to Whom?

Paradoxically, perhaps, it is not the negative concept of unfreedom, but the positive concept of freedom that is to be defined in negative terms, as the absence of impediments and punishment. Social freedom is thus by definition "negative." We shall see later that so-called positive freedom pertains to a different situation. Nor does the proposed definition distinguish between "freedom from . . ." and "freedom to . . .," but covers both aspects, since it refers to situations in which one person or group is free *to* act in several alternative ways and is free to do so *from*, i.e., wrt, another actor.

Construing social freedom as referring to two or more alternative actions open to R will shield us from falling victim to certain rhetorical devices that play on the favorable connotation of 'freedom' and the negative overtone of 'unfreedom'. A speaker who is in favor of a given limitation of freedom tends to say that individuals are free to do what they are unfree not to do. "Freedom to propagate the truth" has been used as a euphemism for unfreedom to spread "error" in the sense of some narrowly circumscribed religious or political orthodoxy. "Freedom to work" has meant compulsory labor in certain dictatorial regimes.

As in the case of control and unfreedom, it is necessary always to specify who is free to do what wrt whom. The same actor may leave me free in some respects and restrict my freedom in others. American voters are free to vote Republican or Democratic, but unfree to vote Communist when that party is not on the ballot. In Belgium, where compulsory voting is well enforced, voters are unfree to abstain, but free to vote for any party on the ballot or even to vote blank. Drivers are officially unfree to exceed the speed limit, but free to drive at any speed up to that limit (unless minimum speeds are also enforced). We have seen that R, who speeded on a particular occasion and remained unpunished, was not officially unfree to speed; he was free either to speed or not to speed.

Also, one actor may make me unfree to do what another leaves me free to do or not to do. Wrt many governments, married couples are free to divorce under certain conditions or not to divorce; but wrt the Catholic church, Catholics are unfree to divorce (to the extent to which religious sanctions are being applied).

There are also situations in which nobody makes it either impossible or punishable for me to act in various alternative ways. If so, I am free to do so wrt everybody. E.g., most are, wrt most everyone else, free to read most anything or to go most anywhere, at least in "free" societies.

4.2.2 Social Freedom and Ability

Social unfreedom and inability are not synonymous; neither are social freedom and ability. Wrt P, R is free to do x or z not only if R can do either with impunity, but also if he cannot do x, and/or if he is unable to do z, provided his inability has not been caused by P. And if R's incapacity to do x is not the result of any human intervention, then (1) nobody has power over R's not doing x; (2) there is nobody wrt whom R is unfree to do x; and (3) R is free to do or not to do x—free wrt everyone. The man who cannot get out of the pit is, wrt everyone, free to climb out or to stay. What he lacks is freedom of action, but that is a different concept, as we shall see. If we explain low wages during the laissez-faire period or high unemployment during the Depression by prevailing economic conditions rather than by actions of specific groups, we must conclude that workers were free to earn higher wages and the unemployed free to find jobs. What they were lacking and demanding was not the freedom they already had, but the opportunity they lacked. Everybody is, indeed, "free to sleep under bridges" or at home, even the homeless, who have no other place to go. These are conclusions from the proposed definition of social freedom, not justifications of laissez-faire—except in the eyes of those who cannot "free" themselves from the laudatory overtones of the *word* 'freedom'. Being free to do what one cannot do is usually of no value to the actor; but having a freedom is not the same as valuing a freedom one has.

Both enabling and not enabling R to do x leave R's previous social freedom unaffected (just as neither is an instance of either power or unfreedom). The inventors of the airplane made it possible for people to fly; but (theoretically) everybody has been free to fly before no less than after the invention of the plane—although in fact the question did not arise prior to the age of air travel.[4] Given the proposed definition, we must agree with Herbert Spencer that government, by not instituting a "free" public school system, failed to enable children of the poor to develop their intellectual faculties, but that "the liberty to exercise the faculties is left intact. Omitting instruction in no way takes from the child's freedom to do whatever it wills the best way it can" (*Social Statics*, chapter 26). It is the continuation of this passage—"and this freedom is all that equity demands"—to which everyone nowadays objects. "Free" and *compulsory* education is what equity demands, a policy that, on the contrary, demands restrictions of freedom. By organizing "free" public schools, government *enabled* all children to go to school and to avail themselves of the freedom they had. As we shall point out later, there is of course often a functional relationship between opportunity and freedom.

Freedom does not imply ability; nor does ability imply freedom. R may be capable of doing x, yet there may be an actor P wrt whom he is unfree to do so. Many people are able to commit all sorts of crimes, but all are officially unfree to do so, to the extent that law enforcement is effective. Crimes are made punishable precisely because people have the capacity of committing them.

4.2.3 Social Freedom and Power

If P has no power over R's doing x, nor over R's not doing x, it follows that, wrt P, R is free to do x or not. But the converse does not necessarily hold. Both power and freedom relationships may hold between the same pair of actors. There is, first, the case of influence. If P succeeds in dissuading or deterring R from doing x, P, while controlling R's actual conduct, does not make him unfree to act differently, but leaves him free either to do what he actually does or to disregard the advice or threat. If P makes it rewardable (instead of punishable) for R to do x, P may thereby persuade R to do x, but—as we have seen—R remains, wrt P, free not to do x or to do x and, in the latter case, free to accept or to decline the reward. Does it seem paradoxical that one actor has control and power over another actor's behavior and at the same time leaves him free to act differently? Not if we keep in mind that we ask the counterfactual question: Had P not succeeded in influencing R—e.g., had R refused to comply with P's threat—would P have carried it out and punished R for having done so? If the answer is negative, then R was free either to do what P caused him to do or to disregard the threat.

Power and freedom also coincide when P has preventive or punitive power over R wrt a specific range of alternatives, but leaves R free to act as he pleases within that range. In wartime, government has the power to compel citizens to serve in the armed forces, but leaves them free either to answer the draft call or to volunteer. Drivers are free to drive at any speed below the maximum and above the minimum speed limit.

Relationships of freedom do not exist in isolation, but usually entail corresponding relationships of unfreedom. To affirm that freedom of speech prevails in a given society is to refer to a whole network of relationships of both freedom and unfreedom: Everybody is free wrt everyone else to say anything (within certain limits). Everybody is free to do so also wrt government officials. In a "free society" government is unfree to restrict any citizen's freedom of speech or any of his other civil liberties. Every citizen is unfree to prevent anyone else from expressing his views not only wrt other citizens, but also wrt a government that makes it punishable for anyone to encroach upon anyone else's freedom of speech. Government does so by protecting everybody's *right* to free speech. Similarly, a property system is a network of relationships of both freedom and unfreedom, translated into corresponding property rights and the corresponding legal duties. The freedom of the majority in a legislature to enact laws binding on all may be limited by certain rights of the minority.

The freedom and unfreedom of citizens wrt government is thus functionally related to the corresponding legal rights and duties. The preceding examples illustrate the importance of the distinction between being, in a behavioral sense, free to do or not to do something and having the corresponding legal right, and between being unfree to act in a certain way and being under a legal obligation not to do so. Social freedom and unfreedom refer to the noninterference and interference by others; legal rights are conferred and legal duties imposed by virtue of some system of positive law. Here the actor variable 'P' is replaced by a variable ranging over legal systems. It is wrt—or by virtue of—the Constitution of the United States that Americans have the right of free speech and the corresponding legal duty not to interfere with the exercise of that right. To what extent they are *free* to say or write whatever they want, especially wrt actors other than public officials, depends on extralegal factors.

4.3 DEGREES OF SOCIAL POWER AND FREEDOM
So far, I have interpreted the ideas of social power and social freedom in a categorical way, This allows us to assert only that P either has, or does not have, persuading or deterring or preventive or punitive power over R's not doing x, or that R is, wrt P, either unfree to do x or free to do or not to do so. Yet, I have had several occasions to point out that, e.g., deterrence, coercion, prevention, and punishment are matters of degree, and that there are, consequently, degrees of control or of unfreedom. But if so, one might object, the precision of all these concepts fades. The reply is that the "real world" is not made up of clear-cut pigeonholes and that science progresses from classification (yes or no) to comparison (more or less) to quantification (to such and such a degree).

We assert that the United States is more powerful than Cuba and that Americans have greater freedom than Cubans. Political scientists and philosophers cannot do without such concepts. One of the two principles that are the capstones of Rawls's system reads, "[E]ach person is to have an equal right to the *most extensive* basic liberty compatible with a *similar* liberty of others" (1971, p. 60; italics added); Rawls explains that "[l]iberty is *unequal* as when one class of persons has a *greater* liberty than another, or liberty is less *extensive* than it should be" (p. 203; italics added). The meaning of these terms is left open; and so the question arises whether it is at all possible to construct definitions for such concepts that are unambiguous and operational even in the largest sense. Here we are faced with two kinds of difficulties.

The concept of 'harder than' refers to a relation between two physical substances, and we can say that diamond is harder than steel. Concepts like 'more powerful than' or 'equal freedom' are also relational, but they are relations between relations, since the concepts of social power and freedom are in turn relational. Someone who asserts that Stalin was more powerful than Roosevelt may believe that he is simply drawing a comparison between two persons, when he is actually establishing a relation between (1) the Soviet premier, Soviet citizens, and some activity such as criticizing the government, and (2) the American president, Americans, and a similar (or perhaps a different) activity. Schematically, he is making an assertion of the type, 'P1 has more power over R1 wrt x1 than P2 has over R2 wrt x2'. Similarly, 'Soldiers have less freedom than civilians' might be interpreted as a shorthand expression for, 'Wrt their officers, soldiers have less freedom, e.g., of movement, than have civilians wrt their government'.

'Harder than' can be defined by reference to a single operation, the scratch test: For any two substances x and y, x is harder than y iff x scratches y but not vice versa. Then we can assert that steel is harder than copper but less hard than diamond. But the relative extent to which R is, wrt P, unfree to do x will have to be construed as a function of several variables, such as the probability *and* the severity of punishment. Furthermore, these several dimensions vary independently. Thus, as judged by the probability of punishment, drivers are perhaps more unfree to speed in Connecticut than in Massachusetts, but from the point of view of the severity of punishment it may be the other way around.

Examining some of the dimensions of power and freedom separately will enable us to ascertain whether it is possible to draw them together and to arrive at such concepts as total power or equal or unequal liberty.

4.3.1 Probability of Responding or Being Punished

The greater the probability that R would choose not to do x as a result of some influence action y of P or that R's attempt to do x would fail because of some preventive action y of P, the greater P's control and power over R's not doing x. As mentioned before, there are no fixed boundaries between P's making a certain alternative unpleasant or difficult or impossible for R. For example, the higher the tariff wall country P erects against imports from country R, the greater the probability that R will not, and ultimately cannot, continue its exports to P and hence the greater P's power over R in that respect. As judged by the probability of success, we may be able to rank various pressure groups according to their relative degree of influence (and hence control and power) over Congress (or over certain members) wrt the passage of certain bills. The power of any member of a committee system such as a legislature over other members "depends on the chance he has of becoming critical to the success of a winning coalition" (Shapley and Shubik 1964, p. 142), that is, on the probability that his vote turns a possible defeat into success.

The degree of P's power over R's not doing x is thus a function of the probability that P has influence over R's not doing x or makes it impossible or punishable for him to do so. The last two factors also determine the extent to which R is, wrt P, unfree to do x. Analogously, R's freedom to do or not to do x wrt P is the greater, the higher the probability that P neither prevents R from either doing or not doing x, nor makes it punishable for R to act either way. Here we see the advantage of comparative over categorical concepts. There is unfreedom in the categorical sense whenever there is even the slightest possibility that P will prevent R from doing x or punish him if he does, and there is no freedom unless it is practically certain that P will do neither. If social freedom and unfreedom become matters of degree, any situation falling anywhere between the two extremes of maximum freedom and maximum unfreedom can be described in terms of such and such a degree of *either* freedom or unfreedom. We can, e.g., ask: Which government is, wrt the Soviet Union, more unfree—or has relatively more freedom—to shape its own foreign policy, Poland or Rumania? If 40 percent of all speeders in a certain state are fined, we can predict that any driver who speeds will be fined with 40 percent probability, and conclude that, as judged by the probability of punishment, drivers are officially unfree to a degree of 0.4 to speed and that their freedom to speed or not to speed is 0.8 [(60 + 100) / 2]. Here is a case where we can speak not merely of the relative degree, but even of the quantity of an actor's freedom or power.

4.3.2 Severity of Punishment

Wrt P, R's unfreedom to do x is the greater (and his freedom to do or not to do x the lesser) the more severely P would punish R if he found him guilty of having done x. This indicator applies, obviously, only to the degree of power and unfreedom by means of punishability. Sometimes it can be measured, e.g., in terms of the amount of fine or length of imprisonment. To refer to a previous example: The greater government P's increase of its oil price, should government R do x, the greater R's unfreedom to do so.

Since the fine for speeding is the same for all, taxi drivers and millionaires are equally unfree to speed; nor does it make any difference whether the driver is on an emergency trip or is speeding "for fun." On the other hand, making speeding punishable by a fine of one hundred dollars makes drivers unfree to a greater degree than imposing a fine of fifty dollars.

One reason for defining punishment this way is to bring out clearly the difference between the degree of someone's unfreedom and the degree of disvalue (negative utility) to him of being unfree to act in a certain way. That speeding is punishable by a fifty dollar fine is more frustrating to a taxi driver than to a millionnaire, and less irksome to the driver on an emergency trip than it would be for him under different circumstances. But the degree of anyone's unfreedom to speed remains unaffected. It is therefore somewhat ambiguous to say that whether punishability "is a significant deprivation of liberty depends to some extent on the character of the course of action to which it is attached—a fine of a thousand dollars may involve an insignificant deprivation of freedom to commit murder, but it would probably be a significant deprivation of freedom to park a car in a certain spot" (White 1970, p. 187). According to the proposed criterion, everybody would be equally unfree to murder and to park illegally if the punishment were the same. The difference is that someone out to commit a murder would consider this punishment an "insignificant" deprivation of his freedom to murder in the sense that he would disvalue his unfreedom to murder very little, whereas being unfree to park there would be greatly disvaluable to drivers if the fine were that high. The degree to which an actor is unfree to act in a certain way is a function of the extent of punishment, but depends neither on the positive utility to him of acting that way nor on the negative utility to him of being punished.[5]

Comparing the relative severity of punishments of the same kind presents no difficulty, e.g., amounts of fine, price of oil, time in prison. But there is no way of deciding which punishment is more severe, a fine of x or y months in jail. (Which of the two is more distasteful to R might be determined, but does not determine which of the two is a more severe punishment.) In such cases, *this* dimension of unfreedom cannot be applied—a price that seems to me well worth paying to preserve the distinction between the degree of a given relationship of unfreedom and its disvalue to R (or value to P). One might generalize that prevention makes R more unfree to do x than punishment (again, without referring to R's preferences). In the former case, R cannot accomplish x, whereas punishment leaves R the choice between doing x and being punished or abstaining. Accordingly, an embargo restricts freedom more severely than a punitive tariff, however high. That R is likely to feel more deprived by an obstacle than by punishment is, again, irrelevant in this connection.

4.3.3 Range of Activities

Other factors remaining constant, P's power over R is the greater, the wider the range of R's possible actions over which P has power. Conversely, the degree of R's freedom wrt P is an increasing function of the alternative actions P leaves R free to engage in. That the army has more power over soldiers than government over civilians usually means that the range of the soldier's activities over which his officers have power is wider, but that there is a smaller range of actions civilians are officially unfree to perform and a wider range of activities wrt which they are officially free. From this perspective, French voters have greater freedom than American voters, since the former are given the choice of a greater number of parties. (Let me add that this statement implies no criticism of the two-party system—nor approbation.) But there is a certain ambiguity. We could also consider as the given alternatives voting for any party or candidate on the ballot or abstaining. Then we must conclude that Americans have as much electoral freedom as Frenchmen. Here, at least, we can easily "count" the alternatives. But there are many situations in which it is not possible to measure the range of an actor's unfreedom or freedom. "Does greater freedom of speech mean freedom to speak more often, or to more people, or about more important objects? Does it mean freedom to deviate more widely from the socially accepted canon of permitted opinions?" (Wolff 1977, p. 90).

In this context, too, we must be careful not to confuse the degree of an actor's freedom with the degree of value he attaches to his freedom. The degree of my freedom is a function of the possibilities left open to me, but does not depend on whether these do or do not include actions I desire to perform. Suppose P1 invites me to the opera and gives me the choice between *Don Giovanni* and *Così fan tutte*, and that

P2 also invites me—to any one part of the *Ring*. In the second case my freedom is twice as great as in the first. It is quite irrelevant that I happen to love Mozart and to dislike Wagner, and that therefore my choice in the second case is between four "evils." Naturally, I do not care for this greater freedom. Incidentally, I may not value my *freedom* to see one or the other Mozart opera either (it is *attending* the performance of one or the other that I value). The choice may be so difficult for me that I would have preferred that P1 had invited me just to one or to the other. Similarly, the greater someone's desire to travel, the greater the positive utility to him of his freedom to travel, but his freedom to travel is not greater than the freedom of someone who prefers to stay home. Conversely, persons who are being denied passports are equally unfree to go abroad, but this restriction of liberty is the more frustrating to anyone, the greater his desire to go abroad.

Similarly, the degree of P's power does not depend on the positive or negative utility P attaches to its exercise, e.g., on how much it would cost him to exercise it. According to Alvin Goldman, the amount of P's power is inversely proportional to the cost of obtaining the outcome (1972, p. 249), e.g., R's compliance. This would imply that P1, who needs to spend only half as much to get reelected in his district as P2 in his, has twice the power of P2. Goldman acknowledges that, "once the element of cost is introduced, however, strength of desire and aversion must be included as well" (1972, p. 248). It seems to me that these are dimensions not of the degree of an actor's power, but of how valuable or disvaluable it is to him to exercise the power he has. If the probability of being elected in their respective districts is the same for P1 and P2, then the degree of their power over their voters is the same, no matter how strong their desire to be elected and no matter how much they must spend to win the election.[6]

How the actor values the alternatives open to him does not influence the extent of his freedom; but that extent is affected by the degree of difficulty others put in the way of his realizing them. Suppose the president of the United States, by urging motorists not to drive on Sundays, succeeds in dissuading 30 percent of those who usually drive on Sundays from doing so. While he has power over those 30 percent (but not over the 70 percent who continue driving), everyone remains free to drive or not to drive. Those who do must at most "pay the price" of a pang of conscience, however slight. But they are not being punished (except figuratively speaking) with a bad conscience. Here it is R himself who lets his conscience become heavier; P merely motivates R to feel guilty. Now suppose the government cannot obtain the same result without increasing the gasoline tax. Again, the government has power over 30 percent of the motorists, and everyone remains free to drive or not to drive (since the tax does not constitute a punishment for driving). However, the government has changed the range of the motorists' freedom thus: they can either not drive or drive and pay the higher tax. It has reduced the motorists' freedom *not* because, subjectively, they would have preferred to drive without paying more, but because it has placed an objective obstacle (but not an insurmountable one) in the way of driving. From this point of view, the higher the tax, the greater the reduction of freedom. The degree of this freedom becomes reduced even further if the government, to obtain the same result, orders gas stations closed on Sundays, since Sunday drivers will have to circumvent this greater impediment. The degree of difficulty a powerholder places in the way of an activity open to a respondent influences the range, and hence the extent, of his freedom. If, however, the government should make it practically impossible or punishable to drive on Sundays, motorists become unfree to do so, and this dimension of *freedom* is no longer applicable.

There is thus a difference between degree of probability of punishment and extent of range of alternatives. The former dimension establishes a sliding scale from maximum freedom (probability of punishment: zero) to maximum unfreedom (probability: one hundred). From the point of view of the latter dimension, there is discontinuity between freedom and unfreedom. If there are two alternatives open to R, x and z, then, the greater the difficulty P places in the way of x, the smaller the range of R's freedom. But once P has made it impossible or punishable for R to do x, R is no longer free to do x or z, not even to the smallest degree; rather, he is unfree to do x.

Let us examine the following statement in the light of these considerations:

> The extent of my freedom seems to depend on (a) how many possibilities are open to me (although the method of counting these can never be more than impressionistic. Possibilities of action are not discrete entities like apples, which can be exhaustively enumerated); (b) how easy or difficult each of these possibilities is to actualize; (c) how important in my plan of life, given my character and circumstances, these possibilities are when compared with each other; (d) how far they are closed and opened by deliberate human acts; (e) what value not merely the agent, but the general sentiment of the society in which he lives, puts on the various possibilities. (Berlin 1969, p. 130, note 1)

I agree that the extent of my freedom is a function of (a), (b), and (d)—except that in (d) I would leave out "deliberate." However, (c) and (e) are considerations influencing the degree not of my freedom, but of the value I attach to the circumstances that certain possibilities are included in the range of my freedom. The extent of my freedom remains unaffected by these valuations.

4.3.4 Number of Actors Involved

We consider the governor of New York more powerful than the governor of Rhode Island (even though they are equally powerful by each of the dimensions examined so far) because the former has power over a greater number of people than the latter. Analogously, the degree to which R is unfree to do x depends, among other factors, on the number of actors P wrt which R is unfree to do so. Someone's freedom of speech may be limited by his government, church, employer, or neighborhood. Certain freedoms of Americans are limited by local, state, and federal authorities (but, since the other dimensions in reality are not constant, Americans have nevertheless more civil liberties than citizens of certain other countries).

In a strictly hierarchical group like an army or a totalitarian dictatorship, we can say, schematically, the higher an actor's position within the power pyramid, the greater the number of persons over whom he has power and the smaller the number of actors who have power over him, and hence the greater his freedom from this point of view. The actor who occupies the top position has the maximum degree of both power and freedom. Actors at the bottom of the power pyramid have no power over anyone and are under the direct or indirect power of everyone higher up. In a more horizontally structured society, nobody has either power or freedom wrt everybody else. It is not the case that there is "more power" in a dictatorship and "more freedom" in a democracy. From the point of view of the dimension we are considering now, both power and freedom are *more equally distributed* in the latter than in the former type of political system. In a democracy, each citizen has less power and less freedom than a dictator, but more power and freedom than subjects in a dictatorship.

4.3.5 An Overall Measure?

It will have become clear by now that these various dimensions are quite incommensurable and that they cannot be aggregated into a single measure of an actor's total power or overall freedom. If "the only sensible way to measure individual liberty is to measure the aggregate net liberty of all the individuals in a given society" (Macpherson 1973, p. 117), that "only sensible way" is an impossible way. It seems to me quite meaningless to speak of "equal freedom" and to define it as "a maximum of equal freedom, as much freedom as possible so long as there is the same amount of freedom for others" (Raphael 1977, p. 544). What does it mean that there is "more freedom" in the United States than in Albania? Americans have greater freedom to criticize their government; but Albanian drivers have perhaps greater freedom of movement (since there are fewer cars, fewer traffic lights and perhaps fewer traffic rules in Albania). Such an assertion does not constitute a "diabolical defence of Albania"

(Charles Taylor 1979, p. 183), but is perfectly compatible with the view that freedom of speech is a far more important, or significant, freedom. But 'importance' or 'significance' indicate a valuational dimension. If the above statement means that Americans have the more important freedoms, i.e., the freedoms they ought to have, we are no longer engaged in descriptive discourse; we are speaking in normative terms. (In some contexts we also mean that Albanians are unfree to a higher degree, as judged by the probability or the severity of punishment or by the range of alternatives the government has closed to them.)

Freedom House's annual "Comparative Survey of Freedom" rates the nations of the world on the degree to which its citizens are "free persons" (Freedom House 1979, p. 2). "Freedom is defined in the Survey in terms of political rights and civil liberties" (p. 5). Each state is rated on separate scales for civil and political freedoms from 1 ("freest") to 7 ("least free") (p. 6).

We have seen that *specific* kinds of freedom can in certain cases be measured, at least in principle. Maximum civil liberty includes unrestricted freedom of expression, of assembly, of organization (e.g., to unionize), of occupation and movement. Censorship and imprisonment for expressing dissident views are restrictions of civil liberties. The survey does not indicate what measure it uses; presumably, the more severe the punishment and the higher the probability of its application, the lower the country's rank on the scale of civil freedom. The survey also rates a country among the "freest" if "[n]o major media are simply conduits for government propaganda" (p. 6), but does not take into account that citizens may be free or unfree to voice certain opinions wrt actors other than government officials. Media such as television networks are often controlled by private interests; certain groups (e.g., political parties) may wield power over government and, implicitly, over mass media.

Under the category political freedoms the survey lists a number of factors that, it seems to me, do not refer to social freedom of any kind. States are rated "freest" on the political freedom scale if they "have a fully competitive electoral process and those elected clearly rule" (p. 6). True, a party that is being *prevented* from being placed on the ballot is made un-free to participate in the electoral process; but a party's or candidate's inability to win a place on the ticket may also be due to circumstances other than the intervention of govern-mental or other actors. We have seen that, from the point of view of the range of choice, the greater the number of parties among which the voters are free to choose, the greater their electoral freedom; but the survey does not seem to take this dimension into account. A more serious defect is its as-sumption that free elections guarantee that "those elected clearly rule." Effective political power—and authority as well—is often held by others than those elected. If this were taken as an indicator of political freedom, even the United States would rank rather low, at least on the municipal level (but in the survey the United States turns up among the "freest" on the scales of both political and civil freedom). Nor does "the absence of periodic shifts in rule from one group to another" necessarily indicate a "weakening of effective com-petition" and hence a limitation of political freedom (p. 6). The same party often stays in power a long time because of continued majority support in periodic free elections.

"[E]xtreme economic inequality, illiteracy, or intimidating violence" lowers the political freedom rating (p. 6). The last does so indeed; but the economically or educationally de-prived are unable, but not necessarily unfree, to take advan-tage of electoral institutions—certainly not unfree wrt gov-ernment. Nor does "a broad informal consensus irrespective of election processes" (p. 8) indicate that citizens are politi-cally free wrt government or socially free wrt any group. There is not even an *empirical* correlation between political freedom and ideological consensus (as there may well be between political freedom and a high degree of economic equality or literacy). Widespread agreement can be found among subjects of totalitarian regimes, often as a result of effective indoctrination. Democratic societies vary in this re-spect. There is a larger degree of agreement on basic political matters among Americans than among Frenchmen, who have been traditionally divided between Right and Left. However, as long as the party system reflects these cleavages, political freedom remains unrestricted.

Combining the two separate scales of civil and political rights, the survey arrives at an "overall judgment of each [country] as 'free,' 'partly free,' or 'not free'" (p. 6). Thus, in 1978 there has been "a .6% drop in the world's percentage of free persons" (p. 2). This leads us back to the principal objection against comparing or measuring "freedom." Possibly, political liberty and civil rights can be measured; but these are not *the* defining characteristics of "freedom"; they are two specific kinds of the social freedom of citizens wrt their government. They are singled out by the author of the survey because he considers them *desirable*.

FIVE
Other Concepts of Freedom

Sous le grand nom de liberté, c'est ainsi que chaque vanité
cherche sa vengeance et sa pâture.
    Henri Taine, *Les origines de la France contemporaine*

AWARENESS OF THE LOGICAL STRUCTURE of the *definienda* is—we remember—the first requirement of an effective conceptual analysis. Such clarity is especially important when analyzing notions of freedom, as the *word* is being used in ordinary language for at least five different concepts, each with its own structure and meaning. Unlike in chapter 3 on power, I will here be criticizing other writers not so much for defining social freedom differently or less adequately as for applying 'freedom' indiscriminately to these various concepts. The positive valuational connotations of 'freedom' are even stronger than the negative overtones of 'power', and this may account for the propensity of speakers and writers to apply it to a variety of situations they wish to commend. Although I believe that social freedom, as I have defined it, is what political scientists have most often in mind when they use the term, I shall not argue that this concept is more important than the others. My point is rather to clear up the confusions resulting from failure to make these conceptual distinctions.

5.1 SOCIAL FREEDOM AND FREEDOM OF ACTION
Like 'power', 'free' and 'unfree' are used in ordinary language not only to designate relationships of interaction, but also as synonyms for being, respectively, able or unable to do something. That student R is free to become a physician may convey that nobody prevents him from going to medical school or would punish him if he did (or forces him to take up medicine or would punish him if he did not). More likely,

however, this phrase is meant to indicate that R *can* study medicine, that he has the mental capacity, the physical stamina, and the financial resources to go through medical school, so that it is up to him whether to become a physician. 'Free' in this sense refers to a relation between *one* actor and an action. This is a different concept of freedom, with a different logical structure and meaning. We may call it freedom of action, in contradistinction to social freedom.[1] That A has freedom of action wrt x (or that A is at liberty to do x) means that he can do x;[2] that A lacks freedom of action wrt x means that he is unable to do x.

The distinction between social freedom and freedom of action corresponds to that between one actor's power over another's activity and an actor's power wrt his own action. It turns out that 'A can do x', 'A has the power to do x', and 'A is at liberty to do x' are synonymous. In the words of Hume, "By liberty, then, we can only mean the power of acting or not acting, according to the determination of the will; that is, if we choose to remain at rest, we may; if we choose to move, we also may" (*Human Understanding*, section 8, part 1). This is not the "only" meaning of liberty (or of power); it is the meaning of one of several concepts of freedom.

Freedom of action is neither a necessary nor a sufficient condition for social freedom. As we have seen, if R can do x but would be punished by P for doing so, he is not socially free either to do x or not; wrt P, R is unfree to do x. Nor is lack of freedom of action either a necessary or a sufficient condition for social unfreedom. R is free (wrt everyone) to do or not to do what he is unable to accomplish, if his inability is not the result of some other actor's intervention.

This analysis is not compatible with the approach of Gerald MacCallum's, who, in an influential article, also construes the concept of social freedom as "a triadic relation," but in a different way:

> Taking the format '*x* is (is not) free from *y* to do (not do, become, not become) *z*', *x* ranges over agents, *y* ranges over such 'preventing conditions' as constraints, restrictions, interferences, and barriers, and *z* ranges over actions or conditions of character or circumstance. (1967, p. 314)

In this formula, 'x' corresponds to 'R' and 'z' corresponds (more or less) to 'x' in mine. The difference is between MacCallum's 'y' and my 'P'. His variable 'y' covers any kind of "preventive condition," regardless of whether it consists in the interference of some other actor or whether the "barriers" are the result of the actor's own inabilities or of impersonal (e.g., physical) conditions.

MacCallum's interpretation leads to the conclusion that one is unfree to do what one cannot do, regardless of whether one's inability has been caused by another actor. He does not think that this distinction needs to be made.

> [I]f one is concerned with social, political, and eco-
> nomic policies, and with how these policies can re-
> move or increase human misery, it is quite irrelevant
> whether difficulties in the way of the policies are or
> are not *due to* arrangements made by human beings.
> The only question is whether the difficulties can be
> removed by human arrangements, and at what cost.
> (P. 325)

He therefore holds that it "makes perfectly good and histori-cally accurate sense" to speak of "freedom from hunger" (p. 318), whether hypothetical food shortages are the result of crop failures or of agricultural policies. While this distinction may not (or may!) be relevant from a moral point of view, there are many contexts, including those of politics, where it does matter whether inabilities or unavailabilities are or are not caused by specifiable persons or groups, even though the distinction is often difficult to make in practice, as we have seen. It is arguable whether unemployment is caused by capitalists or by capitalism or by other factors. But unless one takes the view that capitalists are responsible for unemploy-ment, it cannot be argued that being unable to find work is an instance of social unfreedom—not on the basis of the pro-posed analysis. MacCallum seems unaware that he is defining not the "triadic relation" of social freedom, but the concept of freedom of action.

Once we have made the distinction between social free-dom and freedom of action, we cannot accept without qualification a characterization of the former like the following: "[S]ocial freedom is to be determined by the extent of the range of alternatives available to an agent" (Smith 1977, p. 236; italics added). We have seen that this is indeed *one* of the dimensions of the degree of social freedom. Imposing an extra gasoline tax on Sundays does reduce motorists' social freedom to either not driving or paying the additional tax. A tax is not a punishment. On the other hand, by making Sunday driving illegal, government does not reduce social *freedom* to either not driving or paying the fine (if apprehended); government makes motorists *unfree* to drive on Sundays, and the degree of their social unfreedom depends on such factors as the probability of being punished and the severity of the fine. It is their freedom of *action*, not their social freedom, that has been limited to not driving or driving at the risk of punishment.

Nor can I concur with J. P. Day, who, in a stimulating article, stipulates that "the truth of 'A is able to D' is a necessary condition both of the truth and also of the falsity of 'A is free to D'" (1977, p. 260). It follows that someone unable to do something cannot be said to be either free or unfree to do it. According to my proposal, 'R can do x' is both a necessary *and sufficient* condition for 'R has freedom *of action* wrt x', since I am using these two expressions synonymously (and hence, if R cannot do x, R lacks freedom of action wrt x). On the other hand, someone unable to do something *can* be said to be either socially free or unfree to do it, depending on whether or not his inability has been caused by another actor.

Since the disagreement here is about definitions, we can only ask which one is better. Day uses as an example the question whether people were free to fly, say, from New York to London, before the invention of the airplane, and answers: since they were unable to fly, they were neither free nor unfree to do so. My answer must be: people lacked freedom of action in that respect, but were socially free to do what they could not do. I must concede that it sounds somewhat odd to say that everyone was free (wrt everyone) to go by boat or to fly (perhaps by Concorde!) before no less than since the age of air travel (see 4.2.2)—until I add that it was freedom of action in that respect that they lacked before the invention of the plane. Day, on the other hand, would have to deny, quite generally, that making it impossible for someone to do something is to make him unfree to do so; he must hold, e.g., that R, whom P has locked in a room, is, wrt P, neither free nor unfree to get out. It seems to me that this consequence of Day's analysis is counterintuitive to a much greater degree and that I am paying a relatively small price for the possibility—which I consider a necessity—of subsuming situations of preventing under social unfreedom.

It has been denied that there is a connection between possibility and freedom, and between impossibility and unfreedom.

> [E]veryone always "has a choice" .... "[H]aving a choice" therefore does not make one free since everyone would be always free if that constituted freedom. (Bergmann 1977, p. 78)

> If we allow ourselves to imagine that obstacles or risks make us "unfree" we will conjure up the notion that they make it impossible for us "to act otherwise." (Bergmann 1977, p. 75)

Granted that we sometimes have a choice to do or not to do what is risky or costly (e.g., to voice dissent under a totalitarian regime); but it is surely not mere imagination that there are also obstacles that make it—literally or for all practical purposes—impossible to act otherwise. Having a choice constitutes not "freedom," but freedom of action, and being unable to act in a certain way is to lack freedom of action in that respect.

Here are some further examples of the widespread tendency to use the words 'free' and 'freedom' without making it clear whether one means to refer to social freedom or freedom of action: "[W]hen someone, person or group, has the power to do or not to do something, to act or not to act in a certain way, he is said to be free to do so" (Friedrich 1963, p. 351). He should be said to be at liberty to do so, as he may be unfree to do it wrt some other actor. "[If someone] broke the law he was obviously free to commit the illegal act" (Cassinelli 1966, p. 35, note 4). He was obviously at liberty either to break the law at the risk of punishment or to comply, and obviously officially unfree to commit the illegal act, assuming that he would have been punished if he did. "Consider the many individuals who have performed actions, started movements, and initiated reforms knowing full well that their so doing would cause others to inflict severe, sometimes unjustified punishment on them. Should we, do we in fact, say that such individuals were deprived of their liberty to behave as they did? Of course not" (Parent 1974, p. 156). Of course yes! Wrt those who punished them, they were unfree to perform these actions (and it does not matter whether they knew about the penalties, let alone whether these were justified). But they were "of course not" deprived of their freedom of action to engage in these risky movements. "Is not the assertion 'the blizzard rendered X unfree to continue his travels' perfectly intelligible?" (Parent 1974, p. 159). Yes, as long as we make it clear that the assertion refers to lack of freedom of action, but not to social unfreedom. It is not true that "a man who has inadvertently fallen into a natural pit with unscalable walls is unfree *in the same sense* as the prisoner at night in his cell" (Cassinelli 1966, p. 28; italics added). Both lack freedom of action, being unable to get out. The prisoner in the cell is *also* unfree *in a different sense:* unfree wrt the guards, who make it impossible for him to leave. In *this* sense, the man in the pit is free to leave (wrt everyone). Whether the situation of the workers in the nineteenth century should be compared to that of the prisoner in his cell or of the man in the pit is a matter of factual, not conceptual, controversy.

In his essay "Two Concepts of Liberty," Isaiah Berlin stated, "It is argued, very plausibly, that if a man is too poor to afford something on which there is no legal ban—a loaf of bread, a journey round the world, recourse to the law courts—he is as little free to have it as he would be if it were forbidden him by law" (1969, p. 122). Interestingly enough, in his introduction, written later, Berlin seems to deny the plausibility of this very argument: "If a man is too poor or too ignorant or too feeble to make use of his legal rights, the liberty that these rights confer upon him is nothing to him, but it is not thereby annihilated" (p. liii). So does Rawls: "The inability to take advantage of one's rights and opportunities as a result of poverty and ignorance, and the lack of means generally, is sometimes counted among the constraints definitive of liberty. I shall not, however, say this, but rather I shall think of these things as affecting the worth of liberty" (1971, p. 204). I agree. A social freedom is usually of no value to those unable to take advantage of it, e.g. (to take a previous example), being officially free to attend school when there are no "free" public schools. There is, then, often an empirical connection between these two kinds of freedom. The greater someone's freedom of action—e.g., the more things he can procure—the less is he dependent on others, and hence the fewer the actors wrt whom he is unfree to do as he pleases and the greater the range of his social freedom. Minimum wage laws restrict the "freedom of contract" of both employers and employees wrt government. But being unfree to accept lower wages than the legal minimum enables employees to earn more and to become less dependent on their employers.

The simplest and most effective way of making the distinction would be to dispense with 'freedom of action' altogether, for the same reasons that I suggested not using 'power to do x'. Since 'to be able to do x', 'to be at liberty to do x', and 'to have the power to do x' mean the same, why not use only the first expression, and speak of 'freedom' only in the sense of social freedom? The same suggestion has been made by Partridge:

> The linking of "being free to" with "having the capacity or power" deprives the word "free" of its essential and unequivocal function, which is to refer to a situation or state of affairs in which a man's choice of how he acts is not deliberately forced or restrained by another man. (1967, p. 222)

5.2 Social Freedom and Free Actions

David Raphael speaks of "freedom of action *or* social freedom" (1970, p. 115; italics added), and continues: "[W]e may define the latter as the absence of restraint on doing what one chooses or what one would choose to do if he knew that he could.... [D]oing what we choose to do is usually doing what we want to do, so that freedom, as I have defined it, is most often a matter of being unrestrained in doing what one wants" (pp. 115, 117). My objection is that neither freedom of action nor social freedom pertains to what an actor actually does or wants or chooses or would choose under certain conditions; both concepts pertain to ranges of *alternatives*. And the range of what I am socially either able or free to do may, but need not, include what I want to do. To take a previous example, I am able and free (wrt everyone) to listen to *Don Giovanni*, which I would like to do, or to the *Ring*, which I would not choose to do; yet, my freedom of action and social freedom extend also to the four Wagner operas. I do not think that "there is something paradoxical about saying that a person is either free or not free to starve, to cut off his ears, or to die" (Benn and Weinstein 1971, p. 195). If nobody prevents him from fasting to death or committing suicide, he is free to do so or not (just as I am free to listen to Wagner), however unlikely it may be that he wants to do so.

Perhaps the above passage could be interpreted as specifying the meaning not of freedom of action or social freedom, but of a free action. Hobbes does so explicitly when he speaks of "actions which men voluntarily do: which, because they proceed from their will, proceed from liberty" (*Leviathan*, chapter 21). Similarly, "so long as a man acts of his own volition and is not coerced in what he does, he is free" (Partridge 1967, p. 222). Here 'free' designates a *property*—of an action. But is a free action the same as a voluntary action? Then there would be no unfree actions, a conclusion perhaps reached by Hannah Arendt when she proclaims that "to *be* free and to act is the same" (1961, p. 153). Complying with a gunman's coercive threat is, in the literal sense, a voluntary action; but it is just the prototype of an action we would want to characterize as unfree, and that is why Partridge adds that for an action to be free, it must be uncoerced. But are all uncoerced actions free? Suppose I act in order to comply with a noncoercive threat or to avoid performing a punishable action. In such cases compliance may be held to be unfree because the action is done—to adopt Day's terminology (1977, p. 258)—not willingly in the sense of gladly, but unwillingly or reluctantly. Should we then follow John Stuart Mill's interpretation that liberty, in the sense of acting freely, "consists in doing what one desires" (*On Liberty*, chapter 5)? While 'acting voluntarily' is too broad a characterization, 'doing what one desires' seems to me to be too narrow. I may go to the dentist unwillingly, or stay away—just as reluctantly. Yet, I am inclined to call either action a free one.

My suggestion is therefore to consider an action unfree if it is motivated by a specific desire, namely, to avoid punishment; otherwise it is a free action. A driver who keeps within the speed limit to avoid a fine does not act freely; his doing so to enjoy a leisurely ride or because of his conviction that speeding laws ought to be respected constitutes a free action.[3]

On the basis of this characterization, what are the connections between social freedom and free actions? If R is (wrt everyone) free to do either x or z, whichever action he performs is a free action, regardless of whether it corresponds to his desire or whether he acts reluctantly. If R is unfree to do x, his not doing x may be an unfree or a free action, depending on whether it is motivated primarily by his desire to avoid punishment or not. The victim of a gunman is unfree to keep his money, and drivers are unfree to speed. Not keeping his money but handing it over is an unfree action (contrary to Hobbes), since it is motivated by the desire to avoid punishment (possibly death). This is not the motive of a driver who wants to take a leisurely ride; his not speeding is a free action. Hence, I do not agree with Day that R does x freely if and *only if* R does x and it is not the case that R is unfree to refrain from doing x (1977, p. 270). As I just pointed out, R may do freely what he is unfree to refrain from doing (e.g., keeping within the speed limits for moral reasons). He may also do freely what he is socially unfree to do (e.g., speed).[4] Deliberately committing a punishable offense normally constitutes a free action, since the actor does so in spite of the risk of punishment.

To summarize, let me react to the following statement: "If murder is a capital offense, those who value their lives are not free to commit murder" (White 1970, p. 196). I would say: (1) All are officially unfree to commit murder, regardless of how much or how little they value their lives. (2) Some are capable of murder, and hence have freedom of action in that respect. (3) If someone wants to commit murder but does not because of the death penalty, his abstaining is an unfree action. But a terrorist who values his cause more highly than his life may commit murder quite freely.[5]

5.3 SOCIAL FREEDOM AND FEELING FREE

"It is usually admitted that the slave who always gets what he wants and never wants what he cannot get may properly be described as being free in one of the many senses of the term" (Smith 1977, p. 236). But in which of the many senses? The slave, whether satisfied with his lot or not, is unfree to leave because he would be punished if he did or because he is being physically prevented or because he has been so well conditioned as to be psychologically incapable of conceiving of that possibility. In the latter two cases, he also lacks freedom of action in that respect. If his conduct is not motivated by fear of punishment, it may well be free. However, this statement is more likely meant to refer to the slave's feeling. To the extent that his wants correspond to what is required of him, he *feels* free. "Contentment, or satisfaction, is a *kind* of freedom" (Smith 1977, p. 236). It is not "freedom in general [that] may be defined as the absence of obstacles to the realization of desires" (Russell 1940, p. 251), but the feeling of freedom. Here 'freedom' and 'free' refer to a characteristic not of an action, but of the actor's state of mind. An actor may be said to feel free to the extent that he is not being made unfree to do what he wants to do (or unfree not to do what he does not want to do). "But what of a prisoner who is prevented from leaving and who prefers not to leave? His freedom can no more be said to be impaired than is that of someone who would not choose to throw himself off a cliff and is protected by a high fence from going over the edge" (Dryer 1964, p. 445). No more—and no less! The prisoner who prefers jail to "freedom," and hence *feels* free in his cell, is as unfree to leave as other prisoners who experience their imprisonment as a deprivation. And whoever walks along the fence is, wrt those who erected it, unfree to go over the edge whether he would want to or not. Berlin has argued convincingly that, "[i]f degrees of freedom were a function of the satisfaction of desires, I could increase freedom as effectively by eliminating desires as by satisfying them" (1969, p. xxxviii). A Stoic may have a strong feeling of freedom because he is being left free to satisfy the few desires he has. But Stoics and Epicureans are equally unfree to break into pastry shops.

The objective interaction relationship of social freedom must then not be confused with the subjective feeling of freedom. Protestants during the wars of religion felt free as long as they were not required to change their religion, even if they were officially unfree to do so. There are also situations in which we *want* our social freedom to be restricted, in which we feel free when we are made unfree to act in certain ways. I prefer that everyone, including myself, be compelled to pay taxes to provide for certain public goods, and this limitation of my social freedom does not diminish my feeling free. Some derive a feeling of freedom from their "freedom of participation" in the political process; others feel free when they "escape from freedom" into submission to authority. Subjects of a totalitarian dictator may have been so thoroughly indoctrinated that they derive a feeling of freedom from walking the tightrope of the official party line, and do not care to do any of the things they have been made unfree to do. Dostoyevsky's Grand Inquisitor plays on these two meanings of the same word when he says, "But let me tell Thee that now, today, people are more persuaded than ever that they have perfect freedom, yet they have brought their freedom to us and laid it humbly at our feet" (*The Brothers Karamazov*).

5.4 SOCIAL FREEDOM AND BEING A FREE PERSON

"Liberty is self-determination, autonomy—this is almost a tautology" (Marcuse 1965, p. 86). Again, "liberty" in what sense? Autonomy is certainly not *synonymous* with freedom in any of the senses examined so far. Is it *one* of the defining conditions of any of these concepts? "Social freedom . . . involves the element of autonomy, the capacity to understand and appreciate alternatives, and to make rational choices" (Smith 1977, p. 247). It does not, given the proposed definition. Since an actor's social freedom does not depend on what he does, it cannot depend on whether what he does is based on rational choice. It is therefore not the case that the contented slave "is *socially* unfree because the conditions of his socialization prevent him from developing powers of autonomy and rational choice, a *logically* necessary condition of genuine social freedom" (Smith 1977, p. 247; italics added). Nor are these defining conditions of freedom of action, or of a free action, or of feeling free. Men are able to act irrationally as well as rationally and autonomously. Deliberately defying the law is a free action, but it may be an irrational one. A slave who lacks the powers of autonomy and rational choice may feel free.

Self-determination, autonomy, acting rationally—these are dispositional properties of individuals and may be taken as defining conditions of yet another concept of freedom: being a free person. It is in this sense that we should take statements such as: "A man is free insofar as he is able to act on a judgment because he perceives it to be correct" (Fried 1978, p. 63); "one can be free only when one is self-determining" (Fay 1975, p. 54). A free person is an individual who has the disposition to act rationally in view of goals he has chosen in an autonomous way, i.e., independently. "[A]cting autonomously is acting from principles that we would consent to as free and equal rational beings" (Rawls 1971, p. 516). Self-determination "is the ability to live in accordance with one's own conscious purposes, to act and decide for oneself rather than to be acted upon and decided for by others" (Macpherson 1973, p. 109). This is the capacity a thoroughly conditioned slave is likely to lack; but a slave who resists indoctrination may well be, in this sense, a free person.

The notion of being a free person has also gone under the name of "positive freedom" (see Berlin 1969, p. 131). This terminology has the advantage of making explicit the distinction between this concept of freedom and "negative freedom," which corresponds more or less to what I have called social freedom.

Let us indicate some of the connections between positive and negative freedom. We have seen that, if P persuades R to do x, R remains free either to do or not to do x. If R accepts P's arguments uncritically (e.g., on P's authority), R does not act like a free person. If he adopts them as a result of his own rational deliberation, his decision "depends on himself." I do not agree that "[t]o the extent that A influences B on some matter X, then B is not autonomous in relation to A with respect to X" (Dahl 1976, p. 40).[6] Being influenced by rational arguments is compatible with being an autonomous and hence a free person.

A free person may sometimes perform actions that are not free. His independent and rational judgment may lead him on occasion to the conclusion that the risk of punishment is too great to warrant disobedience—occasionally, but not generally, since by complying to avoid punishment he does "become the instrument of another man's will." A free person is not as a rule motivated in his actions by fear of punishment. His independent and rational deliberation will lead him either to disobey or to comply for different reasons, e.g., because doing so corresponds to his own moral convictions. I disagree with Robert P. Wolff's thesis that autonomy implies "the refusal to be ruled" and that "anarchism is the only political doctrine compatible with the virtue of autonomy" (1970, p. 18). I surely may, on the basis of my own, independent, and rational deliberation, decide to join some private association and to be bound by its future decisions, including decisions of which I might disapprove. No recourse to the fiction of explicit or even "tacit" consent is needed to draw the analogy with the political situation. If I approve of the majority principle (in elections and legislative assemblies), it will be rational for me to comply with majority decisions, including those I oppose, at least up to a certain point. Compliance with governmental enactments one considers legitimate is compatible with autonomy and "positive freedom." Free persons will "refuse to be ruled" only if they disapprove of the political regime as a whole. Here heroic acts of defiance might be needed to preserve one's freedom in the sense of autonomy. Others may have been so thoroughly indoctrinated that they *feel* free even under a repressive regime; but they no longer act as free persons.

"Positive freedom" is thus compatible both with "negative freedom" and with its restriction. "But positive liberty, in its basic sense of ability to form and follow one's own conscious purposes, requires even more clearly than negative liberty that there be no indirect domination by withholding the means of life and labour" (Macpherson 1973, p. 117). Making the basic necessities of life available to enable individuals to act as free persons requires government to restrict the citizen's social freedom in certain areas. Restriction of a person's social freedom in order to restore his own capacity for self-determination may also be necessary in some cases, e.g., compulsory rehabilitation programs for drug addicts (see McCloskey 1965, p. 494). The possible relationships between negative and positive freedom have been well summarized by Isaiah Berlin: "Individual freedom may or may not clash with democratic organization, and the positive liberty of self-realization with the negative liberty of non-interference" (1969, p. lvii).

SIX

Egalitarianism

*Il ne faut pas entendre par ce mot [égalité] que les degrés de
puissance et de richesse soient absolument les mêmes; mais
que . . . nul citoyen soit assez opulent pour en pouvoir acheter un
autre, et nul assez pauvre pour être contraint de se vendre.*

Jean Jacques Rousseau, *Du contrat social*

THE WORDS 'equal' and 'egalitarian' and their contraries
are often used to denote characteristics of persons or
states of affairs. Persons of the same age or income or ability
are said to be equal in such respects. We consider an existing
income distribution relatively egalitarian when the differences between the highest and lowest incomes are relatively small. Here I shall deal with the concepts of
egalitarianism and inegalitarianism in a different sense,
namely, as characteristics of certain kinds of rules—legal or
moral or customary. 'Egalitarian' and 'inegalitarian', like
'just' and 'unjust', can be predicated only of rules of a particular type, which we may call rules of distribution—i.e.,
rules enjoining one actor to distribute a quantifiable benefit
(e.g., voting rights, salaries) or burden (e.g., military service,
tax payments) to at least two other actors. One may ask
whether it is morally right or wrong to legalize or to outlaw
divorce or abortion, but not whether such laws are egalitarian or inegalitarian. The latter terms are applicable to rules
such as voting or draft or tax laws, to salary schedules, to
hiring procedures, to college admission policies.

Before we determine what makes them egalitarian or inegalitarian, let us examine briefly the structure of rules of
distribution. Such rules specify the following, either explicitly or implicitly: (1) a *benefit* (e.g., one vote) or a *burden* (e.g.,
one year's military service) to be allotted; (2) a *reference
group*—i.e., a class of persons to whom the rule is meant to
apply, usually defined by a common characteristic (e.g., all

citizens), (3) a *selected group*—i.e., a subclass of the reference group to whom the benefit or burden is to be allocated (e.g., all citizens of a certain age).

Rules of distribution can be classified into the following types: (A) rules of selection and (B) rules of apportionment. Rules of selection stipulate that members of the reference group who have a certain additional characteristic shall be selected to receive a specified benefit or to be subject to a specified burden; e.g., all citizens above the age of eighteen and fulfilling certain residence requirements shall have the right to vote; citizens who are male and between the ages of eighteen and twenty-six shall be subject to the draft. Rules of apportionment stipulate that the amount of some specified benefit (e.g., salary) or burden (e.g., income tax) to any member of the selected group shall be proportionate to the degree to which he has a certain additional characteristic (e.g., ability, income). Rules of distribution often combine these two types, as we shall see.

We are trying to determine general criteria by which to characterize rules distributing and redistributing benefits or burdens as either egalitarian or inegalitarian or egalitarian to such and such a degree, independently of whether such measures are being advocated or opposed.

6.1 RULES OF SELECTION (CRITERION A)

We shall for the moment disregard possible variations in the amounts to be apportioned and deal only with rules defining the group to be selected out of the reference group to receive a benefit or to be subjected to a burden in fixed amounts. To simplify, we shall take rules that divide the reference group into just two subgroups: those to whom the benefit or burden is to be allotted (the selected group), and those excluded. Whether and to what degree such rules of selection are egalitarian will depend on the size of the selected group relative to the reference group.

6.1.1 Rules of Distribution

We consider, first, rules of distribution in isolation, as it were; later we shall examine them in their "historical" context.

Our first inclination might be to consider such rules of

distribution the more egalitarian, the greater the proportion of those who are "treated equally" by virtue of the rule. The most egalitarian rules would then be those that treat all members of the reference group the same way and that do not select any subgroup for different treatment. In other words, if either the selected or the excluded group is the same as the reference group, the rule is fully egalitarian (strictly speaking, there is then no "selected group"): universal suffrage as well as total absence of elections; universal military training as well as an all-volunteer army (nobody must serve). Such a definition has the advantage of bringing out that a dictatorship without elections is, wrt the treatment of its citizens, just as egalitarian as a democracy based on universal suffrage and protection of everybody's basic rights. Rousseau was well aware of this seemingly paradoxical feature of despotism. "Here is the ultimate stage of inequality, and the extreme point which closes the circle and touches the point from which we started. Here all individuals become equals again because they are nothing" (*Second Discourse*). It seems quite plausible to consider a rule 100 percent egalitarian if it makes the same allotment to either 100 percent or to 0 percent of those to whom it applies. It follows—and this, too, may seem plausible—that a rule treating 50 percent of the reference group one way and the other half differently is 100 percent inegalitarian, e.g., male suffrage or drafting half the male population within a certain age-group. But it follows further that the rule becomes more egalitarian if we move from the 50 percent point *in either direction*. Thus, granting the franchise to, say 25 percent of the population would be fairly egalitarian, since this policy treats 75 percent of the population "equally" by disenfranchising them. Moreover, this rule is egalitarian to the same degree (namely, to 50 percent) as giving the vote to 75 percent. Furthermore, if we start with giving the franchise to 10 percent, the more we increase the number of voters, the more *inegalitarian* the policy becomes, up to the 50 percent point, which is the most inegalitarian policy. Not until we give the vote to more than 50 percent does the rule become more egalitarian. As it often happens, this definition of egalitarianism appears at first to be practical and in agreement with "common sense"—until we draw some of the logical conclusions to which it leads. These are so counterintuitive that we cannot possibly hold on to the definition.

I think the following definition will lead us out of this difficulty.

Definition: Wrt a given reference group, a rule of distribution of fixed benefits or burdens is the more egalitarian, the greater the ratio of the selected group to the reference group.

Accordingly, a rule is fully egalitarian iff it assigns the benefit or burden to all members of the reference group, i.e., if the selected group and the reference group coincide. Let us take again voting laws as an illustration and consider as the reference group all adult inhabitants of a given country. Then, giving the suffrage to all is egalitarian, and the more so, the lower the voting age and the fewer the requirements of citizenship, residence, registration, etc. So far, this definition leads to the same conclusion as the previous one. But now we come to the differences. Manhood suffrage is 50 percent egalitarian (or inegalitarian to 50 percent, but not to 100 percent). Disenfranchising blacks is less inegalitarian than disenfranchising women if fewer than half of all men and women of voting age are black, but more inegalitarian if blacks constitute the majority. Differences as to who should have the right to vote do not affect the judgment that manhood suffrage in Switzerland (when it was in effect) was more egalitarian than voting laws in South Africa, but more inegalitarian than voting practices in Mississippi twenty years ago.[1] Giving only 1 percent of the population the vote is very inegalitarian even though 99 percent are "treated equally." But must we not conclude that a political system without elections is the most inegalitarian? This is surely in better agreement with our common view than calling such a system egalitarian, as would follow from the previous definition. Indeed, in an extreme dictatorship, one actor has absolute power over all others, and the latter have no power over anyone. However, the proposed explication leads to yet another conclusion, and a still more plausible one. Regimes that do not provide for elections cannot be judged to be egalitarian or inegalitarian. In other words, the ratio of the selected to the reference group is zero. By the same criterion, a draft law is the more egalitarian, the greater the ratio of those who are drafted to those who are not; and the more individuals exempted, the more inegalitarian the rule. The institution of an all-volunteer army cannot be said to be either egalitarian or inegalitarian, since there is no rule imposing an obligation to serve on anyone.

But here we encounter another difficulty. Suppose the government exempts farmers or defers students. Could not one say that what is being distributed here are exemptions from the draft? If so, must we not draw the opposite conclusion, namely, that a draft policy is the more *egalitarian*, the greater the ratio of those who are *exempted* to those who must serve? How shall we decide? Certainly not on normative grounds. Some consider being drafted a burden; others view serving one's country in the armed forces a benefit (and being deprived of this honor a burden). Such considerations must remain quite irrelevant in the present context. I think there is a simple solution. Logically and temporally, there must be a draft law before there can be draft exemptions, just as we cannot conceive of disenfranchising some without a prior voting law, or of tax exemptions without tax laws. So we consider what is being given or exacted *first* to be the benefit or burden allocated by the rule. Any exception to the original rule is necessarily inegalitarian, and the more so, the greater the ratio of those covered by the exception.

Another problem has to do with the size of the reference group. Rules of distribution specify the group selected for the allocation of some benefit or burden, but cannot logically circumscribe the reference group. This decision is left to the political analyst. But by what criterion should he be guided? Does the reference group of a voting law consist of all inhabitants of the country? Of all citizens? If we take the former, the voting system in France turns out to be more inegalitarian than that in the United States because the percentage of foreigners in France is (or at least was a few years ago, because of the many "guest workers") greater and there are more obstacles to naturalization. In the latter case, the

United States is less egalitarian in this respect because the residence requirements are more stringent. Logically, it is possible to make any rule fully egalitarian by defining the reference group so narrowly that it becomes identical with the selected group. Conversely, to label any given rule inegalitarian, it is sufficient to characterize the reference group more broadly than the selected group. For example, Dahl takes political equality as one of the defining criteria of 'procedural democracy': decisions must "take equally into account the expressed preferences of each member of the demos" (Dahl 1979, p. 101). Immediately the question arises, "What persons have a rightful claim to be included in the demos?" (p. 100). This reference group can be narrowed down until it coincides with the selected group of decision makers. But "if a demos can be a tiny group that exercises a brutal despotism over a vast subject population, then 'democracy' is ... indistinguishable from autocracy" (p. 112). That is why Dahl adds the stipulation that "the demos must include all adult members of the association except transients" (p. 129). To the extent that a given political system meets the condition of political equality wrt *this* reference group, it fulfills one of the criteria of procedural democracy. A given rule of distribution can be said to be egalitarian or inegalitarian only "wrt a given reference group"; accordingly, the proposed definition of egalitarianism starts with this clause.

But does not the proposed definition lead to the conclusion that a simple majority rule in a voting assembly, e.g., of 100 members, is only 51 percent egalitarian (or 49 percent inegalitarian), since 51 percent of its members can form a "selected group" whose preferences prevail over the excluded minority of 49 percent? Not so. The "benefit" being distributed by this rule is the *chance* of having one's own preference adopted as binding on all. This probability is theoretically the same for every member of the voting assembly. It does not matter whether a simple or a qualified majority rule is operating. Even the requirement of unanimity is 100 percent egalitarian, since every voter has a veto power over the assembly's decisions; i.e., he has the same chance of being the one dissenting member with the power of blocking the vote of all others. The situation is different if there exists some "permanent minority" in the assembly. Suppose that 25 percent of the members are black and that they are regularly outvoted by the other 75 percent. Egalitarianism would require that the former be given three votes to the latter's one; this would give each member the same chance of having his view implemented. This is not to say that giving each voter in an assembly the same probability of being part of a "winning coalition" is a necessary or sufficient condition for equality of political influence. As mentioned before, degree of influence is not a "benefit" that can be allocated by formal rules, but the outcome of many factors over which legislators have no control.

The same considerations apply whenever a limited number of benefits or burdens are to be distributed among a larger number of persons. For example, there are 100,000 men eligible for service in an army needing 50,000. Someone might argue that any "selective service" procedure is bound to be 50 percent egalitarian (or 50 percent inegalitarian), since half of the available men will be selected out of the reference group. But here, too, it is the chance of being drafted that is being distributed. A draft law is fully egalitarian if it gives each eligible man the same chance of being drafted or exempted. Consequently, selection by lottery is 100 percent egalitarian, but selection based on education or occupation would be inegalitarian, since it increases the probability of being drafted for anyone with the specified characteristics. That the most egalitarian policy happens to be considered by many to be the fairest is a mere coincidence.

Let us take as a last example the question of admission to a college. If the reference group is constituted by the applicants and the benefit consists of being enrolled, the only fully egalitarian method would be to admit them all; and the smaller the ratio of those admitted to those who apply, the more inegalitarian the admissions policy. If there are 600 applicants, admitting 400 is more egalitarian than admitting 300, no matter whether admission is based on SAT scores or race or sex or geography or any combination of such factors. Suppose now that the size of the freshman class is given;

e.g., 450 among the 600 applicants can be admitted—a 75 percent egalitarian policy. But the question remains: which method of selecting these 450 students is the most egalitarian? Giving every one of the 600 applicants the same probability of admission would be fully egalitarian—e.g., a random selection such as a fair lottery, however inadvisable such a method of selecting students (unlike soldiers) may be. Any other admissions policy would be inegalitarian by this criterion, including, of course, selection on the basis of aptitude. Any quota system, too, would be inegalitarian, no matter what quota characteristic one might adopt. It is one of the advantages of the proposed definition that egalitarianism and justice remain distinct concepts.

Our interpretation has the merit of construing egalitarianism as a comparative and even as a quantitative concept, making it possible to ascertain that one rule of distribution is more egalitarian, or more inegalitarian, than another, or that a given rule is egalitarian to such and such a degree.

6.1.2 Rules of Redistribution

Rules allocating benefits or burdens, especially those enacted by laws, operate in a historically given context. They are therefore more properly viewed as rules of *re*distribution. There is an existing distribution that may itself be the result of the application of some formal rule of distribution, or it may be the effect of custom. A new rule is introduced (e.g., a law is being enacted) that redistributes the benefits or burdens, i.e., that changes the ratio of the selected to the reference group. As political scientists, we want to determine whether such a rule of redistribution is egalitarian and to what degree. For that purpose, we must compare the historically given distribution with the distribution resulting from the application of the rule.

Definition: Wrt a given distribution (and wrt a given reference group), a rule of redistribution of fixed benefits or burdens is the more egalitarian, the greater the ratio of the selected to the reference group after the application of the rule as compared with the original distribution.

In other words, the more egalitarian the allocation after the application of the rule, the more egalitarian it is. Conversely, a rule of redistribution is the more inegalitarian, the more it reduces the size of the selected group.

Is admitting 400 of the 600 applicants to a college an egalitarian or an inegalitarian policy? It depends. If the year before 300 of the 600 applicants were taken, admitting 400 increases the ratio of the selected group; consequently, this new policy constitutes a more egalitarian rule of redistribution. But this same policy is inegalitarian if previously 500 of the 600 applicants had been admitted. The French Constitution of 1791 was egalitarian not because it substituted property for birth as the criterion for the right to vote, but because it extended the suffrage to a much greater number of citizens (namely, to over half of all adult males who paid a certain amount of taxes).[2] With respect to *this* historical situation, the later introduction of universal suffrage constituted again an egalitarian redistribution of voting rights.

6.2 Rules of Apportionment (Criterion B)

As mentioned before, rules of distribution and redistribution can differ, not only with respect to the relative size of the selected group, but also with respect to the differences in amounts of benefits or burdens to be apportioned. Let us now consider this second type.

6.2.1 Rules of Distribution

Again, we consider, first, rules of distribution in isolation, and we take up only rules that are fully egalitarian by criterion A (i.e., the selected group coincides with the reference group) but that allocate benefits or burdens to members of the selected group in varying amounts. Let us take a simplified example, involving only two persons, X and Y, both of whom initially possess the same number of units (e.g., dollars).[3] Now let us compare the following rules of distribution: (1) X and Y are to receive 1 unit; (2) X and Y are to relinquish 1 unit; (3) X gets 2 and Y 1; (4) X receives 1 and Y pays 1. Obviously, the first two rules are egalitarian and the last two inegalitarian. The criterion is the difference between the amounts X and Y are to receive or to relinquish. If the difference is 0 as in cases (1) and (2), the rule is egalitarian; in all other cases it is inegalitarian, and the more so, the greater the difference. In case (3), the difference between the allotments to X and Y is 1, in case (4) it is 2; hence, (4) is more inegalitarian than (3).

We can infer from these examples that the only fully egalitarian principle of apportionment is that of equal shares to all—or from all—members of the selected group, regardless of any difference in the specifics by which the shares are apportioned. This is Aristotle's conception of numerical equality, "being treated equally or identically in the number and volume of things which you get" (*Politics* 1301b) or you are made to relinquish. It is the idea that "everybody [is] to count for one, nobody to count for more than one" (John Stuart Mill, *Utilitarianism*, chapter 5) when it comes to the distribution of benefits or burdens. Consequently, a rule of apportionment is fully egalitarian iff it allots the same amount of benefit or burden to each member of the selected group.

Otherwise the rule is inegalitarian. Rules that are fully egalitarian, by both criteria A and B, allot a specified benefit or burden to *all* members of the reference group in *equal* amounts. Voting laws, to be 100 percent egalitarian, must not only grant every citizen (fulfilling certain requirements) the franchise, but also give everyone, e.g., one vote; giving some citizens more votes is inegalitarian, just as is disenfranchising some. One vote to each stockholder is fully egalitarian; additional votes to stockholders owning more than x shares is inegalitarian, and so is giving votes to stockholders in proportion to the number of shares they own.

Inegalitarian rules of apportionment may also be called rules of proportionality, since they stipulate that the amount of some specified benefit or burden apportioned to any member of the selected group shall be a function of—or, synonymously, shall be proportional to—the degree to which he has a certain characteristic. It would be misleading to apply to these rules the Aristotelian terminology of proportional *equality*. Rules of proportionality are necessarily *inegalitarian*, since they allot different amounts of benefits or burdens to different members of the selected group. All "patterned principles of distribution" (to use Robert Nozick's phrase) are rules of proportionality, since they stipulate "that a distribution is to vary along with some natural dimension" such as "to each according to his moral worth, or needs, or marginal product, or how hard he tries, or the weighted sum of the foregoing, and so on" (Nozick 1974, p. 156).

On the basis of the foregoing analysis, all such rules of proportionality are inegalitarian. But they are inegalitarian in varying degrees, depending on the degree of the difference. If the difference between the largest and smallest allotments is relatively small, the rule may be considered relatively egalitarian (but not fully egalitarian).

Definition: A rule of proportionality is the more egalitarian, the smaller the difference between the amounts allotted to members of the selected group.

This is Rousseau's sense of equality I have quoted at the beginning of this chapter. According to this definition, the degree of egalitarianism or inegalitarianism of rules of proportionality depends exclusively on the difference between the amounts apportioned, not on the specific criteria by which the difference in allotments is determined. Giving stockholders votes in proportion to the shares they own—or in proportion to their age or height!—is the more inegalitarian, the greater the difference in the number of votes among stockholders.

Rules subdividing the selected group into just two categories also constitute rules of proportionality. One way of giving stockholders votes in proportion to the number of shares they own is to grant all who own less than x shares one vote and all who have more than x, say, ten votes. Is this rule more or is it less inegalitarian than establishing a sliding scale of votes in proportion to the number of shares owned? The answer depends only on the range of votes. If the latter rule gives the richest shareholders more than ten votes, it is more inegalitarian than the former; if less than ten, the former rule is the more inegalitarian one.

Similarly, an income tax and a sales tax are both rules of proportionality, and as such inegalitarian. The former establishes a sliding scale of taxes in proportion to income; the latter correlates tax payments with buying, by establishing two categories: buyers pay the sales tax (buyers of the same product pay the same amount); nonbuyers do not.

6.2.2 Rules of Redistribution

Which is relatively more inegalitarian (or more egalitarian), a graduated income tax or a sales tax? The criterion we just established is not of much help in answering such questions—unless we consider rules of apportionment, too, as rules of redistribution. Again, we compare the historically given distribution with the distribution that comes about after the rule of redistribution has been applied. Whether and to what degree the rule is egalitarian will now depend not on the amounts of benefits or burdens allotted to members of the selected group, but on the amounts they end up with. "[I]t is benefits to persons, not allocation of resources as such, that are meant to be made equal" (Vlastos 1962, p. 42). Accordingly, if the difference between holdings after the operation of the rule has become smaller, the rule is relatively egalitarian; if the difference has increased, it is inegalitarian.

Let us take some further simplified examples, and let us assume that in all of them the original distribution is the same; namely, X possesses 8 units and Y has 2. Now let us examine different rules of redistribution. (For examples [1]–[4], see 6.2.1.) (5) Take 3 units from X, and give 3 units to Y (like [4], a rather inegalitarian rule of distribution). As a result, both X and Y end up with 5 units. The previous difference between the holdings of X and Y, namely 6 $(8 - 2)$, has now been reduced to 0 $(5 - 5)$. Considered as a rule of redistribution, it is fully egalitarian. (6) Take 3 from X and 1 from Y. This rule of redistribution, while not fully egalitarian, may be considered egalitarian to a certain degree, since the difference between the holdings of X and Y has been reduced from 6 $(8 - 2)$ to 4 $(5 - 1)$. (7) Take 1 from X and 1 from Y (the same as [2], an egalitarian rule of distribution). As a rule of distribution, it is neither egalitarian nor inegalitarian, since the difference between holdings remains the same, namely, 6 $(8 - 2 = 7 - 1)$. (8) Take 1 from X and 2 from Y. This is inegalitarian, both as a rule of distribution and as a rule of redistribution (it increases the difference in holdings from 6 to 7). As these examples illustrate, a rule of redistribution can be said to be egalitarian or inegalitarian only wrt some initial distribution.

Definition: Wrt a given distribution, a rule of redistribution of varying amounts is the more egalitarian, the more it reduces the differences between holdings.

A rule of redistribution is then fully egalitarian iff the holdings of all members of the selected group have been fully equalized (example [5]). Whenever the members end up with different amounts, the rule of redistribution is inegalitarian, whether the difference in holdings of the original distribution has been preserved (example [7]) or increased (example [8]) or even reduced but not equalized (example [6]). However, in example (6), the redistribution, while still inegalitarian, may nevertheless be considered egalitarian in a relative sense, and the more egalitarian, the more the gap has been narrowed. Contrarywise, the greater the differences have become, the more inegalitarian the rule of redistribution.

However, this definition is not yet quite satisfactory. Example (7) illustrates a sales tax, since X and Y (in spite of differences in their wealth) pay the same amount when they buy the same amount. Rule (7) is inegalitarian, but not highly so, since it does not increase the difference between the holdings of X and Y. Yet, we are inclined to consider a sales tax rather greatly inegalitarian, since the tax paid by a poorer buyer represents a greater proportion of his wealth. On the other hand, rule (6), an example of a regressive income tax, turned out to be relatively egalitarian. But does not such a tax seem rather highly inegalitarian? While the difference between the holdings of X and Y has been reduced, Y had to relinquish 50 percent of his holdings $(2 - 1)$ whereas X paid less than 40 percent $(8 - 3)$. Although more has been taken away from X than from Y, X started with 4 times more than Y. But *much* more would have to be exacted from X than from Y before we would consider the redistribution egalitarian.

I think a way out of this difficulty is to take percentage differences between the combined holdings as the criterion for deciding whether a given rule redistributes assets in a relatively egalitarian way, and to what degree. I therefore propose to modify the previous definition as follows.

Definition: Wrt a given distribution, a rule of redistribution of varying amounts is the more egalitarian, the more it reduces the percentage differences between holdings.

Let us apply this definition to some of the previous examples, remembering the original distribution: X has 8, Y has 2; total 10. (7a) Taking 1 from X and 1 from Y reduces this total to 8. X ends up with 7/8 of this total, or 87.5 percent, and Y with 1/8, or 12.5 percent. The percentage difference between X's and Y's holdings has increased from 60 to 75. A sales tax now turns out to be rather highly inegalitarian, as indeed it is, since it weighs heavier on the poor than on the wealthy.

RULES OF REDISTRIBUTION

Examples	Holdings of X	Holdings of Y	Difference	The Rule Is:
Rule (5)	8	2	6	
	−3	+3		
	5	5	0	Fully egalitarian
Rule (6)	8	2	6	
	−3	−1		Relatively
	5	1	4	egalitarian
Rule (7)	8	2	6	
	−1	−1		Neither egalitarian
	7	1	6	nor inegalitarian
Rule (6a)	8	2	60% of total	
	−3	−1		Relatively
	$\frac{5}{6}$ (83%)	$\frac{1}{6}$ (17%)	66% of total	inegalitarian
Rule (6b)	8	2	60% of total	
	−3	−0.5		Relatively
	$\frac{5}{6.5}$ (77%)	$\frac{1.5}{6.5}$ (23%)	54% of total	egalitarian
Rule (7a)	8	2	60% of total	
	−1	−1		Highly
	$\frac{7}{8}$ (87.5%)	$\frac{1}{8}$ (12.5%)	75% of total	inegalitarian

(6a) Taking 3 from X and 1 from Y reduces the total to 6. X is left with about 83 percent of this total (5/6) and Y with about 17 percent (1/6). The percentage difference between the combined holdings of X and Y (83 − 17) is now 66—larger than 60, the percentage difference between their initial holdings. According to the revised criterion, such a regressive income tax is relatively inegalitarian. (6b) X again pays 3, but Y pays only 0.5 instead of 1. The total of assets is now reduced from 10 to 6.5. X's holdings are reduced to about 77 percent of this total (5/6.5) and Y's to about 23 percent (1.5/6.5). The percentage difference between their holdings is 54, which is smaller than the percentage at the start, which was 60, and so this rule of redistribution is relatively egalitarian. Indeed, a graduated income tax does not become egalitarian to a certain degree until those in the highest bracket pay proportionately very much and those in the lowest very little (or nothing). Quite generally, when the difference in initial holdings is very great, simply taking more from one who has more than from one who has less does not make the redistribution egalitarian. It does not become so until much more is taken from the former than from the latter, a feature the revised definition brings out more clearly.[4] A graduated income tax with steep brackets now turns out to be more egalitarian (or less inegalitarian) than a sales tax, since the former equalizes (to a certain degree) while the latter increases the differences between holdings among taxpayers "after taxes."

6.3 Combining Both Criteria

Rules of distribution and of redistribution are often a combination of type A and type B. They determine both the relative size of the selected group and the amount to be allotted to its various members. Combining the criteria of egalitarianism for rules of distribution of both types, we arrive at the following.

Definition: Wrt a given distribution and wrt a given reference group, a rule of redistribution is the more egalitarian, (A) the more it increases the ratio of the selected to the reference group or (B) the more it decreases the percentage difference between holdings among members of the selected group.

A rule of redistribution may be egalitarian according to criterion A and inegalitarian according to criterion B (e.g., when universal suffrage is introduced, but men are given two votes and women one), or vice versa (e.g., when the policy is "one *man* one vote", i.e., when only men can vote, but all voters have one vote). It may seem paradoxical that one and the same policy—e.g., universal suffrage—turns out to be egalitarian in one sense and inegalitarian in another. We must keep in mind that criteria A and B are restricted to different parameters of measurement. Criterion A determines the egalitarianism of selection, i.e., whether the application of the rule has increased the ratio of the selected to the reference group. Criterion B determines whether the differences in holdings of members of the selected group have diminished as a result of the application of the rule. Introducing a policy of "one man one vote" affects both these criteria. The degree to which such a rule of redistribution is egalitarian is thus a function of two independent variables (whereas the concepts of degree of power and freedom have at least four dimensions).

We shall now examine some of the most widely discussed principles of redistribution in the light of this definition.

6.3.1 Equal Benefits

Let us take length of schooling as an example of a benefit to be redistributed, and let us take as the given distribution the historical situation existing prior to the introduction of compulsory education—a highly inegalitarian one, since only the "happy few" whose parents could pay for private instruction were educated. With the introduction of "free" and compulsory school attendance, all (i.e., all members of the reference group) are provided with the fixed benefit of schooling from and up to a certain age. Both absolutely and relative to the previous situation, this policy is fully egalitarian by criterion A. It is also egalitarian from the point of view of criterion B, but not fully so. The previous gap between children with and those without schooling has been narrowed, the lower limit having been pushed up from no schooling to schooling for a required minimum number of years. But those who can will graduate from high school, college, or graduate school. A fully egalitarian redistribution of length of school attendance (when we disregard the quality of instruction) would provide the same number of years of schooling for everyone and would prohibit anyone from attending school for a longer time (even at his own expense and even if this policy should mean the end of higher education).

We turn now to the allocation of positions. There is, in any advanced society, a hierarchy of positions with respect to remuneration, status, and of course the task to be performed. For our theoretical purposes, we make two simplifying assumptions: (1) the hierarchical structure of the positions does not change, and (2) a position is assigned to each working member of the society (there are no unemployed) by virtue of formal rules (although this is not usually the case). How are we to determine whether and to what degree such hypothetical rules of distributing and redistributing positions are egalitarian or inegalitarian?

Let us start with criterion B. Since there is a gradation of benefits such as salaries, filling the different positions will necessarily be inegalitarian. Any possible redistribution is bound to remain just as inegalitarian. Persons are being moved from some lower to a higher occupation or vice versa, but the positions themselves remain the same. There can be changes in the difference of salaries between any two job-holders, but the overall difference remains the same. If in the original situation the higher a person's social rank, the higher his office, it makes no difference from the point of view of criterion B whether positions are being redistributed in proportion to wealth or ability—or height.

Criterion A does not, strictly speaking, apply here, since there is a gradation of benefits. To make criterion A applicable, we may, quite arbitrarily, subdivide the pyramid of positions into two levels, made up, respectively, of fifty top posts and of all the lower ones. The reference group consists of all who are assigned to positions, and the selected group of those who are chosen to fill the fifty highest. Then all conceivable policies of allocating and reallocating positions will again turn out to be inegalitarian, and equally so, since the selected group will always consist of the fifty persons assigned to fill the fifty top positions. Again, it makes no difference whether these go to the fifty noblest or wealthiest or tallest or to the fifty with the highest qualifications.

To redistribute the various positions of the pyramid in an egalitarian way would require involving everyone in a musical chair kind of rotation of all positions ("to hunt in the morning, fish in the afternoon, rear cattle in the evening, criticize after dinner").[5] Another egalitarian method would be to flatten the pyramid itself, i.e., to equalize the benefits attached to the various occupations. To be fully egalitarian, every position would give its holder the same remuneration and status, and be equally attractive (or unattractive), just as a completely egalitarian educational system would give each pupil the same length (and perhaps quality) of schooling.

6.3.2 Equal Chance

Suppose now that the benefit to be distributed consists not of the positions themselves, but of the chance of occupying the most desirable ones. The number of persons to be assigned to any position is of course much greater than the number of the positions coveted (which we assume again to be fifty). As the examples of the draft and of admission to college illustrate, a random selection such as a fair lottery is the only fully egalitarian redistribution of the probability to belong to the selected group, i.e., to occupy one of the fifty top posts. All other methods are inegalitarian—e.g., to give fifty persons the certainty of being selected and to exclude all others, or to give some persons or group a greater chance than others. Any quota rule is inegalitarian, regardless of whether the quota characteristic is sex or race or wealth or ability. Whenever a greater number of persons are in competition for a smaller number of some given benefit, a random distribution constitutes the most egalitarian policy, since it equalizes the chances of each to win out.

6.3.3 Equal Access

To give everyone the same access to all positions, including the highest ones, means to open them to everyone not on a chance, but on a competitive, basis. All may enter the competition, and the fifty top positions will go to the fifty applicants who—figuratively speaking—receive the fifty highest marks in the competitive examination. All personal characteristics *other than qualification*, such as sex, race, wealth, connections, are to be disregarded. Giving all an equal access leads to the consequence that the position each person will occupy will be a function of his ability, to the exclusion of all other factors. Thus, while from the point of view of the chance of occupying the highest positions, it is inegalitarian to give the better qualified a better prospect, the principle "to each according to his ability" is egalitarian if the benefit consists of the access to these posts. This is the idea of the French Declaration of the Rights of Man: "All citizens are equally eligible to all public dignities, places, and employments, and without other distinctions than their virtues and their talents." Naturally, the educationally and culturally advantaged—and that usually also means the economically favored—have in general a better prospect of reaching the higher positions. Equal access does not imply equal opportunity, as we shall see.

Here again, quota systems are inegalitarian. It is inegalitarian to open the competition only to whites or only to men or even—theoretically—to allow only college graduates or those with a certain SAT score *to apply*. Fixed quota characteristics are often combined with selection according to ability. All are admitted to the competition, but those with a specified characteristic are given extra points, as it were, so that those with that characteristic have a better access to a given position than someone else with the same, or even a slightly (or even greatly) higher, test score. Here we must consider the selected group to consist not of those who get the top positions, but of those who are given preferential treatment in acceding to them. A quota system of this type is less inegalitarian than a straight one and the less inegalitarian, the greater the number of those who receive preferential treatment (the selected group) relative to all applicants (the reference group). Preferential hiring of blacks is more inegalitarian than favoring whites in the United States, for the sole reason that there are fewer blacks than whites.

(For the same reason, privileges for whites are more inegalitarian in South Africa.) It is about equally inegalitarian to make the access to certain positions easier for men or for women. Let us remember that we are dealing with egalitarianism as a purely descriptive concept, to the exclusion of any normative considerations.

Redistributing a benefit in an inegalitarian way is sometimes a means to a more egalitarian redistribution of another benefit. Admitting blacks to medical school on a preferential basis when admission was previously based only on aptitude constitutes an inegalitarian policy of redistributing access to medical school. Such a quota policy is often adopted with the expectation that black students will, after graduation, set up practice in black neighborhoods previously lacking an adequate supply of physicians. As a result, there will be a reduction in the inequality of access to medical care among the total population.

6.3.4 Equal Satisfaction of Basic Needs

Returning to the field of education, we can ask whether remedial programs for some which were later added to compulsory education for all are egalitarian or inegalitarian. The answer depends on whether we consider educational resources or educational attainment as the benefit being distributed.

Before the introduction of these programs, roughly the same amount of educational resources was spent on every pupil. Now additional funds are provided for a selected group (whose members are, of course, quite different from the selected few who originally were the only ones to receive any education). By criterion A, this is an inegalitarian redistribution of resources, just as is giving educational advantages to gifted pupils. However, remedial programs attempt to raise the educational level of economically and educationally disadvantaged children and thereby to reduce the differences in educational achievement among all. By criterion B and as a redistribution of educational attainment, such policies are egalitarian, just as the introduction of compulsory schooling constituted an egalitarian redistribution of the length of schooling.

This example illustrates that one rule can be said to be more egalitarian than another only wrt some specified benefit or burden. Wrt educational resources, remedial prograns are inegalitarian; wrt educational achievement, they are egalitarian. It makes no sense to ask which of the two principles—equality of educational resources distribution or equalization of educational achievement—is more egalitarian, just as we cannot say that equality of rights is more (or less) egalitarian than, say, equality of opportunity.

Remedial programs are an application to the field of education of the general principle "to each according to his need" in the sense of satisfying to an equal degree the most basic needs of everyone who cannot do so by himself. During the laissez-faire period (which we take as the historically given situation), the basic needs of the poor remained unsatisfied. Later on, minimum wage laws and other social welfare policies were introduced that provided special benefits for the neediest. According to criterion A, such measures are inegalitarian, like special programs for those in need of remedial education. But like the latter, welfare policies are egalitarian by criterion B. By bringing about a more equal satisfaction of everyone's basic needs, they reduce the differences between the holdings of the wealthiest and the poorest. "[U]nequal distribution of resources [is] required to equalize benefits in case of unequal needs" (Vlastos 1962, p. 43). A fully egalitarian redistribution of wealth would—theoretically—provide everyone with the same amount of wealth (including income), just as a complete equalization of educational attainment would leave everyone equally well (or poorly!) educated.

6.3.5 Equal Opportunity

Athletes have an equal opportunity to win a race if they all start from the same line. Quite generally, opportunities are equal if there is a "fair race, where people are even at the starting line" (Okun 1975, p. 76). Those who are initially behind must be brought forward (possibly at the expense of those who are ahead) if there is to be equal opportunity for all contenders. Who turns out to be the winner will now depend only on his ability to run faster than his competitors.

The principle of equality of opportunity thus combines the maxim "to each according to his need" with the idea of equal access, or "to each according to his ability."

> The thought here is that positions are to be not only open in a formal sense, but that all should have a fair chance to attain them.... [T]hose who are at the same level of talent and ability, and have the same willingness to use them, should have the same prospects of success regardless of their initial place in the social system, that is, irrespective of the income class into which they are born. (Rawls 1971, p. 73)

On the other hand, those who differ in ability or motivation have unequal prospects of success. "[D]iscrimination on grounds of capacity there must be, if equal opportunity is to be preserved" (Raphael 1977, p. 546).

Applied to the allocation of positions, we can, quite schematically, distinguish the following phases: (1) In the historically given period, the highest positions go to the noblest or the wealthiest or the most influential. (2) The introduction of the principle of equal access to positions ensures that all occupations are open to all "in a formal sense." (3) Those born into the lowest-income classes are given special benefits, so that everyone's most elementary economic and educational needs are satisfied. This is a necessary condition for bringing everyone up to a common starting line.[6] (4) Only then is the race on, and only then do all (always quite theoretically) have the same opportunity of winning the highest positions. "Differences in natural abilities are generally accepted as relevant characteristics that are being tested in the race rather than as unfair headstarts and handicaps" (Okun 1975, p. 76). (5) The highest positions go to those with the highest qualifications, to the exclusion not only of all other personal characteristics, but also of their "initial place in the social system." Equality of opportunity, rather than mere equality of access, leads to meritocracy. Equal opportunity thus remains compatible with a highly inegalitarian distribution of benefits, e.g., with a steep pyramid of positions. "It says nothing about the need to eliminate sharp distinctions, except insofar as this may be

necessary to give everybody the same chance to compete"
(Frankel 1971, p. 203).

If we consider the *chance* of acceding to the most desirable
occupations, we can establish, again very schematically, the
following rank order: Random selection gives everybody the
same chance and is thus fully egalitarian. Equality of opportunity is less egalitarian, as those with lower abilities have a
smaller chance than the more gifted. Equality of opportunity
is nevertheless more egalitarian than mere formal equality of
access. If all start from the same line, many have some
chance. If there is no common line, those who must start
from way back have very little chance and those who are
already ahead have decidedly better prospects. Quota systems excluding those who lack the quota characteristics from
even competing are still more inegalitarian.

But if quota systems are inegalitarian, why do institutions
practicing preferential hiring of minorities call themselves
equal opportunity employers? Quota systems, even when
combined with selection by ability, are inegalitarian, but
only as a rule of selection. However, giving certain
minorities "extra points" helps them reach the common
starting line. As a rule of apportionment, this is an egalitarian policy, since it eradicates, or at least reduces, the previous differences in starting points among all competitors. In
such cases, equal opportunity at the start does not result in
meritocracy at the end, since who gets what position does
not depend exclusively on his ability.

To call the idea of equality of opportunity relatively egalitarian is not to advocate such social arrangements. It is the
favorable connotation of the word 'equality' which accounts
for the tendency to confuse the descriptive concept of
egalitarianism with the moral notion of justice.

6.4 ARISTOTLE'S CONCEPTIONS OF EGALITARIANISM

Since most discussions about equality go back to Aristotle, it
may be of interest to examine briefly his various conceptions
of egalitarianism. Two of them will turn out to be much
broader than the proposed analysis.

6.4.1 Equal Shares to Equals

It is in connection with the problems of justice that Aristotle deals with the concept of equality. Justice requires "that persons who are equal should have assigned to them equal things" (*Politics*, 1282b). A rule is unjust "when either equals have and are awarded unequal shares or unequals equal shares" (*Ethics*, 1131a). Here we are, of course, not concerned with the normative concept of justice, but with the notion of egalitarianism in a descriptive sense. But Aristotle, at least in one famous passage, seems to take both concepts coextensively: "Now if the unjust is unequal, the just must be equal" (*Ethics*, 1131a). This suggests that he means to characterize a rule of distribution as egalitarian (as well as just) if it allots "equal shares" to "equals," and inegalitarian if either equal shares are distributed to unequals or unequal shares to equals.

Now, whether *shares* are equal or unequal can in many cases be ascertained. The proposed definition, too, is applicable in principle only to benefits or burdens that are somehow quantifiable. But what does it mean to say that *persons* are equal or unequal? In what respect? Aristotle's answer, "To each according to his deserts" (*Ethics*, 1131a) is clearly a normative notion. Descriptively speaking, two persons can be said to be equal only in the sense that they share to the same degree the characteristic chosen by the rule under consideration. But then any conceivable rule of distribution turns out to be egalitarian, and inegalitarianism becomes a logical impossibility. Indeed, rules of distribution necessarily allocate equal shares to all who share a specified characteristic, and give a different treatment to any two persons who are "unequal" in that respect. Universal suffrage usually means that every citizen beyond a certain age shall have one vote, but aliens and minors shall have none. White suffrage gives the right to vote to all white adult citizens, but not to nonwhites or minors. A graduated income tax, whether progressive or regressive, requires those with the characteristic of being in the same bracket to pay the same amount. A sales tax levies the same amount on all buyers of the same product (who are "equal" in *this* respect). It is logically impossible for any rule of distribution to treat either equals unequally or unequals equally, in the sense of allotting the same benefit or burden (in the same amount) to persons who differ wrt the characteristics *singled out by the rule*, or different shares to persons whom the rule places in the same category.

6.4.2 Proportional Equality

The same criticism applies to Aristotle's notion of proportional equality. Aristotle holds that rules of distribution meet this requirement if there is "equality of ratios" (*Ethics,* 1131a; *Politics,* 1301b) between some characteristic of one person and his allotment and the characteristic of another person and his assigned share. In other words, a rule fulfills the condition of proportional equality if the amount allotted to anyone is a monotonically increasing function of the personal characteristic specified by the rule; the more of the characteristic, the greater the share.[7] Any two persons are treated in a proportionally egalitarian way in this sense provided the difference in the amount allotted to each is correlated to the degree to which they differ wrt the specified characteristic. Accordingly, a salary scale based on the principle "to each according to his ability" would be egalitarian in this sense because it pays each person a salary proportional to his ability.

The objection is, again, that every conceivable rule of distribution would turn out to be fully egalitarian. Indeed, every rule not only allots "equal shares to equals" and "unequal shares to unequals," but also distributes them in proportion to the latter's inequalities. In every case, "there will be the same equality between the persons and the shares: the ratio between the shares will be the same as that between the persons" (*Ethics,* 1131a). To each according to his ability, to his income, to his height—all these principles would be fully egalitarian, and so would a graduated income tax, whether progressive or regressive. Even rules establishing only two categories of allotments fulfill Aristotle's criterion of proportional equality, e.g. (to take a previous example), "one vote to stockholders with less than x shares, ten to owners of more than x," as well as "the more shares, the more votes."

The same objection applies to a famous passage in Marx's *Critique of the Gotha Program* in which he predicts that the principle "to each according to his work" will eventually be superseded by that of "to each according to his needs." Marx considers the former (as well as the latter) principle egalitarian, since "[t]he right of the producers [to receive means of consumption] is *proportional* to the labour they supply; the equality consists in the fact that measurement is made with an *equal standard*, labour." It is an egalitarian principle even though "it tacitly recognizes unequal individual endowment and thus productive capacity as natural privileges" (in Marx 1972, p. 530; italics in original). *In this sense*, every conceivable rule of proportionality would be egalitarian, since each lays down a standard ("equal standard" is redundant) that correlates a specified allotment to a specified personal characteristic (labor furnished or need—or height).

According to the proposed interpretation, the only fully egalitarian rules of distribution are those providing the same allotment (in the same quantity) to all members of the reference group (or at least of the selected group). All other rules are inegalitarian, including all patterned principles of distribution, i.e., rules of the type "to (or from) each according to his . . ." Such rules of proportionality, while inegalitarian, may nevertheless be considered relatively egalitarian if they establish a relatively narrow range of discrepancy between allotments. The proposed analysis has the advantage of enabling us to ascertain that one rule of proportionality is relatively more egalitarian than the other, or that a given rule of proportionality is egalitarian or inegalitarian to such and such a degree. As we saw, the degree of equality or inequality of these rules depends not on the standard—i.e., on the personal characteristic singled out—merely on the range of difference between allotments. We cannot ascertain in general whether "to each according to his needs" is less, or more, inegalitarian than "to each according to his work." If we compare a policy of benefits adjusted to needs where the neediest get very much more than the less indigent with a policy of benefits according to work with a relatively equalized salary scale, then the latter is more egalitarian than the former. This is not to deny, of course, that someone may without inconsistency advocate the more inegalitarian policy as the fairer one.

6.4.3 Numerical Equality

There is, finally, Aristotle's concept of "'numerical equality' [which] means being treated equally, or identically, in the number and volume of things which you get" (*Politics*, 1301b). I, too, consider such treatment egalitarian—the only treatment that is fully egalitarian. Alloting the same "number and volume of things" to all members of the reference group ("everyone to count for one") is fully egalitarian, by both criterion A and criterion B.

My only criticism of Aristotle's notion of numerical equality is that it does not take into account the possibility of *relative* egalitarianism. As we have seen, rules of proportionality may be considered relatively egalitarian if the differences between shares are relatively small, and rules of redistribution if they increase the ratio of the selected to the reference group or decrease the differences between holdings.

Even so, it seems to me that Aristotle's concept of numerical equality comes closest to the proposed analysis. To repeat: whether and to what degree a rule of distribution or of redistribution is egalitarian does not depend on the specific characteristic determining the allotment, but on the difference between the amounts allotted and on the ratio of the selected to the reference group.

SEVEN

Self-Interest and
Public Interest

THE NORMATIVE OVERTONES of the concepts of self-interest, and especially of public interest, are even stronger than the normative overtones of those examined before; hence, the difficulty of disentangling evaluative from descriptive aspects is even greater. I believe that it is nevertheless possible to construct descriptive definitions, so that social scientists with different political and ideological perspectives can nevertheless agree whether a certain action is in the actor's own interest or whether a given policy is in the public interest.

7.1 EXPRESSIONS TO BE DEFINED

When dealing with self-interest, I shall take as the *definiendum* 'it is in A's interest to do x in situation S'. As in the case of the concepts of power and freedom, the actor variable A will be understood to range over human individuals or collectivities such as "interest groups" or, when dealing with the "national interest," even over national societies. It is always (if often implicitly) with reference to a given situation S that we speak of an action's being in someone's interest; but we need not always mention S explicitly. Since politics is primarily concerned with political actions, I shall not deal with statements to the effect that some state of affairs not arising from voluntary human behavior is in someone's interest, e.g., that there be sunshine. Nor shall I consider such expressions as 'it is in A's interest that B do x' or 'it is more in A's interest to do x than to do y'; these can easily be defined once we have clarified the expression 'it is in A's interest to do x'.

The concept of self-interest refers to a relationship between actor A and his action x. When it comes to public interest, we are concerned with the three-term relationship between actor A, a policy x, and a public P, and with whether the former's policy is in the latter's interest. So the expression to be defined is 'it is in the interest of P that A do x (in S)'. The variable 'P' stands for a public in the sense of "any group of human beings where the unity of the group is determined by its organization under a common public authority" (Rees 1964, p. 31); hence, we are considering a municipality or a state, as distinguished from smaller collectivities such as parties, trade unions, and other interest groups. The variable 'x' ranges over public policies—for instance, acts of legislation or decisions of economic or foreign policy. 'A' stands for one or several persons or organized groups acting in the role of policymakers, e.g., those who make up the government or one of its branches. 'A' may also stand for some larger political unit; one may ask whether some policy adopted by the European Common Market or by the oil-producing countries or by the United Nations is in the public interest of a group of nations. Again, I shall disregard some other current locutions, e.g., that it is in the public interest that everyone obey traffic laws or that a millionaire who gives his paintings to the National Gallery acts in the public interest. Most questions of public interest do arise, after all, in connection with governmental policies.

7.2 Defining Characteristics
7.2.1 Rationality

Whether A acted in his own interest when he did x, or whether his policy x was in the public interest, depends, first of all, on whether it was rational for A to do x in the given situation. Intuitively, actions not in some sense rational would hardly be considered to correspond to the actor's own or to the public interest. We have, then, no choice but to include this somewhat controversial concept among the defining characteristics. We have used it before, when we tried to distinguish coercive threats from mere deterrence and when we included the disposition to act rationally in the *definiens* of a free person.

Broadly speaking, an action x done by actor A in situation S will qualify as rational if, in the light of the information available to A in S, it is an optimal means to the attainment of some ultimate goal of his. In this broad sense, an actor, to be rational, must—in theory at least—determine, for each alternative course of action open to him in S, all alternative outcomes, specify their relative desirability to him, and choose the alternative action with the most desirable outcome.[1] 'Information available to A in S' refers not to the information in A's personal possession, but to the evidence he could obtain if he used "due care under the circumstances," to use legal terminology. More information (as well as other help) is available to a surgeon in a metropolitan hospital than to a physician performing an emergency operation in the desert.

The concept of rationality must be further relativized, namely, wrt the actor's own intrinsic preferences. Hence, an observer who wants to find out whether it was, or would be, rational for A to do x (and in A's interest to do so) must be cognizant not only of the information that was or is available to A in S, but also of the ultimate goal to which A's doing x is meant to be geared. I do not think that there are objective criteria of rationality when it comes to ultimate preferences; these are a-rational rather than either rational or not. I do not agree with authors who, like Richard Brandt, speak of the rationality of "a basic or intrinsic desire, aversion, or preference" (Brandt 1977, p. 268); this view presupposes the metaethical theory of value-cognitivism that intrinsic valuational principles can be shown to be valid on the basis of objective criteria. For the same reason, I do not subscribe to the following statement:

> [H]ealth and wealth may both be interests of N's, but
> if an action which would produce more wealth for N

would be detrimental to his health, then it is (probably) in N's interest at t to do what is necessary to protect his health, and it is not in his interest at t (indeed, it is—probably—against N's interest at t) to do that act which would produce the added wealth. (Benditt 1975, p. 246).

Which of these alternatives are in N's greater interest depends on N's own ultimate preferences, not on those of the investigator. If N values greater wealth at the cost of impairing his health more highly than preserving his health by foregoing some luxuries, it may well be rational for N to pursue the former goal and in his interest as well, assuming that the other defining characteristics of 'self-interest' are satisfied. Dedicating oneself to the cause of "national liberation" as an aim itself is neither rational nor irrational. But having adopted that goal, it may be quite rational to want to publicize it by highjacking a plane. Thus, the proposed criterion does not imply "a substitution of the analyst's choice for the actor's choices" (Polsby 1980, p. 224). Whether x is in A's interest depends on whether his doing x meets the *objective* criteria of rational choice in terms of A's *own* ultimate goals.

Here someone might object that our actions are seldom geared toward well-circumscribed ultimate goals and that we rarely establish an explicit preference rank-order among possible intrinsically desirable states of affairs. We can hardly expect an observer such as a social scientist to discover the underlying valuations of an actor who himself does not have a clear picture of them. A definition of interest in terms of rationality which, in turn, refers to the actor's intrinsic preferences can hardly be considered "operational" even in the largest sense. To consider unavoidable the inclusion of rationality in the definition of interest is not to deny these difficulties. To point them up is, on the contrary, one of its advantages.

That the criteria of rational choice do not apply to ultimate commitments does not mean that they pertain only to means to given ends. Here are some cases in which the actor most likely failed to apply "due care under the circumstances" in his choice of ultimate goals and, hence, did not act rationally, and not in his own or in someone else's interest: (1) A commits himself to some utopian goal, i.e., to one not attainable by whatever means. If a classless society (in some sense) or world federation is an empirical impossibility, it is not rational to try to bring it about. (2) A espouses several incompatible goals, e.g., maximizing his wealth *and* health, or maximizing welfare in society *and* its equal distribution. (3) A's realizing his goal leads to further consequences whose negative utility *to him* outweighs his positive valuation of the goal itself; e.g., a successful revolution may foreseeably lead to more repression afterward than is acceptable to the revolutionaries themselves. (4) A misjudges his "real" preferences; e.g., he runs after wealth when health is actually more valuable to him. An actor's real preferences may thus differ from those he believes he has, as well as from those (I hold) he should adopt. Everybody is not always the best judge of his best interests. It often happens that an observer knows better than the actor himself what course of action would be rational and in the latter's interest in a given situation. Here again, both actor and observer are faced with the difficulty of determining the latter's underlying intrinsic valuations. (5) A acts irrationally not only when he "neglects to act in accordance with his actual preferences and desires" (Dworkin 1979, p. 92), but also when he assesses the probabilities and utilities of the outcomes correctly in terms of his real preferences without acting accordingly. Instances of weakness of the will fit in here. We tend to indulge in immediate gratification even though we realize that doing so might lead to greater disadvantages, especially when the former are certain but the latter are not. To take a trivial example, I know that wearing seat belts reduces injury in case of accident, and I attach greater negative utility to being injured (taking into account the relatively low probability) than to the (slight) inconvenience of wearing the seat belt. Yet, I often do not.

In the case of public interest, it is A's policy decision x that must be rational, the individuals who make up the public P being merely affected by x, favorably or unfavorably. We shall see, however, that A, to act in the public interest, must take the public's intrinsic preferences into account.

Deciding rationally is a necessary, but not a sufficient,

127

condition for acting in one's own or in the public interest. While the criteria of rational choice can be applied to whatever an actor's ultimate preferences may be, actions that are in one's own or in the public interest pertain to ultimate goals of a certain kind.

7.2.2 Welfare

Only if the agent's action is rational wrt some welfare goal do we say that his action is in his own or in the public interest. In other words, actions or policies must be of a utilitarian kind.

The concept of utilitarianism is familiar from ethical theory. Utilitarianism in its broadest sense encompasses all teleological moral doctrines, those that judge the moral rightness or wrongness of actions by the goodness or badness of their consequences. In contradistinction, deontological moralities hold that certain actions are right independent of their outcomes; they are right if they conform to certain moral principles—e.g., Socrates's injunction (in *Crito*) that citizens should obey all laws under all circumstances, or "justice as fairness."[2] Utilitarianism in a narrower sense is the name of one particular teleological view: those consequences of actions are desirable—and hence those actions are right—that promote utility.

Whereas 'utilitarianism' designates a type of ethical doctrine, 'utility' refers to a certain category of goals. 'Utility', too, has been used in a broad and in several narrower senses. Bentham used it broadly: "By utility is meant that property in any object, whereby it tends to produce benefit, advantage, pleasure, good, or happiness (all this in the present case comes to the same thing)" (*Principles of Morals and Legislation*, chapter 1). Economists have narrowed down the concept to make it a synonym of 'welfare', itself a term with many shades. "'Welfare' is a convoy concept" that may include such things as "food; safety; clothing; shelter; medical care; . . . congenial employment; companionship" (Braybrooke 1968, p. 143). We must, however, avoid interpreting 'welfare' in an all-inclusive sense. It does not comprise the psychological gratification a person may derive, e.g., from a more egalitarian distribution of wealth at the cost of a reduction of his own. Egalitarianism is a nonutilitarian goal; so is individual self-realization or collective dedication to some cause.

I construe the concept of interest as referring to goals that are utilitarian in this narrower sense. Interest "always appears to have carried an emphasis on material advantage and thus to find its home especially in economic and quasi-economic discourse" (Barry and Rae 1975, p. 382). This defining condition narrows down the concepts of self-interest and of public interest in a plausible way. It precludes us from saying that Soviet dissidents who openly champion the cause of human rights at the risk of imprisonment act in their self-interest—or in the public interest (but not from saying that their actions are rational in view of that goal or admirable from a moral point of view). Plato and Rousseau held that the state ought primarily to further the citizens' moral improvement, not their material well-being and, hence, not the public interest. Policies of "national liberation" are not in the public interest if they are in conflict with public welfare, e.g., it they foreseeably lead to a lowering of the people's living standard, as they often do. On the other hand, championing a seemingly nonutilitarian goal like the defense of the French language in Canada or of Flemish in Belgium may be primarily directed at securing better jobs and higher positions for French Canadians and Flemish-speaking Belgians. Justice often conflicts with utility and thereby with the public interest. One may advocate educational advantages for the gifted on public interest grounds if one holds that they contribute in the long run to the well-being of all (as John Stuart Mill might have argued). At the same time, one might consider such a policy unjust and for this reason favor instead Head Start programs for the underprivileged. It is on the grounds of justice rather than of public interest that the latter policy is being defended.[3]

Actors who are primarily concerned with well-being, their own or that of a larger group, are confronted with further choices among various and often conflicting welfare goals. Either drugs or drug rehabilitation may be in A's self-interest; either increasing industrial production or conserving energy may be held to be in the public interest, depending on one's ultimate welfare valuations.

7.2.3 Whose Welfare?

We come now to the point at which the two concepts of self-interest and public interest bifurcate. An individual acts in his own interest only if he aims at promoting his own welfare. Policies, to be in the public interest, must promote the collective welfare of the public.

Having differentiated between utilitarian and nonutilitarian goals, we must make a further distinction among the former, according to whose welfare is to be promoted. Hence, we must distinguish between egoism, altruism, and what John Stuart Mill has called benevolence. An egoistic actor aims at promoting his own well-being, regardless of the effects his action may have on others. The altruist cares more about the welfare of others than about his own. A benevolent actor aims at the welfare of a group of which he himself is a member, attaching to his own utility neither more nor less weight than to that of any other member of the group.[4]

Actions in the actor's self-interest are, by the proposed definition, of an egoistic kind.[5] The drug addict who underwent rehabilitation because, after careful deliberation, he judged that staying healthy was, after all, preferable to him acted in his self-interest; not so if his change of mind was due to his consideration of the hardship his continued addiction would cause to his family. Acting in one's self-interest must then be distinguished from being willing to forego some level of personal well-being, either for the sake of some nonutilitarian goal or to promote the welfare of others. Saint Francis distributed his wealth to the poor out of his altruistic moral conviction that he should sacrifice his own material welfare to increase the well-being of the disadvantaged. He acted out of utilitarian considerations, but contrary to his self-interest. Sometimes the most effective way for A to promote his own interest in the long run is to serve the interests of B, even at his own expense. Since what counts as self-interested activity depends on the actor's ultimate goal, such seemingly altruistic behavior must be sub-sumed under the concept of self-interest.

If actions done in the actor's own interest are egoistic and acting in the interest of others is altruistic, "subordinating one's purely personal interests to the service of interests that one shares with others who are members of the same group" is a benevolent kind of action (Flathman 1975, p. 279). Be-nevolence, too, is often a means to, and even a disguise for, self-interested pursuits. Especially in the political sphere, benevolence as well as altruism are rare occurrences. "Politi-cal man," like "economic man," tends to pursue his own interest, either directly, or *by means of* serving the interests of others or, most often, of a group to which he belongs. Thus, auto workers who support their union's advocacy of tariffs against Japanese cars act in the interest of auto workers generally (and, in this case, of the American auto industry as well), against the interest of American consumers (and Japanese producers), and in their own long-range interest, even though supporting the union may involve material sac-rifices, e.g., going on strike. (Perhaps they do not act in their ultimate self-interest if the tariff causes further inflation.)

Public interest policies belong to the class of actions that are benevolent in this technical sense.[6] Here the actors are usually persons acting in their capacity of members of a gov-ernment and its various branches, and the group for whose benefit they act (and of which they themselves are members) is made up of the public at large, e.g., the citizens of a politi-cal unit such as a state. A policy is in the public interest if it promotes the welfare of the public.

The expression 'welfare of the public', like 'welfare of a group', requires some clarification. To that effect, we must distinguish between two kinds of properties, which May Brodbeck has aptly exemplified by the two propositions 'In-dians are red-skinned' and 'Indians are disappearing'. "In the former, each and every Indian is said to be red-skinned, while in the latter Indians as a group are said to be dis-appearing, that is, diminishing in population." Properties like 'red-skinned', 'Catholic', 'being a citizen of the United States' can be attributed to human groups only *distributively*, as applying to individual members of the group. On the other hand, 'disappearing' or 'cohesive' or 'democratic' are applicable to a group only *collectively*, "so that the group itself is logically the subject of the proposition" (Brodbeck 1968, p. 282). 'Welfare' or 'interest' belong to a third category; these concepts can function both distributively and collectively. Taken in the distributive sense, 'the welfare of the public' means the welfare of every member of the public and 'the public interest' would be synonymous with "the interests which each and every man, upon separate examination, has in common with everyone else" (Rees 1964, p. 24).[7] For reasons I shall point out below, I propose to take 'welfare' in connection with a group (such as a public) in the collective sense. Accordingly, a policy, to be in the public interest, must promote the welfare of the public as a whole rather than the personal welfare of each, or any, of its members.

That I am using the property concept 'welfare' in a collective sense when applied to groups constitutes an implicit denial of "definitional methodological individualism," which maintains that all group properties can be defined by properties of its constituent members.[8] A democratic political system is not reducible—either in the definitional or the explanatory sense—to a society whose members hold democratic beliefs. Similarly, the public interest is not identical with the interest of each member of the public, and I shall later criticize the authors who define the former in terms of the latter.

7.2.4 Whose Welfare Preferences?

Whether A's action x was or is or would be in his self-interest depends on his own egoistic welfare goals, either actual or hypothetical. Either spending more time at the office or in his backyard may be in A's interest, depending on whether his wealth or his health is most valuable to him.

The concept of public interest, too, must be defined in terms of intrinsic preferences, but these pertain to the collective welfare of the public. Whose collective welfare preferences? Not those of A, i.e., not the welfare preferences the policymakers themselves might adopt. Those of P? There is no such thing. While 'welfare' can be meaningfully attributed to a collectivity as well as to individuals, 'choosing', 'preferring', 'valuing', 'acting (rationally)', like 'redskinned', can be predicated only of individuals (or of groups in a distributive way). That Americans value democracy means that most Americans prefer democratic institutions. Governmental decision makers who want to act in the public interest must be guided by the preferences of all members of P, or at least of most of them; they must be guided by their individual desires pertaining not to their own respective personal welfare, but to what they deem beneficial to collective welfare of the group as a whole—or rather by the preferences they would have if they adopted the collective welfare point of view. I agree "that a policy would be in the public interest if its consequences would implement one or more of the established basic values of the community" (Cohen 1962, p. 156), but would add: to the extent that they are of a collective welfare kind. This corresponds also to Braybrooke's view: "If the people cared nothing about recreation. . . . then recreation would not now be a subject in which the public interest is involved" (1962, p. 139).

But what if public opinion is divided as to what is beneficial to the public as a whole? Even if all members of P want to promote the collective welfare, some might favor increasing production at the price of increasing pollution while others might value environmental protection more highly. In many countries there is disagreement as to whether the collective welfare requires legalizing abortion to reduce the number of unwanted offspring or outlawing it to reduce promiscuity (there are, of course, other, nonutilitarian arguments against abortion). Also, there may be so strong an antagonism between rival interest groups that it is not possible to ask, even as a mental experiment, what all or most persons within both groups would consider ultimately desirable if they adopted the collective welfare point of view. In such situations it is just not possible to assert that it is in the public interest to adopt one rather than another policy. In comparison with the concept of self-interest, the notion of public interest unavoidably has a rather limited range of application, if taken in the descriptive sense. The corresponding normative concept is the more important one, as we shall see.

7.3 PROPOSED DEFINITIONS

Actions that are in the actor's own or in the public interest may thus be characterized as being rational wrt promoting the actor's own welfare or the collective welfare of the public, respectively.

7.3.1 Self-Interest

Definition: It is in A's interest to do x iff it is rational for A to do x wrt promoting his own welfare.[9]

The assertion that it is in A's interest to do x thus refers to a hypothetical condition: were A primarily interested in his own well-being, x would be a rational choice for him in S. (Hence, it is reasonable to expect that, if A did x, his own welfare would be enhanced, or at least maintained.) For example, that it is in A's interest to spend more time in his garden and less in his office means that it is rational for A to do so if he values his own welfare most—assuming, of course, that A identifies his well-being with health rather than wealth.[10]

On the basis of this definition, statements about self-interest turn out, at least in principle, to be empirical, even though they involve not predictions of the actor's behavior, but assessments of what it would be rational for him to do in view of his actual or hypothetical preferences. That something is valuable to someone is a factual assertion about his valuations. Once the observer has ascertained them, he is often in a better position than the actor himself to determine the latter's rational course of action. In the words of Kurt Baier:

> Now, in the case of an individual we often know what would promote his welfare (his interest, his good, his advantage) without knowing whether he would choose to do it. The explanation is of course that individuals, even when they have full information, often choose for reasons other than that they wish to promote their welfare. . . . It would be really surprising if his actual choices, determined by his loves and hates for others, by moral, legal, and other considerations, by his inclinations, desires, im-

pulses, and passions, were always to coincide with his choices based solely on his interest, good, or welfare. (Baier 1967, p. 132)

'It would have been in A's interest to do x (even though he acted differently)' refers to the contrary-to-fact condition that A would have done x, had he acted rationally from an egoistic-utilitarian point of view. Such contrary-to-fact assumptions are sometimes easier to deal with than it may seem. While citizens are often divided on what would promote the collective welfare, their egoistic welfare preferences tend to be similar, even their hypothetical ones. True, there are rational suicides and drug addicts, but most prefer life to death, health to immediate gratification, wealth to poverty (but usually not at the price of endangering their health). That is why we can make empirical assertions of a hypothetical kind, like "it would have been in Saint Francis's own interest to keep his wealth (but contrary to his altruistic convictions)."

'It was (or would have been) in A's interest to do x' must be distinguished from 'A acted in his self-interest in doing x'. Unlike the former, the latter assertion is about A's actual past actions, preferences, and motives. It means that A intended to promote his own welfare and that his action x was rational wrt that ultimate goal. Again, this is not to deny the difficulties of finding out A's "real," and perhaps unconscious, motives, especially when there are several. For example, the drug addict may have decided to undergo the cure to preserve his health *and* for the sake of his family *and* for nonutilitarian reasons. We have also seen that people often promote their own welfare in the long run by acting altruistically or benevolently. We may therefore stipulate that A acted in his own interest if concern for his own well-being was his primary motive.

Interpreted this way, the concept of self-interest enables us to make assertions about what kinds of actions are or were in the interest of a given person or group regardless of our own preferences, and to say that it would have been in someone's interest to act differently from the way he did, without implying that he should have done so. It is not self-contradictory to say, "it is in my interest to do x, but I shouldn't" or "you didn't act in your interest—fortunately!"

7.3.2 Public Interest

More than twenty years ago, Walter Lippmann suggested "that the public interest may be presumed to be what men would choose if they saw clearly, thought rationally, acted disinterestedly and benevolently" (1955, p. 40). Adding " . . . for utilitarian purposes" forms a definition close to the one I propose.[11]

Definition: It is in the interest of the public P that A enact policy x iff it is rational for A to enact x wrt promoting the collective welfare of P.

'The collective welfare of P' refers to the preference all or most members of P would have if they valued the collective welfare above all. Policies, to be in the public interest, must be *rational* wrt some outcome desirable to the *members of the public* from a *utilitarian* and *collective* point of view. For example, if the quasi unanimity holds that less pollution rather than more production is most beneficial to the collectivity as a whole, government, to act in the public interest, must give priority to policies of environmental protection.[12] If public opinion is divided, neither reducing pollution nor increasing production can be said to be in the public interest.

Statements about the public interest tend to be contrary to fact to a greater degree than those about self-interest. As mentioned before, most citizens care little about the "common good" and more about their individual and group interests. It will therefore be in many cases more difficult to hypothesize which welfare goal most members of a public *would* adopt if they were inclined to act "disinterestedly and benevolently."

The proposed definition of public interest does not indicate by what method government is to assess public opinion concerning actual or hypothetical collective welfare goals. Voting usually does not provide the answer. Legislative assemblies rarely vote on such "ultimate" goals, and even if they did, their vote would not necessarily reflect public opinion at large.

> The assent of the people on such matters (as on any other) is not expressed in one election, or in one survey, or in one legislative session. It is settled public opinion that counts, something that becomes visible only as the cumulative results of secular change—results, which after a while cease to be seriously challenged, of the whole complex process of popular government. (Braybrooke 1962, p. 139)

Furthermore, our concept of public interest must be applicable to nondemocratic systems as well. A dictator may well aim at the collective welfare of his subjects on the basis of what "the people care about," although he is most likely to want to do so as a means to further his own political interests or ambitions.

Nor must government be guided by democratic procedures when it comes to its choice of "policy x" to implement a quasi-unanimously adopted actual or hypothetical collective welfare goal. Whether a policy promotes the collective welfare, and as such the public interest, depends exclusively on the criteria of rational decision making, and not on the citizens' individual preferences (other than their ultimate collective welfare goal). To determine the public interest, we need not concern ourselves with the problem of how to aggregate individual preferences into a "social welfare function." The theory of collective choice is relevant to the question whether policy decisions have been arrived at through democratic procedures, not whether they are in the public interest.

A government that does not adopt the prevailing (actual or hypothetical) collective welfare preferences (e.g., it misjudges public opinion) or does not implement them in a rational way or adopts some nonutilitarian goal or serves only the interests of some particular group does not act in the public interest.

In analogy to 'A acted in his self-interest in doing x', 'A's policy x was in the interest of public P' implies that A enacted policy x, that A aimed at implementing the (actual or hypothetical) collective welfare preferences of the members of P, and that it was rational for A to enact policy x wrt that particular collective welfare goal.

Contrary to the view that the concept of public interest "makes no operational sense" (Schubert 1960, p. 224), we have now seen that this notion, like that of self-interest, can be defined in descriptive terms and used independently of our own preferences, including those pertaining to the collective welfare. Presumably, the overwhelming majority not only prefers popular TV programs, but also considers it beneficial to the public as a whole (if not to every individual) that these programs serve recreational rather than educational purposes. It follows that it is in the public interest (in the descriptive sense) that programs remain as they are. But conceding this fact need not prevent me from deploring it from the point of view both of my own interest and of what I myself consider desirable from the collective welfare point of view, namely, the promotion of cultural values. However, if it could be shown that the majority does not "see clearly" (in Lippmann's phrase) the effects of recreational programs and fails to realize that educational television is in fact more conducive to the collective welfare, promoting the latter would be in the public interest.

7.4 OTHER DEFINITIONS OF INTEREST
7.4.1 Definitions in Terms of Desires

Political science deals with questions of both self-interest and public interest. In the former case, it is primarily concerned with the interests not of individual actors, but of groups. Classical positivists like Arthur Bentley used 'interest', 'group', 'activity', and 'desire' more or less synonymously. According to David Truman, "shared attitudes toward what is needed or *wanted* in a given situation, *observable as demands or claims* upon other groups in the society . . . constitute the interest [of an interest group]" (Truman 1955, pp. 33–34; italics added).[13] Similarly, 'interest' has been defined by the *Restatement of the Law of Torts* as "anything which is the object of human desire" (quoted by Feinberg 1973, p. 26); by Roscoe Pound as "the claims, demands, or desires which the human beings . . . seek to satisfy" (quoted by Held 1970, p. 23, with other examples); and more recently by LaPalombara as "conscious desire to have public policy... move in a particular general [*sic*] or specific direction" (1964, p. 16; italics in original).[14]

Now, if 'x is in A's interest' were synonymous with 'A desires x (or the outcome of x)', then, whatever a person or group A wants or demands or claims or desires would be in A's interest, and it would be self-contradictory to say that a person or group is mistaken about his or its interest. The proposed definition of self-interest, too, refers to A's desires, but only to ultimate goals of an egoistic welfare kind (actual or hypothetical) and to means it would be rational to adopt in this connection.

With these many restrictions, it remains true that the proposed definition of self-interest does pertain to the actor's own (welfare) preferences, whatever they may be, e.g., good health or more wealth. I do not therefore agree that, "[i]f a man is endeavouring to hang himself, it can hardly be said to be in his interest to be provided with a rope" (Rees 1964, p. 20). According to the proposed defining criteria, someone who gets hold of a rope to hang himself does act in his own interest, provided that, applying the rules of rational choice, he has come to the conclusion that death is better for him than living. Our reluctance to subsume such cases under self-interest stems from our propensity to substitute our own standards of personal well-being for those of the actor. I believe that the concept of self-interest would lose its identity, and hence its usefulness, if it were made to include ends other than egoistic welfare goals, as do interpretations such as the following:

> [A] person might claim to have an interest in a policy of racial integration... because a recommendation for it was derivable from a principle of justice which he approved. (Held 1970, p. 23).

He may have "an interest" in such a policy; but if his support is motivated by nonutilitarian considerations like those of justice, the policy should not be considered to be *in* his interest. Again:

> We... speak of an individual's "interest" in supporting UNICEF, or promoting the civil rights of

others, or working for legislation to aid the poor. I think it appropriate to say that policies favorable to these objectives are "in the interest of" the individuals with these interests, as well as in the interests of those who will benefit more concretely. (Held 1970, p. 23)

I do not think it appropriate to say that such altruistic interests pertain to policies that are "in the interest of" those who work for the benefit of others.

Some writers have questioned the very distinction between egoism and altruism on which my definition of self-interest is based. "If I feel that my satisfaction is reduced by somebody else's poverty (or, for that matter, by somebody else's wealth), then I am injured in precisely the same sense as if my purchasing power were reduced" (Arrow 1967, p. 11). Not in the same sense. To take the positive counterpart, I may derive as much satisfaction—in the psychological sense—from relieving someone else's poverty as from increasing my own purchasing power. But, clearly, the first action is altruistic and only the second is in my own interest.

Nor do I agree with MacIntyre, who holds that these distinctions are not applicable to such situations at all.

> For in most of my dealings with others of a cooperative kind, questions of benevolence or altruism simply do not arise, any more than questions of self-interest do. . . . [I]f I want to lead a certain kind of life, with relationships of trust, friendship, and cooperation with others, then my wanting their good and my wanting my good are not two independent, discriminable desires. It is not even that I have two separate motives, self-interest and benevolence, for doing the same action. I have one motive, a desire to live in a certain way, which cannot be characterized as a desire for my good rather than that of others. (1967, p. 466)

Difficult as it often is in practice to disentangle an actor's various motives, in theory it is possible to ask whether his *primary* motive for acting cooperatively was altruistic (e.g., "promoting the civil rights of others") or benevolent (e.g., promoting the civil rights of a minority to which he himself belongs) or egoistic (doing so to improve his own situation). In the political and economic sphere, most seemingly altruistic and benevolent activities are geared ultimately to the actor's own purposes. To speak of "[o]ther-regarding and social regarding self-interests" (Flathman 1975, p. 280) seems to me a contradiction in terms.

If individual interest is not the same as individual desire, then, a fortiori, the public interest should not be identified with the desires of the individuals who make up the public or with those of the majority. If the public interest were "our interest in the democratic method . . . regardless of the policies it may produce" (Sorauf, quoted by Held 1970, p. 215), it would, again, be contradictory to assert that a democratic majority favors a policy not in the public interest. In fact, most citizens are most often more concerned about their own personal or group interests than about the collective welfare, and even when they adopt a goal of the latter kind, they often advocate policies that are not rational in that respect. True, individual desires are among the defining conditions not only of self-interest, but also of public interest, but these must pertain to the collective welfare and be quasi-unanimous; otherwise, there is no policy that can be qualified as being in the public interest. On the other hand, a specific policy, to be in the public interest, must be rational wrt a given collective welfare goal, regardless of whether that policy is approved by the majority of citizens or in a legislative assembly.

7.4.2 Definitions in Terms of Needs

The concepts of self-interest and public interest have sometimes been taken in the sense of actions satisfying the needs of the actor or the public, respectively. "[O]n this view, a policy would be in someone's interest to the extent that it, by comparison with other alternatives, promoted need fulfillment or increased opportunities to promote need fulfillment" (Connolly 1974, p. 60). 'Need' is a rather vague concept. A need may be "a necessary means to the attainment of a goal of the person who is said to have the need. . . . What people need in this sense is always relative to what they want" (Paul W. Taylor 1959, p. 107). Then 'x is in A's self-interest' would mean that A's doing x is a means to whatever goal A wants to achieve, and the criticisms of section 7.4.1 would apply. E.g., if A needs a weapon to commit murder or suicide, it is in his interest to acquire it, however irrational it is for A to commit murder or suicide, in terms of his more ultimate goals.

A way out of this difficulty might be to equate interest with the satisfaction of *basic* needs, i.e., the acquisition of "primary goods, . . . things which it is supposed a rational man wants whatever else he wants" (Rawls 1971, p. 92). Such an interpretation of 'needs' brings the definition closer to the proposed one, since it refers essentially to *welfare* goods it is *rational* to want in furtherance of any more remote welfare goals. However, it could then never be in anyone's self-interest to secure anything not included in the list of basic needs; e.g., it could not be in the interest of an art lover to travel to Florence or in the interest of the suicide or the murderer to get a weapon, even if these actions were rational. While excluding irrational wants or needs from the concept of self-interest, we must include *anything* it may be rational for anyone to obtain for whatever *egoistic welfare* goal he might adopt, rather than merely *primary goods* it is rational for most people to obtain for the sake of *whatever ends*.

It seems more plausible to identify *public* interest with the fulfillment of basic needs that, by definition, every rational man wants to be satisfied. Even though public opinion is often divided about the priority of competing collective welfare goals, all are likely to agree that the welfare of the community as a whole will increase if the basic needs of each of its members are fulfilled (whether by government regulation or otherwise is another question). But again, there are other policies some might consider to be in the public interest—e.g., saving the Acropolis (the "public" here being worldwide), even though doing so does not satisfy anyone's *basic* needs, and satisfies the luxury needs only of those able to travel there.

There is a more fundamental objection against defining the concepts of interest in terms of either needs or wants. Such approaches tend to confuse the analytical problem of what meaning to attach to these concepts with the empirical question of what actions or policies are in fact in the interest of a given actor or a given public in a given situation. (Benditt [1973, p. 292] makes a similar point.) Equating interest with the fulfillment of basic needs makes it true by definition that, if doing x fulfills a basic need, it is in the interest of A or of the public to do x. The proposed definitions, on the other hand, make it possible to determine empirically (in a broad sense) whether fulfilling some basic need or securing some good that is not "primary" is in the interest of a given person or group or of the public as a whole. One of the criteria of a fruitful explication is to avoid as far as possible making true by definition what can be left open to empirical investigation.

7.4.3 Definitions in Terms of Happiness

According to Bentham, "a thing is said to promote the interest, or to be *for* the interest, of an individual, when it tends to add to the sum total of his pleasures" (*Principles of Morals and Legislation*, chapter 1) or his happiness, since Bentham uses these terms interchangeably. Bentham adopts a purely aggregative view of society. Consequently, the public interest or "the interest of the community is then—what? The sum of interests of the several members who compose it" (ibid.). And since an action is in a person's self-interest when it increases his happiness, it follows that a policy is in the public interest "when the tendency it has to augment the happiness of the community is greater than any which it has to diminish it" (ibid.), that is, when it augments the happiness of each of the members who compose the community.

Bentham's definition of self-interest is not very different from the proposed one. At least implicitly, it refers to rational choice, since a person can be mistaken as to what course of action will increase his pleasure or happiness. I have avoided these terms because they are not only vague, but also too broad. As mentioned before, a person can derive pleasure or happiness from acting altruistically or benevolently or from pursuing non-utilitarian goals; but such actions do not promote his own welfare and are therefore not in his self-interest by the proposed definition.

Another criticism concerns Bentham's expression 'happiness of the community'. I have argued previously that 'welfare' or 'interest' can be predicated of social groups as well as of individuals, but that only individual persons can be said to be happy or to feel pleasure (and pain), just as only individuals can have preferences or make choices. But the most serious objection is to Bentham's aggregative view of society, which leads him to define a community as nothing but the sum of its individual members. And so he comes to the conclusion that the public interest consists not of what serves the collective welfare of the public, but of what promotes the happiness of each of its members.

7.4.4 Public Interest Defined in Terms of Individual Interests

The view that the public interest is equal to the sum of interests of each of its members is not necessarily tied to the identification of interest with happiness. Such has been the thinking of classical liberalism and its modern followers, as given expression in the following: "[T]o say that an action is in the public interest is to judge it consistent with a political situation that is beneficial to everyone, if not immediately at least in the long run, and whether or not everyone realizes it" (Cassinelli 1962, p. 46). In other words, a policy is in the public interest if it is rational for every member of the public to support it as a means to his own welfare. This definition is open to different interpretations.

a) A policy that is "beneficial to everyone" could mean a policy that brings about the *greatest* good for everyone, or at least for "the greatest number." Now, if the public interest meant the greatest benefit for each person, it would not be in the public interest to produce public goods (i.e., goods that, once in existence, cannot normally be withheld from anyone) like schools, roads, parks, transportation, clean air, or police protection. It would be to the *greatest* advantage of each person, and in his greatest interest, if everyone else contributed to the production of such public goods but if he himself were a "free rider."

We can go a step further. Taken in the literal sense, to maximize everybody's utility is logically impossible.

144

It would, no doubt, be to the interest of every man, taken separately, to have twice his present income, on the assumption that the income of everyone else remained more or less the same. But, since such an interest could not be satisfied for everybody at one and the same time, it would be easy to show that the concept of human interests is self-contradictory [if taken in this sense]. (Rees 1964, p. 24)

b) A policy that is "beneficial to everyone" could also mean a measure promoting the welfare of everyone to an equal, rather than to a maximal, degree. The public interest has accordingly been defined as those policies that are in the equal interest of every member of the public. Feinberg applies this idea to public goods:

[*A*]*ll* of the members of a community or group want some good which is in fact in the interests of each individual *equally,* and yet it is in no individual's interest to contribute toward the goal unless all are *made* to do so. (1973, p. 53; second italics supplied)

Indeed, unless the number of individuals in a group is quite small, or unless there is coercion..., rational, self-interested individuals will not act to achieve their common or group interests. (Olson 1965, p. 2)

Consequently, it is in the public interest to have a government with the authority to make everyone contribute to the production of public goods and, more generally, to do what is to the equal interest of everyone. Nobody would be as well off as if he were a free rider, but everyone would be as well off as everyone else and better off than he would be without the existence of public goods.

That there be government rather than anarchy and that there be certain public goods may well be to the advantage of everyone. But there are other public goods, such as fire and police protection or welfare payments or medical care, that provide benefits not to everyone equally, but to *anyone* who might find himself in certain well-defined situations. The formula 'equal benefits to all' would not cover such situations, which we do, however, normally consider as serving the public interest.

c) Such considerations have led certain writers to apply the concept of public interest to policies making certain advantages available to "nonassignable individuals" (Barry 1962, p. 200): "Thus the public interest is the material advantage of a broad and undefinable group of people, as opposed to private interests, which are material advantages confined to particular and specifiable people" (Barry and Rae 1975, p. 382). A similar definition is provided by Benditt: "[S]omething is a public interest if, and only if, it is an interest of anyone who is a member of the public; that is, if and only if it is essential to the protection, and even for the improvement, of anyone's welfare or well-being" (Benditt 1973, p. 301).[15] Since everybody knows in advance that there is a certain probability that he will be in need of the police or a physician, it is in the interest of *everyone*—and hence in the public interest—that certain services be available to *anyone* who might need them.

Here my objection is that we normally would want the concept of public interest to apply to certain public goods that are of benefit not to an "undefined group" but to "specifiable people," and disadvantageous to other groups also capable of being determined in advance. Persons without children of school age have nothing to gain and something to lose from having to pay school taxes. Compelling a factory owner to install antipollution devices is a burden to him without corresponding benefit when he is in his country villa; the direct beneficiaries are those living near the factory. Opening public places to all races in South Africa is to the advantage of well-defined groups and burdensome to another (whites with racial prejudices). Yet, such policies that are in the interest neither of everyone nor of anyone but only of some may well be held to be in the public interest.

There is a further criticism against equating the public interest with the equal interest of every, or even of any, member of the public. This approach is somehow linked to the belief of classical utilitarianism and liberalism in the "harmony of interests," the view that "individual interests, by courtesy of the invisible hand, coincide with the public interest" (Musgrave 1962, p. 107). Contemporary political science, attuned to the existence of conflicts of interests, requires a concept of public interest also applicable to policies that are in the interests of one group and contrary to those of another.

We cannot construct such a concept as long as we use 'benefit' or 'welfare' or 'interest' distributively when applied to groups, as do all the definitions I have criticized in this section. That is why I have taken these terms as referring to collective properties of "the public" as a whole. Only if we define the public interest by reference to the collective welfare of the public is it possible to assert that it may be in the public interest to advantage one group at the expense of another or to strike a compromise between conflicting group interests. It is just because the collective welfare is so often different from personal utility that we must ask the fictitious question: if people were to agree on a collective welfare goal, which policy would it be rational to enact for that purpose?

7.4.5 Public Interest Related to the "General Will"

The proposed analysis of the public interest bears a closer resemblance to Rousseau's idea of the general will than to any other classical theory, provided we give that notion a certain interpretation. Contrary to Bentham and to those who adopted his views, Rousseau denies that the public interest is definable in terms of individual interest.

> In fact, each individual, as a man, may have a particular will contrary or dissimilar to the general will which he has as a citizen. His particular interest may speak to him quite differently from the common interest: his absolute and independent existence may make him look upon what he owes to the common cause as a gratuitous contribution, the loss of which will do less harm to others than the payment of it is burdensome to himself. (Rousseau, *The Social Contract*, I, 7)

For example, Rousseau might have argued that it is in the "particular interest" of each individual to be a free rider; and each individual may rationalize this by arguing that benefiting from a public good without contributing to its costs will increase his own utility more than paying for it would increase the utility of all others—provided, we must add, that a sufficient number of others pay to produce the public good in the first place.

> There is often a great deal of difference between the will of all and the general will; the latter considers only the common interest, while the former takes private interest into account [regarde à l'intérêt privé], and is no more than the sum of particular wills. (II, 3)

Translating this language of "will" into depersonalized terms, we can interpret this passage as contrasting the sum of private or particular interests with the general or public interest.[16]

> [E]ach individual, having no taste for any other plan of government than that which suits his particular interest, finds it difficult to realize the advantage he might hope to draw from the continual privations good laws impose. (II, 7)

Difficult, but not impossible. Individual citizens are able to set aside their particular short-term interests, to determine policies that are in the public interest, to submit to obligations "to a whole of which [they] form a part" (I, 7), and to realize that, "instead of a renunciation, they have made an advantageous exchange" (II, 4), an exchange of their greater immediate, but incompatible, advantages for what is their long-range collective benefit. "Each man, by giving himself to all, gives himself to nobody" (I, 6). By supporting and submitting to policies that are in the public interest, he does not serve the interests of particular persons or groups, but acts for "the public advantage" (II, 3). My own interpretation of the concept of public interest is in substantial agreement with these passages, but not with some of the ideas implied and elaborated in other parts of *The Social Contract*.

I agree with Rousseau that a political society constitutes a whole to which properties such as 'interest' can be attributed, just as they can to individual persons, and that the interest of the former cannot be defined as the sum of the latter. But a political system is not an *organic* whole. Unlike 'interest' or 'welfare', 'will' (like 'preference' or 'happiness') can be predicated of individuals (or of groups distributively), but not of collectivities like Rousseau's "body politic" (at least not in a literal sense). But since Rousseau's general will "wills" the common interest, it seems legitimate to substitute the latter expression for the former, thus abstracting from Rousseau's organic conception of the state, or rather of the desirable polity.

Indeed, Rousseau is not concerned so much with defining a concept as with propounding a normative doctrine about the desirable political society and the citizen's moral duty to work for the common good *in such a society*. My purpose has been to construct definitions of 'self-interest' and 'public interest' that will be serviceable to the formulation of whatever normative as well as descriptive theory.

It is after a bill "has been put to the free vote of the people" that we know whether it is "in conformity with the general will" (II,7), provided their vote is determined by considerations of the common good rather than by their particular interests. According to the proposed interpretation, whether a policy is in the general interest depends on whether it is *rational* to adopt it in view of some generally agreed collective welfare goal; but neither the end nor the means depends on popular vote.

This brings me to the most important difference between Rousseau's conception and the proposed definition. 'Public interest', as I have defined it, pertains only to collective welfare, whereas Rousseau's 'general will', 'public advantage', 'common good' refer primarily to the nonutilitarian goals of egalitarian justice and moral self-development through political participation. If the notion of public interest were taken in so broad a sense, we could not say that a given policy—e.g., providing educational advantages for the gifted—is in the public interest, yet unjust. As in the case of 'power', we must resist the temptation to give the concept of public interest a meaning so broad as to render it useless.

EIGHT

Normative Interpretations

IN THE PRECEDING CHAPTERS, I have been criticizing other definitions of some basic political concepts, thereby indirectly justifying my own analysis. In this chapter I shall have to adopt a more defensive strategy. I must defend my approach against the view that political concepts like those I have been analyzing are not purely descriptive, but have a normative component; that these are two sides of the same coin; and that statements using these concepts are therefore bound to function simultaneously as factual assertions and moral judgments. In the last chapter I shall discuss the thesis of the inseparability of "facts" and "values" in a more general way. Here I shall examine only how this theory affects the interpretation of the concepts we have been dealing with.

8.1 POLITICAL CONCEPTS AS MORAL NOTIONS

The theory I am considering does not deny that there are concepts that are purely descriptive (e.g., 'table', 'driving', 'atom'[1] and others that are entirely normative (e.g., 'right' or 'wrong', 'desirable'). But there is a large gray area (so to speak) of what Julius Kovesi has called "moral notions"; situated "between good and yellow" (1967, p. 1) (e.g., 'murder', 'prejudice', 'charity'), these are both descriptive and normative. "Evaluation is not an icing on a cake of hard facts" (p. 25). Wrongness is part of the meaning of 'murder'; hence, to say that murder is wrong is redundant.

Political concepts, it is now often alleged, fall within the category of moral notions. "[M]ost of the major concepts of political discourse are neither purely empirical nor purely normative" (Held 1973, p. 73). William Connolly is a typical representative of this view, which I shall illustrate mainly by passages from his book. According to him, political concepts "describe from a moral point of view or, less restrictively, from a normative point of view. Such concepts describe while conveying the commitments of those who share them" (1974, p. 6).

Power is one of these concepts. "[T]he attribution of power to a segment of the society functions more as an accusation than as a normatively neutral description of the political process" (p. 126). Accordingly, an increasing number of political scientists have come to the conclusion "that a neutral, operational definition acceptable to all investigators regardless of ideological 'preference' is not forthcoming with respect to *this* concept" (p. 128). Lukes, too, maintains that "power is one of those concepts which is ineradicably value-dependent" (1974, p. 26).

There is no denial that, *in ordinary language,* terms such as 'murder' or 'charity' function both descriptively and normatively. But it is by no means the case that everyone or most people or even most people within the same culture adopt the *same* moral point of view with respect to murder or stealing. Many believe that Brutus did the right thing in murdering Caesar or admire Robin Hood for stealing from the rich to help the poor.

In the area of politics, the differences between various moral points of view tend to be even greater. Contrary to Connolly, those who "share" the concept of power do not necessarily share the same "commitments" with respect to specific power situations. Someone who attributes power to a given person or group P *may* "accuse" P of wrongdoing; and someone else may hold that it is P's moral right or even his duty to dissuade or deter or restrain R from doing x or punish him for doing so, and that R is under a moral obligation to comply. R himself may adopt this latter moral point of view, and citizens in general tend to do so with respect to governmental power they consider legitimate. But then again, moral opinion about the legitimacy of a given government, and hence of its power, is often divided. It therefore seems to me that Connolly is mistaken to speak of "[o]ur shared judgment that there is a moral presumption against limiting or impairing the choices of others" (1974, p. 95). True, this presumption can be "overridden" (ibid.). But what is the use of introducing a presumption that must be defeated in so many instances? Moreover, considerations of who has the burden of defeating a presumption are relevant to court proceedings; in philosophical debates each side has the burden of substantiating its claims and refuting those of the other.

That there can be, and often are, differences in moral outlook would alone justify our attempt to construct a language of political inquiry that could be used by all political scientists regardless of their ethical or ideological views. Now, if it were correct that political concepts necessarily "describe from a moral point of view," such an endeavor would be bound to fail. So the most effective refutation would be to succeed in formulating "neutral, operational definitions acceptable to all investigators regardless of their ideological preference." This is precisely what I hope to have done. The proposed analysis of power and its related concepts should be acceptable not only to defenders as well as critics of existing power structures, but also to political scientists engaged in describing and explaining power phenomena independently of normative considerations.

Or does my attempt to construct an ethically neutral concept of power commit me to a certain moral view after all, implicitly and—worse—unknowingly? It has been alleged that "[t]o understand politics scientifically" and "to build a new scientific politics around a value-free concept [of power]" leads not to a condemnation, but, on the contrary, to an approbation of power acts (Rosen 1977, p. 468). "It was but a short dialectical step from the building of a science of power and influence to the subsequent yearning on the part of political scientists for some measure of camaraderie with the powerful" (p. 469). Accordingly, there is a "logical link" between American political science—"almost exclusively preoccupied with the concept of power"—and Watergate (p. 467)! It is doubtful whether there is even a *psychological* link between studying power politics and wanting to participate in the game; my guess is that most political scientists are happier to remain within the sheltered walls of academe. But surely there is no *logical* or "dialectical" connection between defining and studying power, on one hand, and adopting "an amoral attitude toward power" (p. 467) on the other. Nor do I agree that "[t]he scientific effort to delineate the acquisition and use of power lost sight of the fact that power, particularly in a constitutional system, has normative dimensions" (p. 471). At least, this need not be the case. Defining power concepts descriptively and studying power relations empirically is perfectly compatible with evaluating power phenomena morally, positively or negatively.

Quite consistently, Connolly considers what I have called social unfreedom to be a moral notion, too.

> [W]e are not *simply* purporting to describe a state of affairs when we say that some individual or group is not free in some respect; we are also typically advancing a charge or making an accusation that we expect those we advance it against to deny, rebut or accept. (1974, p. 152)

Just as "we" are blaming any actor whom we assert to be wielding power (at least prima facie), we are making an accusation against P when we affirm that he is making it impossible or punishable for R to do x (an accusation that can be rebutted). But surely there are legal restrictions the enactment and enforcement of which most of us favor, and there are also actors other than those wielding governmental authority wrt whom we want certain individuals or groups to be unfree to act in certain ways.

While power and unfreedom are held to involve blame, "freedom is a benefit" (MacCallum 1967, p. 312), and the concept of social freedom has "positive normative import" (Connolly 1974, p. 143) and should therefore not be taken as a purely descriptive concept.

> In the ordinary language of political life and in more formal systems of political inquiry the normative dimensions in the idea of freedom are not attached to it as "connotations" that can be eliminated; without the normative point of view from which the concept is formed we would have no basis for deciding what "descriptive terms" to include or exclude in the definition. (Connolly 1974, p. 141)

First of all, what is *the* normative point of view allegedly involved in the idea of freedom? Here the variety of moral outlooks is perhaps even greater than in connection with power. Plato thought that government should *not* give its citizens much freedom (which he defined, quite descriptively, as being allowed to do what one likes [*Republic*, VIII, 557]). Furthermore, as mentioned earlier, it is empirically impossible to favor "a freedom" such as freedom of speech without also approving of the necessary limitations of freedom. Also, one kind of freedom deemed desirable must be weighed against other freedoms incompatible with the former, as well as against other goals such as welfare or equality.

For rhetorical purposes, it may be good strategy to use the *word* 'freedom' only in a laudatory way, and to call a freedom one opposes 'license': "If unbridled license of speech and of writing be granted to all, nothing will remain sacred and inviolate.... Thus, truth gradually being obscured by darkness, promiscuous and manifold error, as too often happens will easily prevail. Thus, too, license will gain what liberty loses" (Encyclical *Libertas*, 1888). Here, unfreedom to propagate "error" becomes freedom—to affirm "truth"—and freedom of opinion becomes "license."

My point is this. If 'freedom' is taken by everyone as a moral notion to refer to all, and only to, relationships of *both* freedom and unfreedom of which he approves, everyone will agree on one point only: that "freedom" is something good. But there will be disagreement on what states of affairs are the desirable ones. Meaningful disagreement about the desirable extent and limit of some specific kind of social freedom presupposes agreement about the meaning of 'freedom'. I believe that such agreement is possible on the basis of the analysis of the concept of social freedom I have provided. The proposed interpretation does not even deviate from "the ordinary language of political life," except that it detaches the concept from what I consider to be its moral *connotation*. Since it incorporates no "normative point of view," it can be applied by anyone to determinate states of affairs, regardless of his moral, political, or ideological convictions.

'Equality' and 'egalitarianism' are, like 'freedom', words that have acquired a positive moral connotation in *our* society at the *present* time. Again, I say "connotation" because I believe to have shown that the concept of an egalitarian or inegalitarian rule of distribution can be used in a valuationally neutral way, at least relative to a given distribution and a given reference group. This approach has been criticized by Virginia Held, who maintains that "to *evaluate* whether societies and their components are egalitarian, judgments are needed about a particular aspect of *moral* concern, that of equality" (1973, p. 72; italics added). Accordingly, to determine whether tax systems or educational arrangements are egalitarian "would require judgments concerning the moral significance of various features of them, as well as the degrees to which their various rules impose burdens and provide benefits" (p. 71). I am taking the latter criterion as a sufficient defining condition, and this enables me to say that a given tax law or educational system is inegalitarian but fair, or egalitarian but unjust. In a similar vein, Conrad has objected that the proposed definition fails to take into account "our notion of equality as a moral rather than operational notion" (1976, p. 138), and, more specifically, that it "is not helpful as an answer to the problem of the *merits* of quota systems as compensatory devices for disadvantaged groups" (p. 140; italics added). To me, this is an advantage. My conclusion that quota systems of any kind are inegalitarian has no bearing on whether some particular quota system is just or has other merits.

The concepts of self-interest and public interest, too, are frequently interpreted as moral notions. " 'Interest' is one of those concepts that connects descriptive and explanatory statements to normative judgment" (Connolly 1974, p. 46; cf. also Lukes 1973, p. 34). " 'Interests', then, may have to be understood normatively, and not simply as accounts of actual desires" (Benn 1960, p. 129). I would agree with these views if it were added, "sometimes." Indeed, utterances like 'it is in A's interest to do x' sometimes do function both normatively and descriptively. If I say to a drug addict, "It is in your interest to undergo drug rehabilitation," I may want to persuade him to *change* his intrinsic preferences. And while I may inquire into what is in the interest (descriptively speaking) of a drug addict or a highjacker or a dictator without approving of his pursuing that course, I am not likely to say that a certain policy is in the public interest unless I am also in favor of that policy. (We have seen that the descriptive concept of public interest is applicable only when a quasi-unanimous opinion prevails as to which collective welfare goal is to be implemented.) Unlike concepts such as power or freedom or egalitarianism, those of self-interest and public interest have an unvarying meaning, even when interpreted as moral notions. There may therefore be some justification for introducing them into our reconstructed language, provided we define them adequately and distinguish them clearly from the corresponding purely descriptive concepts. We shall try to do so in the next section, but also point up the drawback of interpreting the notions of interests in a moral sense.

8.2 Political Concepts Normatively Defined

Writers who view political concepts as moral notions sometimes provide definitions. These do, of course, differ from the proposed ones, and I shall have to defend these against their interpretations.

8.2.1 In Descriptive Terms

Some of the definitions to be examined in this connection are couched in descriptive terms, as are those I criticized in the preceding chapters; but they are geared to make the concepts they define applicable to those, and only to those, situations their proponents want to commend (as when they define 'freedom') or condemn (as in the case of 'power').

Certain of the descriptive definitions examined earlier are of this type. For instance, the propensity to define power as comprising deception, manipulation, and the threat and use of force, but as excluding persuasion by rational argument and offers of reward is based not only on (alleged) common usage, but on normative considerations as well. If the attribution of power to an actor functions as an "accusation," the exercise of power can consist only of actions that are ethically wrong. Consequently, to persuade someone to act in a certain way by providing him with good reasons is not to exercise power over him, in contradistinction to manipulation or coercion, which violate the moral injunction of respect for persons. "[F]or those tacitly or explicitly committed to the principle that persons are worthy of respect, the distance between persuasion and manipulation is a moral distance; it reflects the judgment that there is a moral presumption against the latter that does not obtain for the former" (Connolly 1974, p. 94). The same moral presumption holds against "coercion, anticipatory surrender, force, and conditioning" (p. 94). Contrarywise, "persuasion . . . is not a form of power" (p. 95).

I do not think that there is a "moral presumption" against the use of 'power' in Connolly's sense, even as judged by those who subscribe to the ethics of respect for persons. Most of us hold a moral presumption *in favor* of the government's deterrent and punitive power in the area of common crimes or of taxation for the purpose of providing public goods that cannot be made available through voluntary contributions. And while we do not want those occupying official positions to deceive their own citizens, we sometimes approve of such methods when used by one government against another. On the other hand, there are instances of rational persuasion of which most of us would disapprove, e.g., to convince someone else by means of reasoned arguments to highjack a plane in order to publicize some national liberation movement. Here it can be objected that both the highjacker and the persuader violate the principle of respect for persons, since both consider innocent passengers as not worthy of respect, but merely as means for a "cause" (see Ball 1978, p. 611).[2] My reply is that communication, at least on a scientific level, should not be restricted to those who share a common moral point of view. The example illustrates the very need of a definition of power acceptable to all (at least to all political scientists), regardless of their divergent ethical views. Recommending an overarching, as well as ethically neutral, concept of power is not to brush over the dissimilarities— normative as well as descriptive—between its various subcategories.

Another previously discussed interpretation of relevance in this connection is the widespread tendency to consider an actor to be unfree to act in a certain way, even if his inability to do so is not the result of some other actor's intervention.

This notion of unfreedom is used when it is felt that the actor *should* be enabled by some other actor to do so and that the latter's failure to enable him is morally wrong. According to Macpherson, "the unequal access to the means of life and labour *inherent in capitalism* is . . . an impediment to the freedom of those with little or no access" (1973, p. 101; italics added). True, those with little access to the means of life and labor are likely to be unfree to do many things and unfree wrt many actors. But on the basis of the proposed definition, they are not unfree to secure an adequate standard of living if their inability is "inherent in capitalism" rather than caused by any specific group (and I have tried to show the advantages of this definition).

For the same reasons, the concept of social freedom is often restricted to being able to do what others *should* make it possible to accomplish. To give just one example of this familiar conception, "Personal freedom means the power of the individual to buy sufficient food, shelter and clothing to keep his body in good health and to gain access to sufficient teaching and books to develop his mind" (Webb and Webb 1923, p. 45). Such definitions confuse social freedom with freedom of action. Furthermore, they restrict the meaning of the latter to an actor's capacity to bring about something *specific* such as a certain level of well-being.

Denying, as I do, that inabilities resulting from impersonal factors are instances of social unfreedom has been interpreted as a defense of laissez-faire capitalism (see e.g., Macpherson 1973, p. 91). More generally, defining social freedom the way I have done has been tied to viewing society—and approvingly so—as consisting of Hobbesian, isolated, self-interested, utility-maximizing individuals. I do not believe that my interpretation of social freedom and unfreedom has any normative implications, no more so than my attempt to construct a valuationally neutral concept of power. Proponents of this *definition* of negative liberty need not be "[p]roponents of negative liberty" (Macpherson 1973, p. 98). To deny that inabilities caused by capitalism (rather than by capitalists) are limitations of freedom is not to approve of these inabilities or to defend capitalism, and to deny that providing full employment and social benefits are matters of freedom is not to oppose such measures.

Defining "freedom in general" as being able or being permitted to do what one wants—thus confusing social freedom with the feeling of freedom—is also linked to normative considerations, in this case the conviction that people should normally be enabled and permitted to fulfill their desires. The same normative standpoint accounts for the related view that an individual has *more* freedom if the range within which he is free to act includes the alternative he wants to pursue most than if it does not. "Clearly, there can be no simple or direct relationship between the range of available alternatives and the extent of freedom. However numerous the alternatives between which a man may choose, he will not admit himself to be free if the one alternative that he would most prefer is the one which is excluded" (Partridge 1967, p. 223). He may not *admit* or even realize that he remains free to perform any of the actions he wants to perform less or not at all. He may not *feel* free if it is his favored course of action he is being made unfree to pursue. However, we have seen that my not wanting to do something does not count against my being free to do so, that the range of my freedom depends exclusively on the number of alternatives I am free to pursue, and that this range is indeed *one* of the dimensions of the extent of my freedom. Given the proposed definition of social freedom and the ordinary usage of the term as well, it just is not true that "a person who is prevented from doing something which is of some importance to him is suffering a greater curtailment of liberty than [if it is not]" and that "the degree to which his liberty is thereby curtailed depends (other things being equal) on how important the course of action in question is to him" (Loevinsohn 1977, p. 232). Conversely, it is not the case that a person's freedom is greater if what he is free to do happens to include what is important to him and that the degree of his freedom is the greater, the stronger his desire to perform that particular action. As pointed out in chapter 4, we should not confuse the *extent* of my freedom, how much (or how little) I *value* being free in that respect, and how valuable it is to me to be able (as well as free) to pursue *some particular* course of action.

Indeed, even if what I want to do most is included in the

range of my freedom, in most cases the opportunity to do what I desire is what I value, rather than my freedom to do so *or to do something else*, just as, when I am unable but free to realize my desire, I value being given the opportunity I lack, not the freedom I already have. After the revocation of the Edict of Nantes, Frenchmen became free to be Protestants or Catholics. Protestants cared mainly about being no longer unfree to practice their faith, and some would not have minded if Protestantism became the mandatory state religion. Catholics did not value their *freedom* of religion either. The principle of freedom of religion for all was advocated by some philosophers. I mentioned, too, that there are many circumstances in which most prefer being compelled to do certain things, i.e., being made unfree to act otherwise. I deny therefore that "[n]o matter what values men hold, the freedom to pursue these values is important for them " (Bay 1958, p. 15). Being free to do one thing or another becomes important only if one values the possibility of deciding for oneself whether to do this or that. This is the meaning of valuing freedom—or better: valuing some specific social freedom like freedom of opinion—either for oneself or for others or for all. But restricting 'freedom' by definition to doing, or being permitted to do, what one desires is usually a disguise for *advocating* that people *should* be left free to make their own decisions *in some specific area*.

The same normative view—that it is a good thing that people satisfy their desires (including their immediate ones) or needs or happiness—may well account for the tendency to define the notion of self-interest in these terms and for equating the public interest with the wishes of all or of the majority.

Similar criticisms must be directed against Macpherson's conceptual scheme. According to him, "the *whole* of man's power in the general *descriptive* sense" consists of two subcategories: "developmental power," i.e., "whatever ability he may have to use his own capacities," and "extractive power," i.e., "whatever ability he may have to extract benefit from the use of others' capacities" (1973, p. 42; italics added). This distinction corresponds to the one I made between power as an actor's ability to do something and power as an actor's control over another actor's activity. The difference is that Macpherson restricts the former concept to the use of individual capacities for good purposes (as is clear from the context) and the latter to the one activity of "extracting benefit" from someone else, i.e., exploiting him. Hence, developmental power is good and extractive power bad. But surely the concept of power "in the general descriptive sense" must cover other situations, too. Presumably, Macpherson would not subsume an actor's ability to set fire to a building under developmental power. On the other hand, if P dissuades or deters or restrains R from hurting himself, does P not exercise power over R in that respect, even if he derives no benefit from his action? Clearly, social power must be defined to include not only "extractive power," but also power exercised in the interest of the respondent rather than of the powerholder.

Macpherson uses these concepts of developmental power and extractive power to construct his own definitions of positive liberty and negative liberty, respectively. Positive liberty "is virtually the same as . . . a man's power in the developmental sense" (p. 105); i.e., positive liberty is his ability to use his capacities—not for whatever purposes (as I have defined the concept of positive freedom), but to acquire what he ought to be enabled to secure, in the first place the basic necessities of life. This leads us back to freedom conceived as "the power to buy sufficient food," etc. And negative liberty (in Berlin's sense, which is similar to my definition of social freedom) "might well be redefined as *immunity from the extractive powers of others (including the state)*" (p. 118; italics in original). Only when nobody exploits me am I free (to do what?).

From freedom as the ability to secure a decent standard of living it is only a short step to "freedom from want." The first two of the four freedoms of the Atlantic Charter, "freedom of religion" and "freedom of speech," stand for demands that governments should leave their citizens free to adopt any religion and to voice any opinion (within certain limits). But to advocate freedom from want is not to demand that they should be left free to satisfy their basic wants *or to leave them unsatisfied,* nor that they should be able, or even enabled, to secure these necessities. 'Freedom from...' is used in ordinary language to refer to the absence of something unpleasant that was present before, as when someone says that he is free from his headache. 'Freedom from want' means absence of want and *availability* of an adequate standard for all. To advocate freedom from want is to enjoin government to *provide*, e.g., full employment, minimum wages, and certain social benefits. To realize this goal, government must, on the contrary, restrict certain social freedoms such as "freedom of contract." 'Freedom from want' is another way of saying 'welfare'. Of course, those who are "free from" want or from exploitation have, *as a matter of empirical fact*, a greater range of freedom wrt a greater number of actors; but these are indirect consequences of *welfare* policies. The "four freedoms" were good propaganda during the Second World War. From an analytic point of view, civil liberties and social welfare are different concepts, standing for different—and often competing—goals. Admittedly, whether a particular incapacity has been caused by "natural" impediments or by other actors is often a matter of controversy. This is no objection against defining social unfreedom as comprising only obstacles of the latter kind. The proposed definitions of social freedom and unfreedom are neutral on the desirable extent of individual freedom and governmental intervention.

Like freedom from want, so-called freedom of participation does not relate to freedom in any sense. To champion freedom of participation (or participatory democracy) is not to demand that citizens be free either to participate in the political process *or to stay home*, but to urge that they *should* take an active part in it and that the political system should provide them with the opportunities to do so.

The Freedom House survey referred to earlier (4.3.5) provides another illustration for the tendency to apply the notion of freedom to features deemed desirable, even if they have nothing to do with social freedom (or with freedom of any kind). As we have seen, the survey considers a society politically free if "the elected rule," if there are periodic shifts in rule from one party to another, if a broad ideological consensus prevails, or if there is a high degree of literacy and economic equality. On the other hand, the survey does not seem to regard control of the media by nongovernmental groups as restricting freedom of expression (perhaps because otherwise the United States might lose its place among the "freest" countries).

I also used the survey to illustrate that, while specific freedom relations between specified actors can sometimes be measured, it is not even possible to assign any descriptive meaning to 'freedom" without further qualification. Expressions such as 'a free society' can only refer to institutions protecting precisely those social freedoms that *ought* to prevail or which have desirable features of whatever kind. "No society in which these liberties [liberty of conscience, liberty of tastes and pursuits, freedom to unite] are not, on the whole, protected, is free" (John Stuart Mill, *On Liberty*, chapter 1). "Representative government is freedom" (Thomas Paine, *The Rights of Man*).

I have defined a free person as an individual capable of acting autonomously and rationally—for whatever purpose. Philosophers tend to speak of self-determination or of positive freedom in rather dithyrambic tones (even Isaiah Berlin does so), as if a despot or a terrorist could not be a free person in the sense of the definition. Imperceptibly, a free man becomes a man who autonomously and rationally pursues certain specific purposes, those which he *ought* to pursue, and a person who does not act that way is unfree. Philosophers differ as to the goals one ought to adopt as a free person. Some identify freedom with self-realization in the sense of our definition.[3] But there is another tradition going back to Plato that identifies freedom (in the sense of being a free person), on the contrary, with obedience either to one's own "higher" self or to some external authority, or to both if they are the same, as they are according to Rousseau in *The Social Contract:*

> The constant will of all members of the State is the general will; by virtue of it they are citizens and free. (IV, 2)

> [E]ach, while uniting himself with all, may still obey himself alone, and remain as free as before. (I, 6)

> [W]hoever refuses to obey the general will . . . will be
> forced to be free. (I, 7)

> [F]or the mere impulse of appetite is slavery, while
> obedience to a law which we prescribe to ourselves is
> liberty. (I, 7)

In these famous passages, Rousseau uses the form of definition as a rhetorical device to express the moral doctrine that
citizens of the good society ought to comply with its laws,
preferably spontaneously, otherwise under compulsion. And
so freedom becomes its opposite: limitation of desire, restriction of choice, obedience to authority, submission to
(and recognition of) the "general will" or to "natural necessity," and finally unfreedom for purposes deemed justified:
"Liberating tolerance, then, would mean intolerance against
movements from the Right, and toleration of movements
from the Left" (Marcuse 1965, p. 109).

8.2.2 In Normative Terms

Expressions such as 'ability to extract benefits from others',
'unequal access to the means of life and labor', 'ability to do
what one desires', 'freedom to unite', 'representative government' are descriptive.[4] However, the states of affairs
these defining expressions describe are just those the proponents of these definitions happen to value, either positively (as in the case of 'freedom') or negatively (e.g., definitions of 'unfreedom'). Hence, these are normative judgments,
although grammatically they look like descriptive definitions.
In contradistinction, the definitions to be considered now
make explicit use of ethical terms such as 'ought', 'responsibility', 'justified'.

Thus, writers like Connolly not only use the word 'power'
to apply primarily, if not exclusively, to actions they consider
or at least presume to be morally wrong, but also define the
concept of power in terms of 'responsibility' in a moral
sense. "A exercises power over B when he is responsible for
some x that increases the costs, risks, or difficulties to B in
promoting B's desires" (1974, p. 102). Connolly explains that
he means to "refer here to moral responsibility (in a broad
sense of 'moral') . . . [when the actor] is condemned or

praised for the act or condition and (some of) its consequences" (p. 131, note 9). But if one observer condemned A for, e.g., deterring B from doing x and another praised him for doing so, the former would have to affirm and the latter to deny that A exercised power over B wrt his not doing x. And so communication (at least on a scientific level) is bound to break down.

The same idea has also been applied to the concept of unfreedom. "Since freedom is a principle, whatever interferes with it demands to be justified; consequently, only those determining conditions for which rational agents (God or man) can be held responsible, *can qualify as interfering with it*" (Benn and Weinstein 1971, p. 200; italics added). "Responsible" in the sense that the agent (man—or God?) should be blamed for having made someone unfree to act in a certain way? But (to take an extreme counterexample) does not a policeman who overpowers a criminal (perhaps a mad one) interfere with his freedom, even though he would generally be praised for his action? And again, suppose there is disagreement as to whether the policeman acted responsibly. There must then also be disagreement as to whether he interfered with the criminal's freedom—on the basis of this definition.

Freedom has been defined not only descriptively as an actor's ability to do what he wants to do (with the implication that he should be allowed to act as he pleases), but also normatively as doing and being permitted to do what is right. According to Montesquieu, "In governments, that is, in societies directed by laws, liberty can consist only in the power of doing what we ought to will and not being constrained to do what we ought not to will" (*Spirit of the Laws*, XI, 3). But unlike Rousseau, Montesquieu does not tell us (at least not in this passage) what it is that we ought to will. I realize that "can consist" may mean either 'should consist' or 'does consist'. Only if taken in the latter sense does this statement amount to a definition. It would then follow that an actor who is able and permitted to do something he ought not to will is not free to do so! Cicero manages to combine both aspects: "For what is freedom? The power to live as you will. Who then lives as he will except one who follows the things that are right, who delights in his duty" (*Paradoxa Stoicorum*, V, 34; quoted by McKeon 1951, p. 117).

Here is an example of a definition of egalitarianism in normative terms: "The true opposite of equality is arbitrary, i.e., unjustifiable or inequitable treatment" (Von Leyden 1963, p. 67). Accordingly, an inegalitarian rule that is not arbitrary and is justified is egalitarian. It would then be contradictory to say that a differential wage scale is justified *and* inegalitarian or that it is egalitarian *and* unjust to pay the same salary to everyone. And again, what if there is disagreement as to whether a given rule of distribution is justified? Both 'egalitarian' and 'justified' are characteristics of rules of distribution of benefits or burdens. The difference is that 'justified' is a normative and 'egalitarian' a descriptive term. To equate either type of concept with the other by definitional fiat is fallacious.

Defining valuational concepts descriptively is usually called the definist fallacy,[5] as when 'good' is defined by 'conducive to happiness', or 'desirable' by 'desired (e.g., by the majority)', or 'just' by 'egalitarian'—as does Aristotle in his famous statement, "The unjust is unequal, the just is equal" (*Ethics*, 1131a). It would then be self-contradictory to say that a policy promoting happiness is bad or that something approved by the majority is undesirable or that some egalitarian rule is unjust.

To define descriptive terms like 'power', 'freedom', 'egalitarianism' by normative ones like 'responsible', 'ought', is to commit what I would like to call the definist fallacy in reverse, which makes it appear as if factual assertions could be logically derived from normative judgments. Thus, given the definition that freedom means doing what one ought to do and given the normative judgment that A ought to do x (plus the factual assertion that A does x), it follows that A is free. Similarly, if "the opposite of equality" is unjustified inequality and if it is unjustified to pay equal salaries to all, then this policy is inegalitarian. The logic is impeccable; it is the definitional premises that are unacceptable, because they are—once again—not definitions at all, but expressions of normative principles. The same is true of the conclusions. And so the whole "argument" never leaves the domain of normative ethics.

On the other hand, moral notions *must* be defined in normative terms; i.e., words such as *ought* and 'just' must be used to characterize their moral dimension. This way, there is no danger of confusing them with the corresponding descriptive concepts. That it is, in the normative sense, in A's self-interest to do x means that it is rational for A to do x in view of some egoistic welfare goal y that A *ought* to adopt. Statements about self-interest in this sense convey the speaker's moral judgment that it is right, or at least not wrong, for A to look after his own welfare (at least in some particular instance) and that he should adopt some specific egoistic-utilitarian goal y, usually one different from the goal A is now pursuing. Even so, I do not agree with definitions like the following:

> [I]f I say that something is in your interests, I imply that you have a prima facie claim to it, and if I say that 'policy x is in A's interest' this constitutes a prima facie justification for that policy. (Lukes 1974, p. 34)

> To say that a policy or practice is in the interests of an individual or a group is to assert both that the recipient would somehow benefit from it and that there is therefore a *reason* in support of enacting that policy. (Connolly 1974, p. 46; italics in original. See also Flathman 1975, p. 280)

These definitions make it look as if 'interest' always functioned normatively. We do sometimes assert that policy x is in A's interest when we think that there is a prima facie reason to oppose it. I may hold that x is, descriptively speaking, in A's interest, but that A should not do x (and that the corresponding policy should not be enacted) because I believe that A ought to pursue a different egoistic welfare goal or that he should act altruistically or that he should pursue the public interest. To assert that it was in Richard Nixon's self-interest to withhold the tapes (in view of his own intrinsic goal to remain in office) is perfectly compatible with the view that he ought to have acted against his interest. Naturally, if A considers policy x to be in his own interest, *he* may therefore have "a reason" to support it; and if that policy is in conflict with B's interest, B will have a reason to oppose it; and a third person who is not involved may be against policy x because he gives B's interest a higher moral claim than A's or because he favors a policy that serves the public interest rather than the self-interest of A (or B). "Of course, the reason may be overridden by other considerations" (Connolly 1974, p. 46). But these may be so weighty as to eliminate "the reason"—e.g., A's reason—from the start. One might even go further and claim that there is in our society a moral presumption *against* policies serving primarily the interests of a particular group or person. According to the moral standard to which most of us at least pay lip service, egoism is wrong and policies should always promote the general interest.

One further example of taking 'self-interest' exclusively in the moral sense:

> A class of slaves might be apathetic about freedom, perhaps because it never occurs to them that they might be free, perhaps because they have been conditioned to accept their lot. Nevertheless one might say that it would be better for them, *or in their best interests*, if they were free, not because this is what they really want, but because slavery is inconsistent with human dignity, or some other general moral standard of that sort. (Benn 1960, p. 129; italics added)

The word 'or' indicates that 'x is in A's interest' is here equated with 'x is better (or best) for A' not in terms of A's own chosen welfare goal, but in the sense of 'x is right by the moral standard one ought to adopt'. Given (*a*) the definition of self-interest as a moral notion, (*b*) the moral standard that one should strive for human dignity, and (*c*) the fact that slavery is incompatible with human dignity, it does follow that it is in the interest (in the normative sense) of slaves to become free, regardless of their actual preferences. If we use instead the proposed descriptive definition—without giving up the normative and factual premises (*b*) and (*c*)—we are led to the conclusion that it may not be in the interest of well-conditioned slaves to become free, since it may be rational for them to remain in their actual condition, given the preferences they have been indoctrinated to adopt. To the objection that preferences based on "false consciousness" are not rational, it must be replied that alleged instances of false consciousness can hardly be established empirically because "false consciousness' is itself a normative concept. Thus, C. Wright Mills characterized it as "lack of awareness of and identification with one's objective interests" (quoted by Connolly 1974, p. 48). But "objective interests" can here only mean interests based on those intrinsic preferences one *ought* to adopt. It seems to me that the above moral argument could be rendered much more clearly and unambiguously as follows: slavery ought to be abolished; hence, well-adjusted slaves ought to be persuaded to give up their "slave morality" and to shift their preferences from security to freedom, so that it will become in their interest to set themselves free. Or alternatively: society ought to make it possible for all to act as free persons (as defined in 5.4); slaves are not free persons; therefore, slavery ought to be abolished.

That it is, normatively speaking, in the public interest that A enact policy x means that there is some specific collective welfare goal y that A should pursue and that it is rational for A to enact x in view of y. Statements of of this type involve two normative judgments:

1. A should aim at the collective welfare generally rather than at furthering the interests of this or that group or at pursuing some nonutilitarian goal. In this sense it is true that "[w]hen an action is in the public interest, it is worthy of approval; when an action is not in the public interest, it deserves our disapproval" (Cassinelli 1962, p. 45). But this statement need not be true if 'public interest' is taken in the descriptive sense. There may be disagreement even among "public-spirited" people, as to whether the public interest ought to prevail in the first place, e.g., as to whether the building of a rocket range, admittedly necessary for the defense and as such in the public interest, is worth uprooting a number of families and thereby sacrificing their private interests.[6] Or, referring to a previous example, some may feel that considerations of justice should supercede those of col-

lective welfare (and hence of public interest) when it comes to educational policies.

Since justice and welfare are different goals, it does not seem to me correct to identify the public interest, even in the normative sense, with "just and impartial rules and procedures for the treatment of persons" (Blackstone 1973, p. 231). Environmental protection may be judged to be in the public interest either in the descriptive or in the normative sense. How the costs are distributed is a matter of justice, not of public interest.

2. A should adopt collective welfare goal y in particular, which may or may not correspond to the actual (or hypothetical) welfare preferences of all or most members of P. To take a previous example, if most believe that recreational rather than educational TV programs promote the collective welfare, such programs are in the public interest—descriptively speaking. At the same time I may hold that the public interest in the normative sense requires the FCC to promote more educational programs, i.e., that this is the collective welfare goal it ought to pursue and x the policy it should enact to that effect.

We must, then, distinguish between a descriptive and a normative concept of public interest as well as of self-interest. Each of them must be defined narrowly enough to enable them to function properly in a language of political inquiry. Still, I see a disadvantage in using these concepts normatively. Of two speakers with different moral convictions, one is likely to affirm and the other to deny that a given policy is in the actor's own, or in the public, interest. Because these are indicative sentences, this looks like a factual disagreement, when the disagreement is really about whether the policy is morally justified. As illustrated by the example of slavery, it seems to me to make for greater clarity to speak explicitly in terms of 'ought' and 'right' when dealing with moral questions, rather than to use amphibious "moral notions."

8.2.3 In Appraisal Terms
Appraising must be distinguished from describing as well as from expressing a normative commitment. Examples of ap-

praising are: grading apples or student papers, evaluating paintings in terms of their market value, wine tasting. In each of these cases, the objects are evaluated in terms of some well-circumscribed standard. Without accepted criteria, e.g., for superior, good, and inferior cheese, "the question whether some sample of cheese is good will have no answer. After their acceptance the question will have a definite answer," acceptable even to those who hate all cheese (Urmson 1965, p. 403).

Writers often *define* political concepts using terms of appraisal such as 'significant', 'arbitrary', 'relevant', 'harmful' (I shall italicize them in the examples), but do not provide any standards or criteria for their application. Yet, "grading words can only be used successfully for communication where criteria are accepted" (Urmson 1965, p. 406). If none are given, it is up to each interpreter to provide his own standard of evaluation. What looks like an appraisal turns out to be a normative judgment, usually of a moral kind.

For example, Connolly defines power as implying not only that power acts are morally wrong (see 8.1), but also that they are *unnecessary*. He himself points to the following consequences: "If part of the point in saying that A has power over B is to *charge* A with closing B's options unnecessarily, it may turn out that the *criteria* appropriate to establishing such a charge in the society of the local shopkeeper are rather different from those appropriate to the society of the corporate manager" (1974, p. 200). Here I agree completely with Connolly. But is this not a fatal objection against his own characterization? If the shopkeeper estimates that A's closing of B's options is unnecessary and the manager considers A's action indispensable, then the shopkeeper and the manager are bound to disagree as to whether the statement 'A has power over B' is true.

Similarly, if freedom is defined as "that condition of men in which coercion of some by others is reduced *as much as possible* to society" or as "independence of the *arbitrary* will of another" (Hayek 1960, pp. 11, 12), whoever applies these definitions must supply his own criteria. And so a Hitler or a Stalin could claim that he has built a "free" society in which coercion has been reduced as much as possible and is not

171

being exercised arbitrarily, given his own purpose.

'A free person', taken as a moral notion, has been defined not only descriptively as a person acting in specific ways, but also in terms of appraisals. Some examples: "'Freedom' [in the sense of psychological freedom] means degree of *harmony* between basic motives and overt behavior" (Bay 1958, p. 83). Accordingly, a free person "is the personality in which a *successful* solution has been found in the conflict between biological drive and social conscience" (p. 86). "Freedom does not require that I am independent from even myself—it demands the opposite: that I achieve a *harmony* with what I *truly* am" (Bergmann 1977, p. 53). Here the words 'require' and 'demand' indicate perhaps that this statement is meant to be not so much a definition ('A is a free person' means 'A achieves harmony with what he truly is') as an exhortation to achieve that sort of harmony (whatever that means).

One of the descriptive definitions of egalitarianism I criticized earlier was Aristotle's concept of proportional equality as "equality of ratios." Another Aristotelian concept of proportional equality may be mentioned in the present context, "equality proportionate to desert" (*Politics,* 1301a; see also 1317b, quoted in chapter 6, note 7), since 'desert' is clearly a word of appraisal. Aristotle defines an egalitarian rule in this narrower sense as "one in which the relative value of the things given corresponds to those of the persons receiving" (*Politics,* 1280a).[7] The relative value of a benefit to be allotted can usually be appraised quite unambiguously in terms of readily available standard such as its monetary value. A person's ability in the sense of his proficiency at a specific task can also often be assessed and even measured fairly objectively. But by what standard should we evaluate the relative value of a person—i.e., whether that person is more deserving or meritorious than another, and how much more? If a given rule of distribution allots, say, the same amount of money to two persons or groups and if I consider the former to be more deserving than the latter, that rule would be according to this conception inegalitarian to me— but perhaps egalitarian to you.

A more generalized and at present widely adopted version of this view is the following: a rule of distribution is egalitarian iff differences in allotments correspond to *relevant* differences in personal characteristics, in other words, provided the specified characteristic is relevant to the kind of benefits or burdens to be distributed. Thus, age and citizenship are said to be relevant to voting rights; it is therefore egalitarian to limit the franchise to adult citizens. Wealth is relevant to taxation; hence, a flat rate or a graduated income tax is egalitarian. Conversely, a rule is inegalitarian if it is either based on irrelevant differences of characteristics or disregards relevant ones. Sex or color or wealth are irrelevant to voting; restricting the franchise to men or whites or payers of a poll tax is inegalitarian. Differences in wealth are relevant to taxation; hence, a sales tax is inegalitarian, since it taxes the poor and the wealthy buyers at the same rate. Again, no standard of relevance is provided. Hence, whether a given rule is egalitarian or inegalitarian depends not on empirical criteria, but on one's own *moral* evaluation. Indeed, that age is relevant to voting but color not means that it is just to require a minimum age for voting but unjust to base the franchise on race.

Bernard Williams disagrees. He holds that it is "quite certainly false" to claim "that the question whether a certain consideration is *relevant* to a moral issue is an evaluative question" (1962, p. 113). He argues that, "if any reasons are given at all" for racial discrimination, "they will be reasons that seek to correlate the fact of blackness with certain other considerations which are at least candidates for relevance to the question of how a man should be treated: such as insensitivity, brute stupidity, ineducable irresponsibility, etc." (p. 113). I agree that the statement 'color is relevant to intelligence' is descriptive. The meaning of 'relevant' here is not the same as in 'color is relevant to franchise'. The former simply means that intelligence is a function of race, an assertion that can be empirically tested—and refuted. But the racist argues not only that color is relevant to intelligence, but also that intelligence is relevant to franchise. The latter statement is normative; it could mean that the franchise should be denied to persons with an IQ of less than x (and blacks are claimed to be among them). If the racist adopts the definition now under consideration, he will also have to conclude that a policy of racial discrimination is egalitarian. On the basis of my proposed definition, if 20 percent of all citizens of voting age (the reference group) are disenfranchised, the voting law is to that extent inegalitarian, whether the excluded 20 percent are black or illiterate or have a name starting with 'M'.

Robert L. Simon has provided a seemingly convincing argument for the thesis that whether a given rule of redistribution is egalitarian cannot be ascertained "independently of value judgments about the economic *importance* of the changes involved for the lives of those affected" (1974, p. 344), and has criticized the proposed, purely descriptive definition for failing to take this factor into account. He illustrates his point by taking up the question whether the distribution of income between blacks and whites in the United States has become more, or less, egalitarian. He points out that, if my criterion were adopted, we would have to conclude "that inequality of income between blacks and whites was decreasing if the percentage difference between incomes was declining. This might be misleading, however, if such a decrease were accompanied by an increase in the difference between the total holdings of each group" (p. 342). If, as a result, blacks remain on the average below the poverty line and whites can buy color television sets, the rule of redistribution involved should be considered inegalitarian, as it turns out to be if we adopt the criterion I reject and Simon recommends, namely, the absolute rather than the percentage difference between holdings.[8] Simon's approach does take into consideration the economic effects of the redistribution on the groups involved. Nevertheless, it seems to me that the criterion of percentage differences is applicable also in this case and that to apply it has the advantage that Simon's moral concern can be expressed more clearly in normative language. Yes, the redistribution is egalitarian—to a degree. If our goal is to reduce the injustices of extreme differences in wealth and poverty, we ought to reduce the percentage differences much more drastically, i.e., effectuate a redistribution of income that would be egalitarian to a much higher degree.

As a last example of a definition by a term of appraisal, I shall cite Benn's characterization of self-interest, a concept that must "be understood normatively" (see 8.1):

> [A] group may be wrong about its interests. . . . For the group is pursuing its interests correctly (i.e., it is not mistaking them) only if it puts *"more important"* ahead of "less important" ones; and what is more important involves questions of standards, and need not be what the group itself *thinks* important. (1960, p. 129)

I quite agree that an interest can be said to be more important than another only relative to a given standard; but here again, the criteria of importance are left open. My proposed definition relates a group's interest to its own ultimate egoistic welfare goals. *In this sense,* the standard *is* "what the group itself thinks important." The group is "wrong about its interests" if it fails to act rationally relative to *this* standard. However, Benn implicitly invites his readers to adopt not only his definition of 'interest', but also his moral point of view, so that an utterance like 'x corresponds to A's more important (hence, real) interest' is another way of proclaiming that it is rational for A to do x in view of a goal that is "correct" by *this* moral standard.

I conclude that, if a writer interprets a political concept as a "moral notion," his definition always turns out to be not a definition at all, but an expression of his commitment to a specific (if often not explicitly stated) moral norm. This is the case whether the alleged definition is stated in descriptive or normative terms or in terms of appraisal.

But did not I myself use at least one appraisal term, namely, 'rationality', to define several of the concepts I claimed to be descriptive? Both self-interest and public interest were defined in terms of policies it is *rational* to pursue, and coercive threats as those with which it is *rational* to comply. Whether a choice is rational is, indeed, a matter of appraisal, but of appraisal in terms of a specific standard. The rationality of the actor's predictions (of alternative outcomes) is to be assessed by the standards of inductive and deductive logic, and the rationality of his preference by their compatibility with his own ultimate goals. Furthermore, the standard is not a moral one, since, theoretically, a choice can be rational or not wrt any ultimate goal the actor may have adopted. As we saw, my qualifying an actor's decision or action or policy as rational does not imply that I approve morally of what he is doing.

There is the further possible objection that I have been using the language of appraisal when speaking *about* the definitions I have been defending or criticizing. For instance, I have been claiming that the distinction between influence and coercion is more *significant* than the difference between rational persuasion and other forms of influence, and I have been arguing against those who find the latter distinction more *important*. I have been claiming that the proposed definitions are *better* or more *fruitful* than others, and that it is more *practical* to dispense with certain concepts (e.g., with the concept of freedom of action). Here again, there is a clearly implied standard of evaluation; and the criterion is again not one of normative ethics, but in this case one of effective scientific communication. Like every standard, this one cannot simply be applied mechanically. Hence, to contend that a proposed definition is to be preferred by that standard is often a matter of controversy (like appraising a particular wine or manuscript); otherwise, a study like this one would be unnecessary. Also, the standard itself is not acceptable to all; it will be rejected by those who adopt the standard of ordinary language philosophy. This controversy will be taken up in the last chapter.

NINE
Reconstructionism Defended

The argument all bare is of more worth
Than when it hath my added praise besides.

Shakespeare, Sonnet 103

I HAVE POSTPONED the justification of the general method I have adopted until the last chapter. Having, so to speak, delivered the goods, I am able to refute counterattacks by pointing to results.

The method I have applied is based on the conviction that ordinary language is in general too blunt a tool to be of use for scientific investigation and that the language used in political life (and in most political writings) is especially ill suited for the purposes of political inquiry. It is therefore necessary to construct a language as free as possible of the imperfections of ordinary usage, or rather to *re*construct its basic concepts (and I shall explain why this latter term characterizes more accurately what I have been doing). Admittedly, this is only a preliminary task. "But recently there has been a growing conviction that although armchair reflection does not provide a sufficient basis for substantive conclusions about what is or ought to be, it *is* fitted to bring about greater clarity and explicitness concerning the basic concepts we employ in thinking about the world and human life" (Alston 1967a, p. 388; italics in original). Accordingly, it has been the aim of this study to contribute, however indirectly, to knowledge about what is and what ought to be in the area of politics.

One of the principal sources of the reconstructionist approach is Ludwig Wittgenstein's *Tractatus Logico-Philosophicus* (1961, written in 1922), which Wittgenstein himself rejected in his later writings; these later writings became one of the most important sources of what has been lately perhaps the most influential view, especially among social and political philosophers. This "ordinary language philosophy" maintains that everyday discourse is often adequate even for scientific purposes and that deviating from it often does more harm than good. To quote Wittgenstein himself:

> On the one hand, it is clear that every sentence in our language is "in order as it is." That is to say, we are not *striving after* an ideal, as if our ordinary vague sentences had not yet got a quite unexceptional sense, and a perfect language awaited construction by us. —On the other hand, it seems clear that where there is sense there must be perfect order. —So there must be perfect order even in the vaguest sentence. (1968, p. 45; italics in original)

Given the predominance of ordinary language philosophy, I have admittedly been trying to swim against the stream or—what is even more ambitious—to reverse its current, which, I am convinced, is flowing in the wrong direction. Referring to the explications I have proposed should enable me to refute the arguments of the ordinary language proponents that reconstructionists try to impose an arbitrary language, that their approach is "positivistic," and that the implied thesis of the separability of "facts" and "values" is mistaken.

9.1 RECONSTRUCTIONISM AND ARBITRARINESS

Ordinary language philosophers accuse reconstructionists of engaging so to speak, in arbitrary acts of legislation: brushing aside well-established usages, replacing them with artificial constructions, and wanting to thrust them on others.

9.1.1 The Explicative Nature
of Reconstructed Definitions

Ordinary language philosophy admits of two kinds of definitions, reportative and stipulative. The former are not, strictly speaking, definitions at all, but reports about the way certain groups of individuals use certain expressions. Reports of linguistic behavior are empirically verifiable. E.g., 'democracy' as used in the United States refers above all to a competitive party system; 'freedom' as it is used in Rousseau means obedience to the general will. Since scientists, or at least social scientists, should use language reflecting common usage as faithfully as possible, their definitions should be of a reportative kind.

Definitions that are not reportative, and that means all genuine definitions, are considered stipulative. They stipulate that an expression to be defined (the *definiendum*) shall be synonymous with another expression (the *definiens*) whose meaning is already clear. Stipulative definitions have their place in the social sciences when new technical terms are introduced, as when Dahl decides to use the term 'polyarchy' "to refer to political systems with widespread suffrage and relatively effective protection of [certain] freedoms and opportunities" (1976, p. 81) and assumes that the words occurring in the *definiens* are already understood. Stipulative definitions do not increase our store of knowledge. Ordinary language philosophers would consider the definitions I have been formulating to be stipulative. But then, is it not all simply a matter of terminology? What right do I have to impose my own "vocabulary of politics" on others and to criticize *them* for not using political terms the same way I do? The only alternative view would be that of essentialism, which considers definitions a mode of cognition of the "true" meaning of what a term stands for, as when Socrates in Plato's *Republic* claims to discover the essential nature of justice by means of defining the concept.

Reconstructionists agree that definitions do not add to our knowledge of "reality," but merely stipulate linguistic equivalences. But they hold that there is a third type of definition; this type is neither wholly reportative nor merely stipulative, but *explicative*. Like stipulative definitions, explications are not verifiable as either true or false; but unlike the former, they can be appraised as good or bad in terms of their suitability for scientific communication.

One of the criteria I have used for guidance is to remain as close to ordinary language as possible, deviating from common usage only when necessary for the sake of clarity. "To handle [conceptual questions] adequately we must reflect on what we normally mean when we employ certain words, and what we had better mean if we are to communicate effectively, avoid paradox, and achieve general coherence" (Feinberg 1973, p. 2). Ordinary language thus remains the starting point. Indeed, both the expressions to be defined and their defining expressions have been couched in the vocabulary of ordinary language. Political thought and action have been, by a long tradition, tied to such nontechnical terms as 'freedom' or 'equality', and political science does not have at its disposal an entirely technical vocabulary. as does physics or even economics. That is why I consider what I have been doing not a construction, but a *re*construction or *re*interpretation of political concepts, and the language I have been elaborating not an artificial or ideal, but a reconstructed or reformed language whose function is "clarification, rather than replacement" (Rorty 1967, p. 16). I have criticized a number of definitions for having implications in conflict with commonly accepted usage. E.g., if 'coercion' were taken as including 'deterrence', it would follow that a legal speed limit coerces motorists to slow down.

On the other hand, explicative definitions are not the same as reportative ones. "Conceptual analysis aims at clarification and systematization of concepts and is not bound to reflect usage where that usage is confused and liable to mislead" (Raz 1970, pp. 303–4). For the purpose of clarification, some of the proposed explications had to diverge from common usage. E.g., I concluded that it makes for greater clarity to define the concept of social power as including rational persuasion and as excluding, e.g., P's beating R "for no reason"; to say that assigning positions by lot is more egalitarian than by ability; or to deny that "freedom from want" refers to social freedom.

Another of my guidelines has been to avoid definitions that would be so broad as to make the *definiendum* synonymous with another well-established locution and thereby to render the former expendable. E.g., equating (by definition) exercising power over someone's action with causing him to act that way; or social freedom with ability; or self-interest with wants or with need fulfillment. I also criticized this last definition for violating yet another standard of adequacy: to avoid making true by definition what had better be left open to empirical investigation.

We have here a similarity between constructing good explicative definitions and good scientific theories. The adequacy of an empirical theory, too, must be judged by "standard criteria," e.g., "accuracy, consistency, scope, simplicity, and fruitfulness" (Kuhn 1977, p. 322). But evaluations are open to challenge, even when there are well-defined criteria. "When scientists must choose between competing theories, two men fully committed to the same list of criteria for choice may nevertheless reach different conclusions" (p. 324). The same is true of political scientists confronted with the choice of alternative definitions. Each may have its drawbacks, and we must decide which seems to us the lesser evil, e.g., defining the exercise of power as covering only intended or also unintentional actions of influence or coercion. This does not mean, however, that the choice between competing theories or explications is "subjective." "[S]cientists may always be asked to explain their choices, to exhibit the bases for their judgments. Such judgments are eminently discussable, and the man who refuses to discuss his own cannot expect to be taken seriously" (p. 337). Similarly, if I propose some explicative definition, I have the burden not of proving that it is true, but of justifying it in terms of standards that themselves are not under discussion. This is what I have been trying to do.

Even so, these definitions are mere proposals, and I have made it a point always to characterize them as such and to qualify statements I have been deriving from them as true only in the limited sense that they are valid, given the proposed definitions. E.g., given my definition of the concept of power, it follows that rational persuasion is a form of power. Inabilities not caused by another actor do not constitute limitations of freedom if the latter concept is taken in the sense of the proposed definition. I have compared the implications of the proposed conceptual scheme with those of other definitions, and weighed their respective advantages and shortcomings. I agree with Brian Barry: "I do not think that there is anything much to be gained from simply picking a definition and saying 'That's the one everybody ought to use'. But I do think that it is useful to see the implications of alternative definitions and to notice the way in which the choice of a definition is affected by what it is that we want to explain" (1976, p. 94).

9.1.2 The "Essential Contestability" of Political Concepts

It is often held that it is impossible to construct explicative definitions of *political* concepts because they belong to the class of those which are "essentially contestable." This means that speakers and writers committed to different political outlooks are bound to use them in different senses, and that there is no justification for singling out one or the other and no possibility of overbridging such ideological gaps. "Recognition of a given concept as essentially contested implies recognition of rival uses of it (such as oneself repudiates) as not only logically possible and humanly 'likely', but as of permanent potential critical value to one's own use or interpretation of the concept in question" (Gallie 1964, p. 188).

Political concepts are held to be contestable because they reflect rival value commitments and because they are inherently vague, open-ended, and ambiguous. For the moment, I shall deal with these latter alleged characteristics.

Many words of ordinary usage—e.g., 'middle-aged'—are vague in the sense that "on either side of the area of clear application there are indefinitely bounded areas of uncertainty" (Alston 1967*b*, p. 218). Words referring to political matters are often vague. E.g., there are clear instances of deterrence and of coercion; but how "severe" must a threat be to the "average man" before it ceases to be deterrence and becomes coercion? On the other hand, how prevalent must the actor's own motivation be for his compliance to be considered autonomous and no longer under someone else's control? Or how steep must a graduated income tax be to become egalitarian? Now, it seems to me that it is precisely reconstructionism that points the way from vagueness to precision, and hence away from this kind of contestability. It does so not with the help of rigid and arbitrary dichotomies, but by replacing the categorical notions of ordinary discourse by comparative concepts. Then we are able to say, e.g., that a certain rule is more egalitarian than another, or that R is, wrt P, the more unfree to do x, the heavier the penalty (all other dimensions of unfreedom remaining constant). We have seen that in certain cases these comparative concepts become quantifiable, enabling us to say, e.g., that a given rule of redistribution is egalitarian to such and such a degree. Overcoming vagueness is one of the justifications of reconstructing political concepts.

Vagueness must be distinguished from open-endedness, i.e., the impossibility of defining a concept by a set of necessary and sufficient conditions of their application (see Waismann 1968). Many political concepts are open-textured in this sense. One may define 'democracy' by a combination of criteria such as periodic elections, competitive parties, representation, freedom of expression, diffusion of political power, implementation of collective preferences; but the presence of all these traits is neither necessary nor sufficient to characterize a given political system as democratic. Is Turkey a democracy? Was France under de Gaulle? Also, "we can never exclude altogether the possibility of some unforeseen situation arising in which we shall have to modify our definition" (Waismann 1968, p. 39). Suppose formal elections should be replaced by a perfected system of electronic expression of preference on concrete issues. Would such a "direct" democracy still be a democracy as defined? Nevertheless, even an opponent of reconstructionism like MacIntyre holds "that in normal circumstances and in standard conditions we can behave *as if* there were such a finite and determinate set [of defining conditions] and we do indeed so behave. Otherwise every question of fact would be indefinitely debatable" (MacIntyre 1973, p. 2)—debatable because of the open-endedness of the terms involved.

Furthermore, open texture is a characteristic of some, but by no means all, empirical concepts. None of the basic political concepts I have been explicating are open-ended. Conceivably, new methods of brainwashing or telepathy might be invented; but I have no doubt that these could be subsumed under either influencing or coercing, the two alternative defining characteristics of exercising control, and hence of power. Nor can I conceive of any "unforeseen situation" that would constitute a reason to alter the proposed conceptual scheme according to which, if R is, wrt P, neither unfree to do x nor unfree not to do x, he is free in this respect.

Ambiguity is another characteristic of many words in ordinary language, including political words. We have seen that 'power' can be understood in at least two ways, and 'freedom' in many more. Ambiguity enables poets to "play on words"; in scientific discourse using ambiguous words easily leads to using them in different senses in the course of the same argument without being aware of the shift of meaning. Ambiguities thus lead to inconsistencies; but these are sometimes viewed as an asset. "If language is seen as human activity rather than as a collection of labels for categories or phenomena, then we will no longer be surprised to find systematic inconsistencies in it—not as a fault or liability, but as essential to its functions" (Pitkin 1972, p. 4). Inconsistencies—i.e., statements that contradict one another—can of course be expressed in any language, even the most artificial one, and their joint assertion is the fault not of the language, but of its user. But can there be any doubt that it is a fault? Is not the first requirement of a conceptual scheme to exclude the possibility of deducing statements from its definitions that are logically contradictory? Here the reconstructionist remedy is to distinguish between different concepts when they are expressed by the same word. Someone may ask: why do you use the expression 'social freedom' in so restrictive a sense? Why not apply it also to what you have been calling 'freedom of action', 'free actions', 'feeling free', and 'being a free person'? My answer is: because using one term to refer to these various situations leads to confusing them with one another, and hence to ambiguities that in turn promote inconsistencies. To keep the distinctions between these various relations and properties clear, it is practical to call them by different names. Which label one attaches to which concept is of little importance. It is merely for reasons of convenience that I have proposed to reserve the expression 'social freedom' for what we have most often in mind when we speak of freedom in a political context. That certain expressions in ordinary usage are vague or open-ended or ambiguous may indicate that such concepts are in fact contested, but not that they are *essentially* contest*able*. "[I]f power is held [e.g., by Lukes] to be essentially contestable, no one view of power can be said to be theoretically superior to any other. The claim that a concept is 'essentially contestable' commits the claimant to a radical relativism about essentially contested concepts in general" (Clarke 1979, p. 125).

9.1.3 Political Concepts and "Self-Understanding"

Writers like Peter Winch, Charles Taylor, A. R. Louch, and A. MacIntyre are opposed to reconstructionism for a reason closely related to the thesis of essential contestability, namely, that political concepts must be interpreted in terms of the actors' own perceptions of political phenomena (for references, see Pitkin 1972, p. 241, and Connolly 1974, p. 44). Their views may be summarized as follows: Politics consists of human actions; actions are intentional; intentions are based on the actor's beliefs and preferences. Furthermore, political actions are in general "rule governed"; activities like commanding, obeying, voting, representation, and taxation involve the actor's awareness of the practices, rules, and institutions involved. Hence, political actions and their outcomes "must be understood in terms of the intentions of the actors and in terms of the conventions of his society, which specify the meaning or significance of particular acts" (Moon 1975, p. 155). Beliefs are "constitutive" of political actions and institutions, and political scientists cannot identify them except in terms of the "self-understanding" of the participants. It is therefore illegitimate to introduce concepts that are not part of the conceptual framework of the actors themselves, and impossible to construct a conceptual system capable of overbridging the differences of "world views" prevalent in various societies and often among various groups within the same political culture. Thus, MacIntyre answers the title question of his article, "Is a Science of Comparative Politics Possible?" in the negative, because the meaning of a concept like political party differs radically in the minds of the participants in different political societies and because it is doubtful whether one can identify "institutions in different cultures as 'the same'" (1972, p. 18). Reconstructionism makes for a static view of politics, incapable of capturing the changing historical and ideological aspects of the political process. "[It does] not encourage, to say the least, exploration of the links between political concepts on the one hand and the changing structure of society on the other" (Siedentop 1977, p. 588).

I do not deny that political concepts refer to factual beliefs and valuational feelings of the actors involved, and often also to the rules in which the actors participate. This is the way I myself have explicated the political concepts I have selected. But I have defined them in terms of the perceptions not of particular actors, but of *any* actor, and this makes them applicable to *any* situation. For example, the concept of self-interest has been defined by reference to *whatever* is conducive to any given actor's own real welfare goal. The proposed definition of public interest is similarly applicable to welfare preferences any given group might adopt. To be influenced is to be made to *choose* to do x, and the variable 'x' ranges over *any* action. Punishment involves P's *belief* that R committed offense x, and also P's action y that R *feels* as a deprivation. The concept of offense in turn refers to some system of legal or customary *rules*. Egalitarianism can be predicated of *rules* of distribution—of *any* such rule. The proposed language makes it possible to *compare* various rules of distribution in different societies (from primitive to post-industrial) as to the degree to which they are egalitarian or inegalitarian.

Granted that there are cases in which it is not feasible to construct such overarching concepts. Possibly there is no single feature that "parties" in the Soviet Union, the United States, and even France have in common. But this seems to me no reason for tying social scientists to the linguistic habits of the actors they study and for requiring that definitions be acceptable to the latter as well as the former. The anthropologist who describes as a "rain dance" certain bodily movements of a tribe cannot be faulted for using a term which may be meaningless to the dancers. Conceptual relativism is an obstacle to scientific explanation.[1] A scientific study of political actions, thoughts, and institutions in their variations in time and space requires the construction of a solid and general conceptual scheme by which to express such comparisons. Provided this precondition is fulfilled, a science of comparative politics *is* possible, and so is a scientific study of politics in general.

But such a rarefied and antiseptic language—it has been argued—while possibly suitable for communication among political scientists, does not capture the subtle shadings of political life and does not reach its protagonists, the actors involved.

> [I]n the attempt to carry out such a project [of "pure description"] systematically, we would find ourselves with an artificial and emasculated vocabulary bearing little or no relation to the ways in which we—and social scientists—speak about human action. (Bernstein 1978, p. 78)

My reply is: we need a language in which social scientists *had better* speak—social scientists yes, but not "we" as political actors. Reconstructed or "ideal languages have only rarely been intended to be a medium of actual communication...; rather, the contention has been that what an ideal language is, would be, can be, or must be like is philosophically revealing" (Caton 1967, p. 169). A reconstructed language of political inquiry is not meant to take the place of the language of political rhetoric, but to reveal the structure of political concepts and to facilitate the formulation of generalizations about political matters, on the normative as well as the empirical level. After all, nobody reproaches atomic physicists or microbiologists for writing and speaking in a language understandable only to fellow scientists. Since a reconstructed language of political inquiry remains relatively close to ordinary discourse, the gap between the language of political science and political action is relatively small.

9.1.4 Political Concepts and Political Theories

The objection I consider the most serious against reconstructionist endeavors such as mine can be found in statements like the following: "[C]oncept formation and theory formation in science go hand in hand" (Kaplan 1964, p. 52). "[T]he meaning of every term we use depends on the theoretical context in which it occurs" (Feyerabend 1968, p. 33). Yet—so the objection would go—I have constructed explicative definitions without relating them to any theories; I have not even been concerned with empirical generalizations about politics. More specifically, I have taken scientific fruitfulness as the standard by which to appraise explicative definitions; but the fruitfulness of an explication can be judged only in the context of particular scientific theories. Benn has made the point forcefully: "I doubt whether one can usefully manufacture concepts for theories not yet constructed, to solve problems not yet posed. . . . It is as if some seventeenth-century philosopher, without glimpsing the theory of gravitation . . . had set out to produce a serviceable definition of 'mass' for any future Newton who happened to have a use for it" (1964, p. 238). In these passages, the term 'theory' is used in the specific sense of a systematically related set of empirical laws. Just as given occurrences are explained by reference to general laws, general laws are in turn explained by subsuming them under more inclusive theoretical principles. For example, Newton's theory of gravitation explains both Galileo's law of falling bodies and Kepler's laws of planetary motion (see Hempel 1965, p. 343). The theory of evolution and of relativity are theories in this sense.

Are there such theories in political science? There are isolated laws or, better, lawlike generalizations about political behavior, processes, and institutions, and about their relations to economic or social or cultural factors. But neither Aristotle nor even Marx has drawn his separate hypotheses together into a full-fledged theoretical system; and it is doubtful whether a Newton of political science will come along in the future, and for no other reason than the nature of the subject matter. (Later I shall deal with the objection that a deductive-nomological political science is not even desirable as an ideal to be approximated.) In the absence of political theories in the strict sense, we are left with the choice of either leaving our basic political concepts unexplicated at the price of remaining entangled in the web of ordinary language, or explicating them independently of any theories with the purpose of clarifying whatever isolated generalizations have been made or may be asserted.

There is a further argument. The term 'theory' is also used more broadly to apply to "a fundamental conceptualization of a field" (Moon 1975, p. 141). In words of Anatol Rapoport:

> In the stronger sense, a theory must contain logically deduced propositions, which, if referring to portions of the real world, must be in principle verifiable. In its weaker sense, a theory can be simply a preparation of a conceptual scheme in which a theory in the stronger sense will one day be developed. In this sense, a theory is concerned with the singling out of presumably important concepts. (1966, p. 132)

This task seems to me worthwhile, even when a theory in the stronger sense is not likely to be developed in the future. Again, I have no better justification than to point to the results of this study. It seems to me of interest for any kind of political inquiry to clarify the various dimensions in terms of which the varying degrees of power or freedom or egalitarianism can be compared; to illuminate the connections between power, freedom, and ability; to distinguish between self-interest, public interest, and other political goals. Such insights seem to me to be of significance, even though they are valid only within a proposed conceptual framework.

9.2 RECONSTRUCTIONISM AND "POSITIVISM"

The reconstructionist method I have been advocating and applying has been criticized not only for leading to arbitrary definitions, but also for being an outgrowth of "positivism," a philosophy once fashionable and even salutary in its day, but now thoroughly antiquated and discredited. Placing "positivism" in quotation marks indicates how I intend to answer this objection. This philosophy has been criticized most effectively by those who continue to be labeled "positivists." "Positivism" continues to live on only in the imagination of certain political scientists who seem to enjoy the easy task of knocking down the straw man this philosophy has become (e.g., Miller 1972). I know of no contemporary philosopher of science who subscribes to the kind of operationalism, behaviorism, and causalism these critics impute to "positivists," and none of these views is taken or implied in the present study.

9.2.1 Operationalism and Behaviorism

In its original form, operationalism required that every expression in a language of empirical science be defined by reference to definite testing operations. These must be stated in "observation terms" designating characteristics that are directly and intersubjectively observable. E.g., defining 'x is harder than y' by the scratch test satisfied the operational requirement (see 4.3). Classical behaviorism is an application of strict operationalism to human behavior, to be defined in terms of observable bodily responses to external stimuli.

None of our basic political concepts has been defined operationally or behavioristically in this sense. For example, 'exercising power' was defined by 'influencing', 'restraining', and 'punishing', and these were in turn defined by 'doing', 'choosing', 'attempting', 'depriving'—the elementary building blocks of the proposed conceptual scheme. I made it clear at the start (see 1.2.3) that even the relatively most concrete of these terms, 'doing x', refers not to bodily behavior, but to actions, and that actions pertain to beliefs, preferences, and rules. Nothing of what I said would imply that, e.g., 'voting' could be defined by 'a hand opening and a paper falling into a box' (assuming that these are observational and behavioral terms). I also indicated that actors are often characterized by their offices or roles.

I did not try to explicate these action concepts in turn, but considered them as given. This is perfectly in line with modern empiricism, which takes as the basis of the conceptual scheme of a given field not observation terms, but an *"antecedently available vocabulary,"* i.e., terms "which have a well-established use in science and are employed by investigators in the field with high intersubjective agreement" (Hempel 1973, p. 372; italics in original).[2] Accordingly, political scientists may take the meaning of action concepts for granted and leave it to psychology and philosophy to probe deeper into them. There are other, far from "observational" concepts I have considered as given—e.g., those of rationality and welfare, which I have used to define the notions of self-interest and public interest. And the very abstract notion of causation figures in the defining expressions of all power concepts. Furthermore, I have interpreted having power as well as social unfreedom and freedom in a dispositional sense. Such explications would have been ruled out by strict operationalism, since they refer not to actual occurrences (let alone to observational or behavioral ones), but to hypothetical and contrary-to-fact conditions. I have not dealt with many concepts referring to political collectivities such as parties or legislatures or states; but I did have occasion to criticize the reductionist view that group concepts are definable in terms of the behavior of their individual members when I pointed out that the public interest cannot be equated with the aggregate of individual interests (which, in turn, do not refer to overt behavior but to—often unexpressed—welfare preferences).

Among political scientists, both operationalism and behaviorism have long been abandoned. "As far as I know, there is probably no one in political science who would consider himself a behaviorist, . . . I know of no one associated with political research who has advocated a position that even begins to approximate so rigid an exclusion of subjective data. Ideas, motives, feelings, attitudes, all appear as important variables" (Easton 1967, p. 12)—but not just as "intervening variables" between stimuli and responses. This behavior*alist* view is concerned not with political behavior, but with political action and interaction. Our approach has been behavioralistic, not behavioristic, and hence not "positivistic."[3]

No further argument seems to me to be required to show that the proposed analysis, rather than being a "fact-minded, anti-conceptual view" (Wolin 1968, p. 329), constitutes an implicit denial of the thesis that "facts" do "exist" independently of theories (in a broader sense) and that there is a natural demarcation line between observational and theoretical terms. On the contrary, everything in this study is compatible with the view that "[t]here is more to seeing than meets the eyeball" (Hanson 1967, p. 91; similarly Popper 1972, p. 71). I therefore disagree that "[t]he assumption that there can be some kind of purely empirical theory [of politics] derives from the naive positivist assumption that facts can be known accurately if only we could lay aside our prejudices and biases" (Wolin 1968, p. 328). It is quite true that "observations themselves represent theory-laden facts" (ibid., p. 329); but this is no obstacle in the way of an empirical science of politics. Otherwise, there would be no science of any kind, since none is based on the "positivist" assumption that facts are known independently of theory.

9.2.2 Causation

Causation is another of the concepts I have taken as given. I have analyzed it only as far as required to indicate that it should be taken in the sense of a probabilistically sufficient condition in the defining expressions of the various power concepts. I need therefore not take sides in the debate between "causalists," who consider the actor's reasons and motives as causal determinants of his actions (e.g., that my intention to vote is a cause of my voting), and "intentionalists," who hold that intentions merely redescribe actions and are therefore conceptually a part of their meaning (e.g., that 'voting' refers to both my intention to vote and to the physical action involved) (cf. von Wright 1971, p. 95).[4]

However, a power concept like exercising influence refers to R's intention or choice not only in relation to his *own* subsequent behavior (and this relation may or may not be causal), but also in relation to some *other*, antecedent action y of P. There can be no doubt that such relationships of *interaction* are causal. "We most naturally speak of causes where some agent does something which results in an interference with the natural operations or conditions of some *other* agent or substance" (Alston 1967a, p. 408; italics added). Even intentionalists must interpret P's influence action y as causing R to choose to do x, even if they deny that R's choice in turn causes him to do so. As pointed out (3.2.2), my affirmation that P influenced R to do x provides a (partial) causal explanation of why R did x. Causality is not a "positivistic" concept, but an indispensable building block of a conceptual scheme of political inquiry—whatever one's philosophy of action.

Even so, it has been objected that the idea of causation is tied to the "covering model of causal explanation." According to this view, to say that C causes E is to refer, at least implicitly, to some general causal law, at least of a probabilistic kind, to the effect that, if some event of kind C occurs, an event with characteristic E will happen—always or probably. Yet, so the argument goes, there are not only no theories, but not even laws of human interaction; hence, the concept of causality can have no place in the field of social and political inquiry.

Here the counterargument is that causal language is appropriate even in the absence of causal laws (assuming, for the sake of argument, that there are none in this field). "The statement that one person did something because, for example, another threatened him, carries no implication or covert assertion that if the circumstances were repeated the same action would follow" (Hart and Honoré 1959, p. 52).[5] Or, to take a previous example, we do say, quite correctly, that the dropping of the atomic bomb on Hiroshima was a cause (perhaps the principal cause) of Japan's decision to capitulate, even though we can hardly refer to any generalization from which this particular statement could be derived. Given this causal relation and given the definition of influencing in terms of causing others to choose to act in certain ways, it follows that the United States exercised influence and hence had power over Japan in this respect. Thus, I agree that "we may have good reasons for believing that two events are causally related even though we cannot provide the appropriate covering law" (Fay and Moon 1977, p. 217). The use of 'causing' in the defining expressions of power concepts does not commit us to the covering law model of explanation in political science.

The question whether there are causal laws of political behavior lies outside the purview of this study. Let me just point out that political scientists want to account not only for political actions and interactions, but also for their unintended consequences. Such explanations do of course involve causal generalizations, as do explanations of political phenomena by reference to geographic, demographic, economic, and other nonpolitical factors. But lawlike generalizations are also often invoked to explain one actor's political behavior as a response to *actions* of others. E.g., that drivers tend to stop at traffic lights is to be explained not by the normative rules of traffic, but by the descriptive law of human behavior that such regulations are in general obeyed (and that propensity can in turn be causally explained). How do we explain that congressmen tend to vote as their constituents want them to (disregarding the influence of pressure groups, etc.)? We explain this tendency not teleologically, but causally; not by pointing out that congressmen do so *in order to* be reelected, but by pointing to the empirical law that people, or at least politicians, tend to act in ways that maximize their chances of attaining their goals.[6]

Political theorists are sometimes so eager to steer clear of the Scylla of old-fashioned positivism that they come close to being shipwrecked by the Charybdis of skepticism and irrationalism. Our reconstructionist approach has avoided the latter danger no less than the former. That political concepts are often contested in political life is no reason that they should remain "essentially contestable" in political science. Vagueness, open-endedness, and ambiguity are not assets to be preserved, but obstacles to be overcome. To reject operationalism and behavioralism is not to abandon empiricism in the broad sense. To point out that causation is not tied to explanation by covering law is not to deny that there are empirical laws, or at least lawlike generalizations, in the area of politics.

9.3 RECONSTRUCTIONISM AND THE SEPARATION OF "FACTS" AND "VALUES"

The last objection to be considered is the claim that reconstructionism in political inquiry implies the mistaken view that "facts" and "values" can be separated. Here my reply will be that this separability thesis, unlike positivism, is indeed linked to our reconstructionist approach, but that it is correct and its denial, the inseparability thesis, mistaken. However, critics attribute certain views to the "separatists" that the latter do not hold and I myself do not share.

First, a word of terminological clarification. To speak of "facts" and "values" in a literal way would be to commit the fallacy of reification (hence the quotation marks)—as if facts and values were things to be "allocated" like pieces of pies. The affirmation and the denial of the separability of facts and values are opposing theories about the meaning of concepts and the verifiability of statements; as such they belong to the philosophy of language.

9.3.1 The Inseparability Thesis

I have dealt implicitly (in chapter 8) with the inseparability thesis as far as it pertains to political concepts, the view that most, if not all, of them are "moral notions" and as such inextricably both descriptive and normative. Here I need only to add that this thesis has the support of ordinary language philosophy: political concepts are contestable not only because they are vague, open-ended, and ambiguous, but also—and perhaps principally—because of their valuational dimension. "[T]he major part of what makes a concept essentially contestable is that criteria for its correct application embody normative standards, and that disputes about the propriety of these standards cannot be settled by rational argument alone" (Gray 1977, p. 339). Since different actors, and different investigators as well, are committed to different moralities and ideologies, it is not possible to come up with definitions embracing such irreconcilable "world views." The related theory that political concepts must be interpreted in terms of the actors' "self-understanding" leads to the same conclusion, since these must differ among actors with different outlooks.

If the descriptive and the valuational ingredients of political concepts cannot be separated, then statements in which such concepts figure cannot be qualified as either factual or evaluative. If so, the distinction between 'is' and 'ought' breaks down. "Psychology and social science are moral sciences; ethics and the study of human action are one" (Louch 1966, p. 235).[7] And so the inseparability thesis "puts an end to any aspiration to a value-free or 'ideology-free' science of man" (Charles Taylor 1971, p. 48). It leads not only to conceptual relativism, but also to cognitive relativism—the view that truth is relative to anyone's value system or "paradigm."[8] This is a denial of the possibility of a "value-free science of man" as well as of an empirical science of society and politics generally. Knowledge of political phenomena is to be gained not by the "scientific method," but through the intuitive method of interpretation or hermeneutics, which "cannot but rely on insight" (Charles Taylor 1971, p. 46).

I have tried to refute the inseparability thesis as it applies to the meaning of political concepts, and I have also argued against the related theories of their essential contestability and subjectivity. Without denying that the same speech act in daily (and political) life sometimes (but by no means always) functions both in a descriptive and an evaluative way, these two dimensions can and must be separated when we redefine political concepts for the purpose of political inquiry. One additional argument fits in at this point. That actions must be charactized by reference to the actor's purposes and preferences is no obstacle, since assertions about an actor's valuations (e.g., about his welfare preferences in connection with his self-interest) are descriptive, not evaluative. Again, the most effective way to refute the inseparability thesis is not to argue in a general way that it is possible to explicate political concepts in a descriptive way, but actually to carry out such a program successfully, as I hope to have done.

If political concepts can be redefined descriptively, then statements in which they appear are descriptive; the phenomena they describe can in principle be explained causally (whether or not by reference to causal laws); and an empirical science of politics *is* possible; and it is possible to distinguish between descriptive and normative statements about politics. To do so, we cannot, of course, go by their grammatical appearance in ordinary language. "If the distinction between 'descriptive' and 'prescriptive' is taken to describe features of discourse that can be detected, as it were, by immediate introspection, it is radically misleading" (Frankel 1976, p. 19). Statements, as we find them, must of course be interpreted within their context (but not in the

196

sense of the proponents of the interpretive method) and "translated" into the constructed language. "All men are created equal," if taken literally, i.e., as a factual assertion, would be either meaningless (men are "equal" with respect to what characteristic?) or false (men differ with respect to practically every characteristic). Obviously, the framers of the Declaration of Independence used the indicative form as a rhetorical device to proclaim that all men have the same natural rights, and this apparently descriptive statement in turn implies that all men *ought* to be given the same corresponding legal rights by their respective governments.[9] We have seen that when political thinkers define concepts such as freedom or egalitarianism in normative terms (and sometimes descriptively), we must reinterpret such "persuasive definitions" as expressing normative principles. In our reconstructed language, words such as 'ought' or 'good' or 'desirable' are to be used only to express the *advocacy* of some policy or goal; the advocated course of action or state of affairs to be realized is to be characterized exclusively in descriptive terms. The same applies to the explanation of political phenomena. This recommendation has been criticized by MacIntyre:

> [T]o insist that political science be value-free is to insist that we never use in our explanations such clauses as "because it was unjust" or "because it was illegitimate" when we explain the collapse of a policy or a regime. (1972, p. 25)

I do insist on both. 'Just' and 'legitimate' and their contraries are normative terms; at least their normative components clearly predominate over their descriptive elements. They do not so much characterize empirical features of policies or institutions as they express moral convictions of speakers or writers. So the *fact* that a regime has collapsed cannot be explained by the *normative judgment* that it was unjust or illegitimate—according to whose judgment? According to the moral point of view generally adopted in Western democracies? Here we have an explanation, but obviously a mistaken one. Would that it were generally the case that regimes *we* consider unjust will collapse (sooner than "just" ones), and *because* we consider them unjust! However, the view MacIntyre criticizes (and to which I subscribe) does not entail "that justice plays no part and can play no part in political life" (ibid.), but is perfectly compatible with the (true) generalization that justice—in the sense of people's (at least some person's) normative judgments of what policies or rules are just—does play an important part in political life.

9.3.2 What the Separability Thesis Does Not Imply

Reconstructionism and the separability thesis are connected; but neither of them entails any of the following views.

a) That political science is "value-free." There is no denial that the investigator's moral valuations often affect his empirical research. His ethical and ideological commitments tend to influence the choice of his topic, of the hypothesis to be tested, of the data to be selected, of the meaning to be attached to certain concepts (at least to genuinely contestable ones, like 'democracy') and sometimes even to his findings. We have seen that the question whether an actor's inability to satisfy certain needs was caused by some other actor (and hence is an instance of social unfreedom in the proposed sense) tends to be answered differently by political scientists of the Left and Right. Social scientists should be self-conscious of their normative premises, spell them out, and as far as possible not let them influence their empirical findings. Value judgments of a nonmoral kind, too, are involved in the very procedures of science, including political science. "[I]n accepting a hypothesis the scientist must make the decision that the evidence is *sufficiently* strong or that the probability is *sufficiently* high to warrant the acceptance of the hypothesis" (Rudner 1970, p. 541; italics in original). Such decisions are based on intrinsic value judgments, not on appraisals in terms of a given standard, unlike assessments of the fruitfulness of definitions or of the significance of conceptual distinctions (see 8.2.3).[10] That a political scientist's moral point of view and any scientist's nonmoral valuations are bound to be reflected in his work is no argument against the separability thesis and against the possibility of an empirical political science or of any science.

b) That political ethics is "fact-free." There is no denial that factual considerations are relevant to moral judgments (which does not imply that normative principles can be derived from factual statements alone). Here again, we cannot go by grammatical appearance. Just as 'all men are created equal' expresses a normative principle, 'ought' statements often constitute so-called instrumental value judgments, and these are descriptive. Indeed, statements to the effect that something should be done as a means to a given end can be translated without loss of meaning into cause-effect statements, e.g., Machiavelli's advice that "in capturing a state, the conqueror should consider all the injuries he must inflict and inflict all of them at once" (*The Prince*, chapter 8). We have seen that appraisals in terms of a given standard, too, are descriptive. E.g., John Stuart Mill's assertion that policies forbidding marriage among indigents "are not objectionable as violations of liberty" is factual (*On Liberty*, chapter 5)—an appraisal in terms of the moral principle (previously propounded) that society may restrict a person's liberty in order "to prevent harm to others" (chapter 1) (in this case to the offspring), but for no other purpose. The only genuine value judgments are those proclaiming that a certain kind of action is right in itself or that some state of affairs is intrinsically good or desirable or preferable. Political ethics does not merely propound such ultimate normative principles, but also investigates how to go about implementing them. We have seen that the criteria of rational action include both judgments of means to given ends and appraisals, hence considerations of fact. The separability between descriptive and normative statements does not imply that there is a corresponding separability between political science and political ethics. The "policy sciences" belong to both.

c) That value judgments are "meaningless." The separability thesis is most often linked to value-noncognitivism, and this metaethical theory is interpreted as claiming that value judgments are meaningless. Here we have another instance of the attack against an outdated and now imaginary form of positivism. Positivists at one time did hold that statements, to be meaningful, must be either analytic or empirically verifiable and that intrinsic value judgments are neither, and must therefore be devoid of meaning. Value-noncognitivists have long abandoned this position; otherwise, they would also have to consider as meaningless, e.g., stipulative and explicative definitions like the proposed ones, since such statements, too, are neither analytic nor synthetic.[11] According to contemporary value-noncognitivism, intrinsic value judgments have no *cognitive* meaning; i.e., they cannot be said to be either true or false, and for the following reason: concepts such as intrinsically good or right or desirable do not stand for any property of anything, but express the speaker's valuational attitude or commitment. "In using moral language we do not, at least typically, tell someone *that* something is the case; we tell someone to *make* something the case. . . . Fundamental moral claims are not matters of knowledge but expressions of attitude, decisions of principle, or declarations of intention" (Nielsen 1967, p. 129).

The opposite metaethical theory, value-cognitivism, holds that value words stand for objectively ascertainable characteristics—e.g., of actions and outcomes of actions—and that statements of the type 'x is intrinsically desirable' can be shown to be true or false, either empirically (naturalism) or on the basis of moral or religious insight (intuitionism).

The disagreement between the two metaethical views is not about the cognitive status of instrumental value judgments or of appraisals in terms of a given standard or of judgments of the rationality of some course of action relative to some given goal—and that includes all of the policy sciences and, hence, most of political ethics. The only question under dispute is whether *intrinsic* value judgments and moral principles can be demonstrated or verified. In other words, the disagreement between the two metaethical theories arises only when there is an issue that is "'irreducibly' moral, [i.e.,] disagreement on moral matters that is not due to mistaken reasoning, lack of adequate facts, or a failure of imagination in envisaging the consequences of an action but stems from genuine 'difference in values'" (Gettner 1977, p. 163). In politics, such "irreducibly moral" issues are usually of the following type: which of several alternative *total* outcomes (of alternative policies) is intrinsically *more* valuable (or a lesser evil)? This may involve questions such as: how much freedom should be given up for how much "more" national security or equality of welfare? (I am now using these terms quite loosely.) Suppose two persons agree on all the relevant facts (existing and predicted) but evaluate the intrinsic worth of such alternatives differently. Value-cognitivism claims that it is possible to show that one of these alternative states of affairs is objectively more desirable than another. According to value-noncognitivism, there is no objective decision procedure by which to settle such irreducibly normative disagreements.

Stressing the diversity of moral outlooks among persons, groups, and cultures inclines proponents of the inseparability thesis not toward value-noncognitivism, but toward the intuitionist version of value-cognitivism. If there is no distinction between 'is' and 'ought', and if political phenomena can be apprehended through "insight" as claimed by the interpretive method, then this way must lead to knowledge of both political facts and political values. Somewhat paradoxically, the inseparability thesis is conducive to subjectivism and relativism as to the knowability of political facts and to objectivism as to insight into political values—in spite of the alleged inseparability of the two.

Proponents of the separability thesis like myself must disagree with the naturalistic version of value-cognitivism for reasons I have indicated previously. Intrinsic moral principles can be neither deduced from empirical generalizations alone ('ought' cannot be derived from 'is') nor based on descriptive definitions of value terms. Defining, e.g., 'good' by 'conducive to happiness' involves the definist fallacy, just as descriptive concepts are not definable in normative terms (e.g., 'freedom' by 'what we ought to do'). (See 8.2.2.)[12]

Theoretically, there is no incompatibility between the separability thesis and intuitionism, the other form of value-cognitivism. One could hold that "facts" are describable and explainable by the empirical method and "values" discoverable by correct moral insight. Empiricists are not likely to admit such different sources of knowledge in different areas; they tend to adopt the position that intrinsic value judgments are not meaningless, but devoid of cognitive status. I sided with value-noncognitivism in connection with the discussion of the notion of rationality, and I have defended this metaethical position elsewhere (Oppenheim 1976). Empiricism, the separability thesis, and value-noncognitivism are aspects of the same "world view." That descriptive statements and intrinsic normative judgments differ with respect to their logical status and linguistic function is one more reason for drawing clear distinctions between descriptive and valuational concepts.

d) That political science should exclude political ethics. Proponents of the separability thesis are often pictured as holding not only that normative judgments are meaningless, but also—perhaps for that reason—that political science should confine itself to empirical investigation and leave it to philosophy to handle the normative aspects. But to repeat, the thesis of the separability of "facts" and "values" does not imply the separability of political science and political ethics; consequently, such a division of labor is not even possible. Nor does the thesis imply that "values" are somehow less significant than "facts." Throughout this study, I have been guided by the conviction that descriptive and normative aspects of politics are of equal importance, and that the kind of reconstruction I have attempted will be equally useful to both. Meaningful disagreement about the desirable extent of public power relative to individual freedom or of egalitarianism or of policies serving the public interest presupposes agreement on what it is one disagrees about; and that in turn requires an agreed system of descriptive definitions of the concepts involved. Effective reconstruction of basic political concepts is a prerequisite for effective political inquiry in all its aspects.

Notes

1. Hence, it is not an updated version of Weldon's *Vocabulary of Politics* (1953) or even of Lasswell and Kaplan's *Power and Society* (1950).

2. I do not deal with legal or institutional concepts (such as rights, representation, political party, the state) or with terms referring to beliefs (e.g., nationalism, paternalism, socialism).

3. It seems to me preferable to state the views of writers I am criticizing in their own words rather than to paraphrase them. And to illustrate that my own proposals are often in agreement—however implicitly—with the interpretations of other writers, it again seems preferable to quote them directly. These two reasons account for the rather large number of citations.

4. Following standard procedure adopted by logicians, I have placed single quotation marks around an expression (word or sentence) whenever something is said about that expression (e.g., about its logical structure or its meaning), as distinguished from the concept it expresses as well as from what it refers to. For example, (1) 'freedom' and 'liberty' are synonyms; (2) the concept of freedom may be expressed by 'freedom' or 'liberty'; (3) freedom of religion prevails in the United States.

5. I apologize for adopting the "modish" tendency "to amputate from the main words of a recurring phrase their initial letters and then, stringing these initials together, to use the resultant cryptogram as a printed proxy for that integral phrase. After their first appearances the phrases 'Three Blind Mice' and 'See How They Run' would then be abbreviated into 'TBM' and 'SHTR'" (Ryle 1976, p. 78). My defense for confronting the reader with "the monster of Initialization" (ibid.) is that the phrase 'with respect to' recurs so often throughout the text that not resorting to such a device would result in a longer (and hence more expensive) book. At least, I am not capitalizing 'wrt' and am not using other initializations, except 'iff' ('if and only if'); but that is common practice.

CHAPTER TWO

1. In the next chapter, I will examine the meaning of 'cause' in connection with power and its related concepts.

2. Because it is a bound variable, 'y' occurs in the *definiens*, but not in the *definiendum*.

3. Sometimes P's manipulation of R's environment constitutes an exercise of influence rather than of restraint. E.g., by placing R in a racially mixed group, P may influence him (through implicit persuasion) to adopt a more favorable attitude toward minority groups and to act accordingly.

4. I owe it to Terence Ball.

5. This example, too, comes from Terence Ball.

6. Here there is again a reference to the idea of rationality. That a difficulty is "unreasonable" means that any rational person would rather not confront it. By refusing someone a passport, the government does not make it literally impossible, merely unreasonably difficult, for anyone in that situation to travel abroad.

7. The only option P forecloses to R is not doing x and being rewarded; but that option was not available to R before P made it rewardable for R to do x. Contrariwise, punishability closes an option previously open to R: doing x without being punished.

8. Actually rewarding someone for what he did is not an exercise of power (unlike punishing him), since rewarding is a subclass of rewardability. But *promising* a reward may be an instance of exercising influence, and hence of power.

CHAPTER THREE

1. I myself once defined power this way: "To have power is to be capable of exercising power" (Oppenheim 1961, p. 100).

2. Braybrooke is the only author I know of who explicitly makes this distinction.

3. As do many contributors to the *Nomos* volume on coercion. E.g., "Coercion . . . in the wide sense . . . is the result of any threat of evil" (Gert 1972, p. 33). "A coerces B when A uses or threatens to use deprivations" (Wertheimer 1972, p. 222). "Coercion is best defined broadly as the use of sanctions to influence the behavior of others" (McIntosh 1972, p. 270; see also Bayles 1972, p. 17).

4. We have seen, however, that not all causal relationships among actors constitute power relationships.

5. Steven Lukes is inclined to answer "both yes and no" to the question whether rational persuasion is a form of influence and power. Yes, because P causes R to act in a certain way; "[n]o, because B autonomously accepts A's reasons" (1974, p. 33). My answer is yes, because R's compliance is the causal effect of P's persuasive arguments as well as of R's own decision.

6. A relation is symmetrical if its truth properties do not change when the order of the variables is reversed. Examples: 'x is married to y'; 'y is similar to x.'

A relation is asymmetrical if, when it holds between two individuals, the validity of its converse is excluded. Examples: 'x is the father of y'; 'x is larger than y.'

A relation is nonsymmetric if R(x,y) and R(y,x) hold for some, but not for all members of the field of R. Examples: 'x is the brother of y' (y may be x's brother or sister).

7. If we disregard the *actions* of A and B, exchange relations are symmetrical, but only in the trivial sense that, whenever an exchange takes place between A and B, an exchange takes place between B and A.

8. Unavoidably, I have myself defined influence in terms of intentions; but I am referring to those of R, not of P (P causes R to *choose* x). I shall deal with R's intentions in 3.5.3.

9. Lukes acknowledges this possibility but is "inclined" to reply that, "if and when B recognizes his real interests, the power relation ends" (1974, p. 33). According to my interpretation, it does not.

CHAPTER FOUR

1. That P punishes R for having done x implies that R did x, or at least that P believes that R did.

2. With rewardability, it is the alternative of not complying and being rewarded that has been excluded.

3. Gerald Dworkin has proposed the following definitions: "A is free to do x, iff it is not the case that A is unfree to do X . . . A is free with respect to doing X, iff A is free to do X and A is free to refrain from doing X" (1970, p. 380). This looks elegant; but where is the other actor? To include him, we would have to say, "Wrt P, R is free wrt X." This sounds awkward.

4. This example is adapted from Day (1977, p. 260). However, my interpretation differs from his, as I shall point out later.

5. This interpretation contradicts and, I believe, rectifies an earlier analysis I now consider to have been mistaken (Oppenheim 1961, pp. 188–92).

6. Of course, if both P1 and P2 spend the same amount, the *probability* that P1 will be elected is greater than the probability that P2 will win; hence, from the point of view of *this* dimension, P1 has more power over his voters than P2 over his constituents.

CHAPTER FIVE

1. Freedom of action must also be distinguished from freedom of choice. Whether we are free to choose between alternative courses of action has to do with the philosophical problem of free will versus determinism, a question of no concern to us here. We want to find out what it means to say that an actor is free to carry out what he has already chosen or decided to do (see Raphael 1970, p. 114).

2. Whenever A can do x, there is at least one alternative action z (e.g., not doing x) also open to A, so that A has freedom of action wrt x or z.

3. I need not enter the free will versus determinism controversy. I need not deny that motives are among the causes of actions, that unfree actions are caused by the actor's desire to avoid punishment and free actions by different motives.

4. "[T]he man who submits to the law does so as freely, no more, no less, than the man who deliberately defies it" (Benn and Weinstein 1971, p. 207). I would say that the latter acts freely and so does the former, *unless* his submission is motivated by fear of punishment; in that case, his compliance is an *unfree* action.

5. The concept of an unfree action could be extended to actions consisting of giving up an attempt to do something that, the actor finds out, is impossible. Take an unemployed person who comes to realize that it is of no use to try to find employment; his forced idleness is unfree. But idleness constitutes a free action on the part of an unemployed person who would have shunned work even under conditions of full employment.

6. Besides, 'autonomous' is a dispositional characteristic of a person, not a relationship between two persons.

CHAPTER SIX

1. One might argue that, on the contrary, Switzerland was less inegalitarian in this respect than Mississippi, because married men in Switzerland tended to take the views of their wives into consideration whereas no group in Mississippi represented the interests of the blacks. However, this only indicates that political *influence* was more widely spread in the former country. But influence, unlike the right to vote, is not a benefit that can be allocated by formal rules. The passage in the text, taken (with minor changes) from Oppenheim (1977), expresses a view rejected there but to which I now subscribe.

2. However, only the fifty thousand wealthiest of these "active citizens" were permitted to vote for the legislative assembly.

3. Most rules of distribution apply to large groups or to the whole population within a given political system. We want to determine, e.g., whether and to what degree a distribution of income is egalitarian. Such problems are usually examined with the help of the so-called Gini Coefficient (see Musgrave 1959).

4. Difficulties arise in the application of this definition to situations in which the combined holdings (e.g., of A and B) themselves increase while the percentage differences remain the same (see Robert L. Simon 1974, p. 341).

5. Karl Marx, *The German Ideology* (in Marx 1972, p. 124). Marx later abandoned this view of the future Communist society.

6. It is not a sufficient condition, surely not as long as society is based on the institution of the family (see Frankel 1971, p. 206). This is why, from the point of view of justice, Rawls adds the "difference principle," which involves what I have called a flattening of the pyramid of positions. Discrepancies, e.g., in salaries, should not be greater than necessary to benefit "the least advantaged" (Rawls 1971, p. 83).

7. It is true that Aristotle has only one characteristic in mind, desert or merit, and hence speaks only of "proportionate equality on the basis of desert" (*Politics,* 1317b). However, the notion may be generalized to apply to any characteristic, at least to any quantifiable one.

CHAPTER SEVEN

1. If the probabilities and utilities of the alternative outcomes can be specified numerically, the rational actor "makes that decision whose expected utility (the average utility of the alternative outcomes each weighted by its probability of occurring) is highest" (Baumol 1961, p. 368).

2. "[U]tilitarianism is a teleological theory whereas justice as fairness . . . is a deontological theory, one that either does not specify the good independently from the right, or does not interpret the right as maximizing the good" (Rawls 1971, p. 30).

3. The same distinction is made by some other authors. "Desegregation, for example, is not an issue for which considerations of public interest is

decisive; it is an issue that turns on direct considerations of humanity and justice and freedom" (Braybrooke 1962, p. 131). "Considerations such as fairness, equality, and others compete with considerations of the public interest in determining what to do" (Benditt 1973, p. 300).

4. 'Utilitarianism' as an ethical doctrine is sometimes used in a still narrower sense than the two mentioned previously—namely, as a synonym for 'utilitarianism' (in the second sense) of a benevolent kind, that it is morally obligatory to promote "the greatest happiness of the greatest number" rather than one's own welfare or that of some other person or group. According to the terminology adopted here, utilitarian goals may be of an egoistic or altruistic or benevolent kind.

5. Egoism is sometimes defined as acting out of self-interest (e.g., Rawls 1971, p. 124). For our purposes, such a definition would be circular.

6. The distinction between egoistic and altruistic welfare goals resembles Fishkin's dichotomy between "private- and public-regarding wants" (1979, p. 27). But whereas self-interested actions are private-regarding, pursuing the public interest involves actions that are benevolent rather than altruistic or "public-regarding" in Fishkin's sense.

7. This is not the view Rees himself adopts.

8. Cf. Brodbeck (1968), Lukes (1973), Mandelbaum (1973). Definitional methodological individualism in turn leads to to reductionism, the view that all social phenomena can be explained by laws of individual behavior.

9. The proposed explication is very similar to the definition Barry gave at one time but later abandoned: "To say that x is in A's interests is to say that he would want it if he were rational and not altruistic or principled in a certain way" (Barry 1962, p. 191)—"not altruistic" as distinguished from egoistic, not "principled" as distinguished from utilitarian. Barry's subsequent definition of 'interest' (1964, p. 4) will be taken up later.

10. If we take into account that A may have the choice of several welfare goals, we must adopt the following, somewhat more complex, definition: it is rational for A to do x wrt some goal y that promotes his own welfare. The assertion that it is in A's interest to do x refers then to two hypothetical conditions: (1) were A primarily interested in his own well-being, he would adopt y as a goal (e.g., health rather than wealth); (2) were A to adopt y as a goal, it would be rational for A to do x (e.g., to cultivate his garden).

11. However, this passage does not bring out Lippmann's value-cognitivist view that ultimate political purposes are not to be chosen by man, but are prescribed by the principles of natural law "in the sense that all men, when they are sincerely and lucidly rational, will regard them as self-evident" (Lippmann 1955, p. 95).

12. To take into account the possibility that "the public" may have the choice of different collective welfare goals (e.g., reducing pollution or increasing production), we may amend the definition as follows: it is rational for A to enact x wrt some goal y that promotes the collective welfare of P, i.e., that would be chosen by all or most members of P if they adopted the collective welfare point of view. Here there are implicit references to three hypothetical conditions: (1) were the members of P to adopt the collective welfare point of view, they would choose y (e.g., clean air); (2) were A to aim

at the collective welfare of P, A would adopt collective welfare goal y; (3) were A to adopt y as a goal, it would be rational for A to enact policy x (e.g., making antipollution devices on cars mandatory).

13. Truman considers it an advantage of this interpretation that the concept of interest is linked to "overt behavior" and, as such, to data that are "directly observable," thanks to "the modern techniques for the measurement of attitude and opinion" (1955, pp. 34–35).

14. Curiously, Barry "suggests" a similar definition contrary to the earlier one I quoted with approval (7.3.1): "[A] policy, law or institution is in someone's interest if it increases his opportunities to get what he wants—whatever this might be" (Barry 1964, p. 4). However, Barry seems to abandon this view in the latter part of this article.

15. Benditt calls this account "a *collective* conception of the public interest" (1973, p. 306). It seems to me that, in the expression 'anyone's welfare' just as in 'everyone's welfare,' the predicate 'welfare' functions distributively (as an attribute of individuals), not collectively (as an attribute of 'the public' as a whole).

16. See also, "What makes the will general is less the number of voters than the common interest uniting them" (II, 4).

Chapter Eight

1. I am concerned with the distinction between 'descriptive' and 'normative,' not between 'descriptive' and 'theoretical.' 'Atom' has both of these latter characteristics.

2. Ball bases the distinction between rational persuasion and coercive manipulation on other than normative grounds (1978, p. 612). I agree with him that utterances of the former kind are predictive (e.g., "if you don't stop smoking, you will get sick"), while the latter are performative (e.g., the gunman's coercive threat).

3. Macpherson's concept of positive freedom also fits here, except that the goal—availability of the basic necessities—is to be realized by others than the actor himself.

4. So is, perhaps, 'obedience to the general will'; "perhaps, " because it is doubtful whether Rousseau's general will can be given any empirical reference, since it is the will not of each or all or of the majority, but of the personified "body politic."

5. See Frankena (1973, pp. 97–102).

6. This example is adapted from Benn and Peters (1965, p. 119).

7. This is actually the defining expression of "a just distribution" (*Politics*, 1280a). But since "the just is equal," the above passage could also be taken as the definition of proportional equality.

8. The following fictitious example might illustrate the problem: Suppose at time T1, the average income of whites is $12,000, that of blacks $3,000 (total, $15,000; difference, $9,000; percentage difference, 80% − 20% = 60%). At time T2, the average income of whites is $24,000, that of blacks $12,000 (total, $36,000; difference, $12,000; percentage difference, 66⅔% − 33⅓% = 33⅓%). The income of whites has doubled, that of blacks quadrupled. Even so, the difference between their incomes

has *increased* from $9,000 to $12,000. But the percentage difference has *decreased* from 60% to 33⅓%. Simon considers the redistribution inegalitarian; I characterize it as egalitarian. This does not imply that it is *sufficiently* egalitarian, from the ethical point of view of equity and social justice.

Strictly speaking, however, no *rule* of redistribution is involved when there are changes in the distribution of incomes. Furthermore, I have previously applied the proposed criterion of egalitarianism only to situations in which the total amount to be redistributed remains unchanged.

CHAPTER NINE

1. Conceptual relativism is aptly criticized by Trigg: "Truth is made to depend on concepts, and as concepts are relative to 'forms of life', truth must be as well" (1973, p. 25).

2. Note that Hempel says "a well-established use *in science*," but not necessarily in ordinary language.

3. Behavioralism has in turn been challenged by "postbehavioralism," which is sympathetic to the views examined in 9.1.3: Actions, including political interactions, must be interpreted in terms of the actor's own conceptions. I have pointed out why I do not believe that this is the right approach to a *reconstruction* of political concepts.

4. Here is an example for each of these opposing views. "I wish to contend that wants can properly be understood as causes of acts, and that an adequate theory of human action can be worked out within a causal framework" (Goldman 1970, p. 55). "[T]he connection between will and behavior is a logical and therefore not in the humean sense a causal relation" (von Wright 1971, p. 93).

5. This thesis has been elaborated, e.g., by Davidson: "Ignorance of competent predictive laws does not inhibit valid causal explanation, or few causal explanations could be made" (1968, p. 91). "We are usually far more certain of a singular causal connexion than we are of any causal law governing the case" (ibid., p. 92). "[I]t is an error to think no explanation has been given until a law has been produced" (ibid.).

6. I.e., "the rational choice model of human behavior" (Moon 1975, p. 195) is applicable to such situations. This is not to deny that political behavior is often irrational. Irrational actions, too, can often be explained causally in terms of general laws, e.g., of psychology.

7. Here is an elaboration of this view: "Inasmuch as the units of examination of human behaviour are actions, they cannot be observed, identified, or isolated except through categories of assessment and appraisal. There are not two stages, an identification of properties and qualities in nature and then an assessment of them, stages which then could become the business of different experts. There is only one stage, the delineation and description of occurrences in value terms" (Louch 1966, p. 56).

8. If there are no theories of political science, there can be no paradigms in Kuhn's sense either, since these are models for theories, "models from which spring particular *coherent* traditions of scientific research" (Kuhn 1970, p. 10; italics added).

9. That these are natural rights also implies that the above 'ought' statement is demonstrably true (in this case it is claimed to be "self-evident"). The natural law thesis is the metaethical theory of value-cognitivism applied to certain norms of political ethics (see Oppenheim 1976, p. 49).

10. However, Rudner considers the value judgments involved here to be of an ethical rather than of a nonmoral kind. The quoted passage continues: "Obviously our decision regarding the evidence and respecting how strong is 'strong enough', is going to be a function of the *importance*, in the typically ethical sense, of making a mistake in accepting or rejecting the hypothesis" (1970, p. 541; italics in the original).

11. Furthermore, a statement can be said to be analytic only wrt a given system; e.g., 'the sum of angles in a triangle is 180 degrees' is analytic within the system of Euclidean geometry; 'all bachelors are unmarried' is analytic, given the definition of bachelor as an unmarried male. The whole analytic-synthetic dichotomy has been questioned, e.g., by Quine (1953, p. 43).

12. That naturalism (at least in its definist version) is incompatible with both the separability and the inseparability thesis is perhaps one further argument against this metaethical theory.

References

Translations Used

NOTE: Translations from Montesquieu, *De l'esprit des lois,* and Rousseau, *Discours sur l'origine et les fondements de l'inégalité parmi les hommes,* are the author's.

Aristotle. *Nichomachean Ethics.* Trans., with Introduction and Notes, by Martin Ostwald. Indianapolis and New York: Bobbs-Merrill, Library of Liberal Arts, 1962.

———. *The Politics of Aristotle.* Trans., with Introduction, Notes, and Appendixes, by Ernest Barker. New York and London: Oxford University Press, 1946.

Dostoyevsky, Fyodor. *The Brothers Karamazov.* Trans., by Constance Garnett. New York: Random House, Modern Library (n.d.).

Machiavelli, Niccolò. *The Prince.* Trans. and ed. by Mark Musa. New York: St. Martin's Press, 1964.

Marx, Karl. *Critique of the Gotha Program.* In *The Marx-Engels Reader.* 2d ed. Ed. by Robert C. Tucker, New York: W. W. Norton & Co., 1972.

———. *The German Ideology.* In ibid.

Plato. *The Republic of Plato.* Trans., with Introduction and Notes, by Francis MacDonald Cornford. New York and London: Oxford University Press, 1941.

Rousseau, Jean Jacques. *The Social Contract.* In *The Social Contract and the Discourses.* Trans., with Introduction, by G. D. H. Cole. New York: E. P. Dutton, Everyman's Library, 1950.

Wittgenstein, Ludwig. *Philosophical Investigations.* 3d ed. Trans. by G. E. M. Anscombe. New York: Macmillan Co., 1968.

———. *Tractatus Logico-Philosophicus.* Trans. by D. F. Pears and B. F. McGuiness. London: Routledge & Kegan Paul, 1961.

General References

Alker, Hayward R., Jr. 1969. "Statistics and Politics: The Need for Causal Data Analysis." Pp. 244–313 in *Politics and the Social Sciences,* ed. by Seymour M. Lipset. New York: Oxford University Press.

Alston, William P. 1967a. "Motives and Motivations." Pp. 399–409 in *The Encyclopedia of Philosophy,* vol. 5, ed. by Paul Edwards. New York: Macmillan Co. and Free Press.

———. 1967b. "Vagueness." Pp. 218–21 in *The Encyclopedia of Philosophy,* vol. 8, ed. by Paul Edwards. New York: Macmillan Co. and Free Press.

American Law Institute. 1932. *Restatement of the Law of Contracts.* St. Paul: West.

211

Arendt, Hannah. 1961. *Between Past and Future*. New York: Viking Press.

Arrow, Kenneth J. 1967. "Public and Private Values." Pp. 3–21 in *Human Values and Economic Policy*, ed. by Sidney Hook. New York: New York University Press.

Bachrach, Peter, and Baratz, Morton S. 1970. *Power and Poverty: Theory and Practice*. New York: Oxford University Press.

Baier, Kurt. 1967. "Welfare and Preference." Pp. 120–35 in *Human Values and Economic Policy*, ed. by Sidney Hook. New York: New York University Press.

Baldwin, David A. 1971. "The Power of Positive Sanctions." *World Politics* 24:19–38.

———. 1978. "Power and Social Exchange." *American Political Science Review* 72:1229–42.

Ball, Terence. 1975. "Power, Causation, and Explanation." *Polity* 8:189–214.

———. 1978. "'Power' Revised: A Comment on Oppenheim." *Journal of Politics* 40:609–18.

Barry, Brian M. 1962. "The Use and Abuse of 'The Public Interest.'" Pp. 191–204 in *Nomos*, vol. 5, *The Public Interest*, ed. by Carl J. Friedrich. New York: Atherton Press.

———. 1964. "The Public Interest." *Proceedings of the Aristotelian Society* (suppl.) 38:1–18.

———. 1976. "Power: An Economic Analysis." Pp. 67–101 in *Power and Political Theory*, ed. by Brian Barry. London: John Wiley & Sons.

Barry, Brian, and Rae, Douglas W. 1975. "Political Evaluation." Pp. 337–401 in *Handbook of Political Science*, vol. 1, ed. by Fred I. Greenstein and Nelson W. Polsby. Reading Mass.: Addison-Wesley.

Baumol, William J. 1961. *Economic Theory and Operations Analysis*. Englewood Cliffs, N.J.: Prentice-Hall.

Bay, Christian. 1958. *The Structure of Freedom*. Stanford, Calif.: Stanford University Press.

Bayles, Michael D. 1972. "A Concept of Coercion." Pp. 16–29 in *Nomos*, vol. 14, *Coercion*, ed. by J. Roland Pennock and John W. Chapman. New York: Atherton Press.

Benditt, Theodore M. 1973. "The Public Interest." *Philosophy and Public Affairs* 2:291–311.

———. 1975. "The Concept of Interest in Political Theory." *Political Theory* 3:245–58.

Benn, S. I. 1960. "'Interests' in Politics." *Proceedings of the Aristotelian Society*, n.s. 60:123–40.

———. 1964. "Some Reflections on Political Theory and Behavioural Science." *Political Studies* 12:237–42.

———. 1967. "Power." Pp. 424–27 in *The Encyclopedia of Philosophy*, vol. 6, ed. by Paul Edwards. New York: Macmillan Co. and Free Press.

Benn, S. I., and Peters, R. S. 1965. *The Principles of Political Thought*. New York: Free Press.

Benn, S. I., and Weinstein, W. L. 1971. "Being Free to Act, and Being a Free Man." *Mind* 80:194–211.

Bergmann, Frithjof. 1977. *On Being Free*. Notre Dame, Ind.: University of Notre Dame Press.

Berlin, Isaiah. 1969. *Four Essays on Liberty*. New York: Oxford University Press.

Bernstein, Richard J. 1978. *The Restructuring of Social and Political Theory*. Philadelphia: University of Pennsylvania Press.

Blackstone, William T. 1973. *Political Philosophy, an Introduction*. New York: Thomas Y. Crowell Co.

Blau, Peter M. 1964. *Exchange and Power in Social Life*. New York: John Wiley.

Brandt, Richard. 1977. "The Concept of Rationality in Ethical and Political Theory." Pp. 265–79 in *Nomos*, vol. 17, *Human Nature in Politics*, ed. by J. Roland Pennock and John W. Chapman. New York: New York University Press.

Braybrooke, David. 1962. "The Public Interest: The Present and Future of the Concept." Pp. 129–54 in *Nomos*, vol. 5, *The Public Interest*, ed. by Carl J. Friedrich. New York: Atherton Press.

——. 1968. *Three Tests for Democracy: Personal Rights, Human Welfare, Collective Preference*. New York: Random House.

——. 1973. "Two Blown Fuses in Goldman's Analysis of Power." *Philosophical Studies* 24:369–77.

Brodbeck, May. 1968. "Methodological Individualisms: Definition and Reduction." Pp. 280–303 in *Readings in the Philosophy of the Social Sciences*, ed. by May Brodbeck. New York: Macmillan Co.

Cartwright, Dorwin. 1965. "Influence, Leadership, Control." Pp. 1–47 in *Handbook of Organizations*, ed. by James G. March. Chicago: Rand McNally.

Cassinelli, C. W. 1962. "The Public Interest in Political Ethics." Pp. 44–53 in *Nomos*, vol. 5, *The Public Interest*, ed. by Carl J. Friedrich. New York: Atherton Press.

——. 1966. *Free Activities and Interpersonal Relations*. The Hague: Martinus Nijhoff.

Caton, Charles E. 1967. "Artificial and Natural Languages." Pp. 168–71 in *The Encyclopedia of Philosophy*, vol. 1, ed. by Paul Edwards. New York: Macmillan Co. and Free Press.

Clarke, Barry. 1979. "Essentially Contested Concepts." *British Journal of Political Science* 9:122–26.

Cohen, Julius. 1962. "A Layman's View of the Public Interest." Pp. 155–61 in *Nomos*, vol. 5, *The Public Interest*, ed. by Carl J. Friedrich. New York: Atherton Press.

Connolly, William E. 1974. *The Terms of Political Discourse*. Lexington, Mass.: D. C. Heath and Co.

Conrad, Thomas R. 1976. "The Debate about Quota Systems." *American Journal of Political Science* 20:135–49.

Crenson, Matthew. 1971. *The Un-Politics of Air Pollution: A Study of Non-Decisionmaking in the Cities*. Baltimore: Johns Hopkins University Press.

Dahl, Robert A. 1957. "The Concept of Power." *Behavioral Science* 2:201–15.

———. 1968. "Power." Pp. 405–15 in *International Encyclopedia of the Social Sciences*, vol. 12, ed. by David L. Sills. New York: Macmillan Co. and Free Press.

———. 1976. *Modern Political Analysis*. 3d ed. Englewood Cliffs, N.J.: Prentice-Hall.

———. 1979. "Procedural Democracy." Pp. 97–133 in *Philosophy, Politics, and Society*, 5th ser., ed. by Peter Laslett and James Fishkin. New Haven: Yale University Press.

Dahl, Robert A., and Lindblom, Charles E. 1953. *Politics, Economics, and Welfare*. New York: Harper & Brothers.

Davidson, Donald. 1968. "Actions, Reasons, and Causes." Pp. 79–94 in *The Philosophy of Action*, ed. by Alan R. White. London: Oxford University Press.

Day, J. P. 1977. "Threats, Offers, Law, Opinion, and Liberty." *American Philosophical Quarterly* 14:257–72.

Dryer, D. P. 1964. "Freedom." *Canadian Journal of Economics and Political Science* 30:444–48.

Dworkin, Gerald. 1970. "Acting Freely." *Nous* 4:367–83.

———. 1979. "Paternalism." Pp. 78–96 in *Philosophy, Politics, and Society*, 5th ser., ed. by Peter Laslett and James Fishkin. New Haven: Yale University Press.

Easton, David. 1953. *The Political System*. New York: Alfred A. Knopf.

———. 1967. "The Current Meaning of 'Behavioralism.'" Pp. 11–31 in *Contemporary Political Analysis*, ed. by James C. Charlesworth. New York: Free Press.

Eckstein, Harry. 1973. "Authority Patterns: A Structural Basis for Political Inquiry." *American Political Science Review* 67:1142–61.

Fay, Brian. 1975. *Social Theory and Political Practice*. London: George Allen & Unwin.

Fay, Brian, and Moon, J. Donald. 1977. "What Would an Adequate Philosophy of Social Science Look like?" *Philosophy of the Social Sciences* 7:209–27.

Feinberg, Joel. 1973. *Social Philosophy*. Englewood Cliffs, N.J.: Prentice-Hall.

Feyerabend, P. K. 1968. "How to Be a Good Empiricist—A Plea of Tolerance in Matters Epistemological." Pp. 12–39 in *The Philosophy of Science*, ed. by P. H. Nidditch. London: Oxford University Press.

Fishkin, James S. 1979. *Tyranny and Legitimacy*. Baltimore and London: Johns Hopkins University Press.

Flathman, Richard E. 1975. "Some Familiar but False Dichotomies concerning 'Interests': A Comment on Benditt and Oppenheim." *Political Theory* 3:277–87.

Frankel, Charles. 1971. "Equality of Opportunity." *Ethics* 81:191–211

———. 1976. "The Autonomy of the Social Sciences." Pp. 9–30 in *Controversies and Decisions*, ed. by Charles Frankel. New York: Russell Sage Foundation.

Frankena, William K. 1973. *Ethics*. 2d ed. Englewood Cliffs, N.J.: Prentice-Hall.

Freedom House. 1979. "The Comparative Survey of Freedom—IX." *Freedom at Issue* 49:1–34.

Fried, Charles. 1978. *Right and Wrong*. Cambridge, Mass.: Harvard University Press.

Friedman, Richard B. 1973. "On the Concept of Authority in Political Philosophy." Pp. 121–45 in *Concepts in Social and Political Philosophy*, ed. by Richard E. Flathman. New York: Macmillan Co.

Friedrich, Carl Joachim. 1963. *Man and His Government*. New York: McGraw-Hill.

Gallie, W. B. 1964. *Philosophy and the Historical Understanding*. New York: Schockan Books.

Gert, Bernard. 1972. "Coercion and Freedom." Pp. 30–48 in *Nomos*, vol. 14, *Coercion*, ed. by J. Roland Pennock and John W. Chapman. New York: Atherton Press.

Gettner, Alan. 1977. "Hare and Fanaticism." *Ethics* 87:160–64.

Gibson, Quentin. 1971. "Power." *Philosophy of the Social Sciences* 1:101–12.

Gill, John G. 1971. "The Definition of Freedom." *Ethics* 82:1–20.

Goldman, Alvin I. 1970. *A Theory of Human Action*. Englewood Cliffs, N.J.: Prentice-Hall.

———. 1972. "Toward a Theory of Social Power." *Philosophical Studies* 23:221–68.

Gray, J. N. 1977. "On the Contestability of Social and Political Concepts." *Political Theory* 5:331–48.

Hanson, Norwood Russell. 1967. "Observation and Interpretation." Pp. 89–99 in *Philosophy of Science Today*, ed. by Sidney Morgenbesser. New York: Basic Books.

Hart, H. L. A. 1958. "Legal and Moral Obligation." Pp. 82–107 in *Essays in Moral Philosophy*, ed. by A. I. Melden. Seattle: University of Washington Press.

Hart, H. L. A., and Honoré, A. M. 1959. *Causation in the Law*. London: Oxford University Press.

Hayek, F. A. 1960. *The Constitution of Liberty*. Chicago: University of Chicago Press.

Held, Virginia. 1970. *The Public Interest and Individual Interests*. New York: Basic Books.

———. 1972. "Coercion and Coercive Offers." Pp. 49–62 in *Nomos*, vol. 14, *Coercion*, ed. by J. Roland Pennock and John W. Chapman. New York: Atherton Press.

———. 1973. "The Terms of Political Discourse: A Comment in Oppenheim." *Political Theory* 1:69–75.

Hempel, Carl G. 1965. *Aspects of Scientific Explanation*. New York: Free Press.

———. 1973. "The Meaning of Theoretical Terms: A Critique of the Standard Empiricist Construal." Pp. 367–78 in *Logic, Methodology, and Philosophy of Science*, vol. 4, ed. by P. Suppes et al. Amsterdam: North-Holland Publishing Co.

Kaplan, Abraham. 1964. *The Conduct of Inquiry: Methodology for Behavioral Science*. San Francisco: Chandler Publishing Co.

Kovesi, Julius. 1967. *Moral Notions*. New York: Humanities Press.

Kuhn, Thomas S. 1970. *The Structure of Scientific Revolutions*. 2d ed. Chicago: University of Chicago Press.

————. 1977. *The Essential Tension: Selected Studies in Scientific Tradition and Change*. Chicago and London: University of Chicago Press.

LaPalombara, Joseph G. 1964. *Interest Groups in Italian Politics*. Princeton, N.J.: Princeton University Press.

Lasswell, Harold D., and Kaplan, Abraham. 1950. *Power and Society*. New Haven: Yale University Press.

Lindesmith, Alfred R. 1968. "Punishment." Pp. 217–22 in *International Encyclopedia of the Social Sciences*, vol. 13, ed. by David L. Sills. New York: Macmillan Co. and Free Press.

Lippmann, Walter. 1955. *Essays in the Public Philosophy*. New York: Mentor Books.

Loevinsohn, Ernest. 1977. "Liberty and the Redistribution of Property." *Philosophy and Public Affairs* 6:226–39.

Louch, A. R. 1966. *Explanation and Human Action*. Berkeley and Los Angeles: University of California Press.

Lukes, Steven. 1973. "Methodological Individualism Reconsidered." Pp. 119–29 in *The Philosophy of Social Explanation*, ed. by A. J. Ryan. Oxford: Oxford University Press.

————. 1974. *Power: A Radical View*. London and Basingstoke: Macmillan Press.

MacCallum, Gerald C., Jr. 1967. "Negative and Positive Freedom." *Philosophical Review* 76:312–34.

McCloskey, H. J. 1965. "A Critique of the Ideals of Liberty." *Mind* 74:483–508.

McIntosh, Donald. 1972. "Coercion and International Politics: A Theoretical Analysis." Pp. 243–71 in *Nomos*, vol. 14, *Coercion*, ed. by J. Roland Pennock and John W. Chapman. New York: Atherton Press.

MacIntyre, Alasdair. 1967. "Egoism and Altruism." Pp. 462–66 in *The Encyclopedia of Philosophy*, vol. 2, ed. by Paul Edwards. New York: Macmillan Co. and Free Press.

————. 1972. "Is a Science of Comparative Politics Possible?" Pp. 8–26 in *Philosophy, Politics, and Society*, 4th ser., ed. by Peter Laslett, W. G. Runciman, and Quentin Skinner. New York: Harper & Row.

————. 1973. "The Essential Contestability of Some Social Concepts." *Ethics* 84:1–9.

McKeon, Richard. 1951. "Philosophic Differences and Issues of Freedom." *Ethics* 61:105–35.

Macpherson, C. B. 1973. *Democratic Theory: Essays in Retrieval*. London: Oxford University Press.

Mandelbaum, Maurice. 1973. "Societal Facts." Pp. 105–18 in *The Philosophy of Social Explanation*, ed. by A. J. Ryan. Oxford: Oxford University Press.

March, James G. 1966. "The Power of Power." P;. 39–70 in *Varieties of Political Theory*, ed. by David Easton. Englewood Cliffs, N.J.: Prentice-Hall.

Marcuse, Herbert. 1965 "Repressive Tolerance." Pp. 81–123 in *A Critique of Pure Tolerance*, ed. by Robert Paul Wolff, Barrington Moore, Jr., and Herbert Marcuse. Boston: Beacon Press.

Miller, Eugene F. 1972. "Positivism, Historicism, and Political Inquiry." *American Political Science Review* 66:796–817.

Moon, J. Donald. 1975. "The Logic of Political Inquiry: A Synthesis of Opposed Perspectives." Pp. 131–228 in *Handbook of Political Science*, vol. 1, ed. by Fred I. Greenstein and Nelson W. Polsby. Reading, Mass.: Addison-Wesley.

Musgrave, Richard A. 1959. *The Theory of Public Finance*. New York: McGraw-Hill.

————. 1962. "The Public Interest: Efficiency in the Creation and Maintenance of Material Welfare." Pp. 107–14 in *Nomos*, vol. 5, *The Public Interest*, ed. by Carl J. Friedrich. New York: Atherton Press.

Nagel, Jack H. 1975. *The Descriptive Analysis of Power*. New Haven and London: Yale University Press.

Nielsen, Kai. 1967. "Problems of Ethics. Pp. 117–34 in *The Encyclopedia of Philosophy*, vol. 3, ed. by Paul Edwards. New York: Macmillan Co. and Free Press.

Nozick, Robert. 1969. "Coercion." Pp. 440–71 in *Philosophy, Science, and Method*, ed. by S. Morgenbesser, P. Suppes, and M. White. New York: St. Martin's Press.

————. 1974. *Anarchy, State, and Utopia*. New York: Basic Books.

Okun, Arthur M. 1975. *Equality and Efficiency*. Washington, D.C.: Brookings Institution.

Olson, Mancur. 1965. *The Logic of Collective Action*. Cambridge, Mass.: Harvard University Press.

Oppenheim, Felix E. 1961. *Dimensions of Freedom*. New York: St. Martin's Press.

————. 1976. *Moral Principles in Political Philosophy.* 2d ed. New York: Random House.

————. 1977. "Equality, Groups, and Quotas." *American Journal of Political Science* 21:65–69.

Pap, Arthur. 1949. *Elements of Analytic Philosophy*. New York: Macmillan Co.

Parent, William A. 1974. "Some Recent Work on the Concept of Liberty." *American Philosophical Quarterly* 11:149–67.

Partridge, P. H. 1967. "Freedom." Pp. 221–25 in *The Encyclopedia of Philosophy*, vol. 3, ed. by Paul Edwards. New York: Macmillan Co. and Free Press.

————. 1970. "Some Notes on the Concept of Power." Pp. 18–38 in *Contemporary Political Theory*, ed. by Anthony de Crespigny and Alan Wertheimer. New York: Atherton Press.

Pitkin, Hannah Fenichel. 1972. *Wittgenstein and Justice*. Berkeley and Los Angeles: University of California Press.

Plamenatz, J. P. 1968. *Consent, Freedom, and Political Obligation*. 2d ed. London: Oxford University Press.

Polsby, Nelson W. 1980. *Community Power and Political Theory*. 2d ed., enlarged. New Haven: Yale University Press.

Popper, Karl R. 1972. *Objective Knowledge*. London: Oxford University Press.

Quine, Willard von O. 1953. *From a Logical Point of View*. Cambridge, Mass.:

Harvard University Press.

Raphael, D. D. 1970. *Problems of Political Philosophy*. London and Basingstoke: Macmillan and Co.

———. 1977. "Tensions between the Goals of Equality and Freedom." Pp. 543–58 in *Equality and Freedom: International and Comparative Jurisprudence*, vol. 2, ed. by Gray Dorsey. Dobbs Ferry, N.Y.: Oceana Publishers.

Rapoport, Anatol. 1966. "Some System Approaches to Political Theory." Pp. 129–41 in *Varieties of Political Theory*, ed. by David Easton. Englewood Cliffs, N.J.: Prentice-Hall.

Rawls, John. 1971. *A Theory of Justice*. Cambridge, Mass.: Harvard University Press.

Raz, Joseph. 1970. "On Lawful Governments." *Ethics* 80:296–305.

Rees, W. J. 1964. "The Public Interest." *Proceedings of the Aristotelian Society* (suppl.) 38:19–38.

Riker, William H. 1964. "Some Ambiguities in the Notion of Power." *American Political Science Review* 58:341–49.

Rorty, Richard. 1967. "Metaphilosophical Difficulties of Linguistic Philosophy." Pp. 1–40 in *The Linguistic Turn*, ed. by Richard Rorty. Chicago: University of Chicago Press.

Rosen, Paul L. 1977. "Science, Power, and the Degradation of American Political Science." *Polity* 9:463–80.

Rudner, Richard. 1970. "The Scientist qua Scientist Makes Value Judgments." Pp. 540–46 in *Readings in the Philosophy of Science*, ed. by Baruch A. Brody. Englewood Cliffs, N.J.: Prentice-Hall.

Russell, Bertrand. 1940. "Freedom and Government." Pp. 249–64 in *Freedom, Its Meaning*, ed. by Ruth Nanda Anshen. New York: Harcourt, Brace.

Ryle, Gilbert. 1976. "Improvisation." *Mind* 85:69–83.

Schubert, Glendon. 1960. *The Public Interest*. Glencoe, Il.: Free Press.

Shapley, L. S., and Shubik, M. 1964. "A Method for Evaluating the Distribution of Power in a Committee System." Pp. 141–50 in *Game Theory and Related Approaches to Social Behavior*, ed. by Martin Shubik. New York: John Wiley.

Shubik, Martin. 1964. "Game Theory and the Study of Social Behavior: An Introductory Exposition." Pp. 3–77 in *Game Theory and Related Approaches to Social Behavior*, ed. by Martin Shubik. New York: John Wiley.

Siedentop, L. A. 1977. "Whither Political Theory?" *Political Studies* 25:588–93.

Simon, Herbert A. 1957. *Models of Man: Social and Rational*. New York: John Wiley.

Simon, Robert L. 1974. "Egalitarian Redistribution and the Significance of Context." *Ethics* 84:339–45.

Smith, G. W. 1977. "Slavery, Contentment, and Social Freedom." *Philosophical Quarterly* 27:237–48.

Steiner, Hillel. 1975. "Individual Liberty." *Proceedings of the Aristotelian Society*, n.s. 75:33–50.

Taylor, Charles. 1971. "Interpretation and the Sciences of Man." *Review of Metaphysics* 25:3–51.

————. 1979. "What Is Wrong with Negative Liberty." In *The Idea of Freedom: Essays in Honour of Isaiah Berlin,* ed. by Alan Ryan. Oxford: Oxford University Press.

Taylor, Paul W. 1959. "Need Statements." *Analysis* 19:106–11.

Trigg, Roger. 1973. *Reason and Commitment.* London: Cambridge University Press.

Truman, David B. 1955. *The Governmental Process.* New York: Alfred A. Knopf.

Urmson, J. O. 1965. "On Grading." Pp. 381–409 in *Logic and Language,* 1st and 2d ser., ed. by Antony Flew. Garden City, N.Y.: Doubleday & Co.

Vlastos, Gregory. 1962. "Justice and Equality." Pp. 31–72 in *Social Justice,* ed. by Richard B. Brandt. Englewood Cliffs, N.J.: Prentice-Hall.

Von Leyden, W. 1963. "On Justifying Inequality." *Political Studies* 11:56–70.

von Wright, George Henrik. 1971. *Explanation and Understanding.* Ithaca, N.Y.: Cornell University Press.

Waismann, Friedrich. 1968. "Verifiability." Pp. 35–60 in *The Theory of Meaning,* ed. by G. H. R. Parkinson. London: Oxford University Press.

Webb, Sidney, and Webb, Beatrice. 1923. *The Decay of Capitalist Civilization.* 3d ed. Westminster: Fabian Society.

Weber, Max. 1947. *The Theory of Social and Economic Organization,* trans. by A. M. Henderson and Talcott Parsons. New York: Oxford University Press.

Weldon, Thomas D. 1953. *The Vocabulary of Politics.* Baltimore: Penguin Books.

Wertheimer, Alan P. 1972. "Political Coercion and Political Obligation." Pp. 213–42 in *Nomos,* vol. 14, *Coercion,* ed. by J. Roland Pennock and John W. Chapman. New York: Atherton Press.

White, D. M. 1970. "Negative Liberty." *Ethics* 81:185–204.

Williams, Bernard. 1962. "The Idea of Equality." Pp. 110–31 in *Philosophy, Politics, and Society,* 2d ser., ed. by Peter Laslett and W. G. Runciman. Oxford: Basil Blackwell.

Wolff, Robert Paul. 1970. *In Defense of Anarchism.* New York: Harper & Row.

————. 1977. *Understanding Rawls.* Princeton, N.J.: Princeton University Press.

Wolin, Sheldon S. 1968. "Political Theory: Trends and Goals." Pp. 318–31 in *International Encyclopedia of the Social Sciences,* vol. 12, ed. by David L. Sills. New York: Macmillan Co. and Free Press.

219

Index of Subjects

matively, 153, 158, 162; degrees
of, 69–81, 85, 154, 201; dimensions
of, 71, 85, 159; and feeling free,
91–93, 159, 184; and free actions,
88–91, 93, 205; and free persons,
79, 93–95, 125, 163, 169, 172, 184;
and freedom of action, 8, 53, 82–
88, 91, 93, 158, 176, 184, 205; as
a relational concept, 7–8, 53, 64;
and social power, 40, 68–69
Social power: degrees of, 69–81, 189,
205; dimensions of, 71; exercising,
10–20, 161, 165, 180–81, 190, 204;
having, 20–28, 191, 193; as a relational concept, 6–7, 53; and social
freedom, 40, 68–69
Social unfreedoms, 7–8, 53–64. *See
also* Social freedom
Social welfare function, 137
Speech acts, 9, 11, 196
Statements: analytic, 199, 210; synthetic, 200, 210
Suffrage, 98, 111, 119

Tax, income, sales, 106, 109, 110,

119, 120, 182
Theories, political, 188–89
Threats: coercive, 15, 40, 63, 125,
182, 208; of punishment, 13, 27,
39–40

Unfreedom. *See* Freedom
Utilitarianism, utility, 127–28, 136,
144, 146–47, 167, 207

Vagueness. *See* Concepts, vague
Value-cognitivism, 125, 200–202,
207, 210
Value judgments, 198–202, 210. *See
also* Concepts, valuational
Value-noncognitivism, 199–202
Variable, variables, 8, 12, 124, 186,
191, 203

Wants, 142, 180
Welfare, 128–33, 139, 142, 162, 167,
175, 191, 201, 207–8. *See also*
Collective welfare
Will: general, 147–49, 164, 179, 208;
weakness of the, 127

Index of Names